FOR TWO PINS

BY

BILL FLANNIGAN

authorHOUSE®

AuthorHouse™ UK Ltd.
500 Avebury Boulevard
Central Milton Keynes, MK9 2BE
www.authorhouse.co.uk
Phone: 08001974150

First published by AuthorHouse 4/23/2009

ISBN: 978-1-4389-3577-5 (sc)

Printed in the United States of America
Bloomington, Indiana

This book is printed on acid-free paper.

This book is dedicated
to my Nanna.
She died in 1943 aged only 47

I was just past my 7th birthday, but the memory
of that awful day is as vivid and as painful
as it was those sixty odd years ago.

My Mother and her sister Betty(Liz) have also
passed on and since embarking on this book
my youngest aunt, Dot(Doreen) has tragically
left this life, so my dedication must be
extended to include them all.

All of the names and dates are entirely from
my own recollections and totally uncorroborated.
Age may have clouded my memory and distorted
some of the facts but it is not intentional.
What I have written I believe to be true
and if I have made mistakes I apologise
only to my family.

Nanna Mills with Mam on her knee

Chapter One

"Biiillleee!"

It sounded like the cry of a not so talented opera singer straining to reach top 'C'.

That shrill note could strike fear into the heart of the bravest of souls. It certainly struck fear into mine. I knew the danger signals that echoed from that cry. I was late, it was after ten o'clock and the tone of the voice spelled trouble!

My mother was a fiery tempered woman and had to be 'handled' with utmost caution. If she decided that you had broken the rules there was no placating her. Excuses or explanations were a complete waste of time. Once she had made her mind up that you were in for a good hiding, you got one. That was just a fact of life.

I ran into the house just as she was closing the kitchen door.

"Should ah lock the front door?" I shouted down the passage.

"Yes, you might as well, it's after ten o'clock", she replied icily.

The old dead lock thumped home into the metal keep as I turned the huge key. It was the only time we ever locked the door, it always stayed open from early morning until bedtime.

"Where have you been till this time? I told you 9 o'clock at the latest."

Ma's voice had a distinct edge to it and the warning bells were ringing loud and clear.

My mind began to race, what could I say? I couldn't tell her

I'd been playing 'chasey' round the gents urinals on Scotswood Road, she would go berserk.

"Aiirr…Chrissy Thorburn fell going round the corner opposite Annie James' shop. He was carrying two milk bottles and he fell right on top of them. He's got over twenty stitches in his hands and arms. What a mess he's in, but the worst thing is, he bit his tongue when he hit the ground and he's had to have six stitches in that as well."

That did the trick; she lost interest in where I had been.

"Eee, the poor little bugger, is he all right then?"

The story was true and had happened earlier that day, exactly as I had told it. Only, I omitted to say what time the incident had taken place and its relevance to my being late for curfew. I discovered at a very early age that if you told your story with conviction and maintained a certain demeanour, you could get away with almost anything.

Ma was kind and maternal a lot of the time, but her quick temper frequently let her down.

It couldn't have been easy for her during the war. My father was conscripted into the army on the 24th of November 1940; leaving her to earn her living, run the house and bring me up at the same time. I'm sure frustration must have played a big part in her mood swings.

My earliest recollection of life was sometime in 1937 when the King and Queen visited the Northeast after their coronation. Although I was very young, I can remember being wrapped in a blanket and carried out to see the cavalcade of vehicles as they passed along Scotswood Road. Cars were a rarity in those days, and to see five or six together was a spectacle indeed.

My mother's family lived a few doors down from where we lived in Cannon Street. There were her four sisters, Grace, Jenny, Betty (who I called Liz), Doreen (who we all called Dot) and Robert, her only brother. My four aunts and one uncle were more like brother and sisters to me. I have always called them by their first names, only referring to them as aunt or uncle in a jocular manner. Grace, the eldest after my mother, was a lot like my Nanna (her mother) always considerate and much quieter than the others. Jenny was a very smart girl, confident and very attractive. She always seemed to be in charge of whatever the other girls were doing.

Betty was a little different from the others. She used to tell such tall stories; how this or that man had bought her a box of chocolates; (she worked for Hamilton's, a local confectioner's on Scotswood Road and I think we all knew where the chocolates were coming from) how her boss was going to put her in charge of her own shop; (at 15 years of age) how every male customer asked her for a date.

My Granda (her father) often used to say...
"If our Betty told me it was day-light I would have to go outside and see for meself before ah believed it." But I loved her dearly and I like to think the feeling was mutual.

Dot, was the youngest of my aunts and certainly the daftest (in the nicest possible way) always full of fun and 'carry on'. I don't know if this is from memory or from my imagination but I'm sure it happened.

It was a lovely summers day and Ma had just finished dressing me, she handed me to my 'Auntie Dot' who was about seven or eight years old at the time and she carried me through to the front room. Then she sat me on my high chair and fastened me to it with a pale blue silk muffler (worn by most men in the 1940's). The chair had no tray or safety arms so the scarf was obviously a precaution to prevent my falling. I must have been no more than six months old. I think she preferred me to one of her dolls.

One thing I know happened one day in 1942, which I will never forget; my first day at school.

I stayed at my Nanna's house on the night before. Robert (my uncle) and I shared the single bed in the front room; my Nanna and Granda were in the double bed. The fire had been lit earlier and the room was lovely and cosy. Rob and I talked for a long time after the gas light was turned off, and I remember clearly telling him there was no way I was going to start school next day.

Next morning, Nanna washed my face and neck and plastered my hair down with Brylcreem. I had a new fairisle pullover and a pair of short pants made out of a black skirt, which had belonged to one of the girls. I put on my first ever cap, not new, and my coat, which was traditionally a navy blue Burberry, again not new.

The walk to school was all up hill via Glue House Lane, St. John's Road, and James Street, to Elswick Road School. From the bottom of James Street the big red brick building looked more like Colditz. The black spike tipped railings seemed to be saying 'Once you're in here, you'll never get out.'

The sight of this chamber of horrors that I had already conjured up in my mind was the last place I wanted to spend the next nine years of my life, so I turned and ran.

At that moment a very strange phenomenon took place. I was conscious of a tightening in my shirt collar and although I took several swift strides I didn't seem to be getting anywhere.

The voice of my Auntie Dot seemed very close to my left ear, in fact so close I could smell the pear drops she had in her mouth.

"No you don't Willix," she said as she suspended me by my shirt collar.

"This is the way to school."

I was dragged towards the school gate kicking and screaming and trying with all my strength to escape. Although I was quite strong for my age I could not break free. Then Dot's friend, Pat, came to her assistance, and between them they carried me bodily, by the arms and legs, and dumped me into an empty classroom to await my fate. My two captors then stood guard at the door, until a teacher arrived.

Miss Collins was a very nice lady. She was wearing a tweed skirt and a bright red jumper. Her smile was warm and friendly as she asked...

"And what is your name?"

But I was a little horror. I refused to give her my name or address or co-operate in any way.

"Now this is very silly," she said, her mouth tightening ever so slightly as she spoke.

"You must tell me who you are and where you are from?"

"Al not!"

I could here the sharp intake of breath, as she fought to keep control. I sensed she was dying to strangle me, but her kindly image was too precious to her, and I knew it. After several more attempts she finally cracked. She bent down and put her nose about two inches from mine and with another sharp intake of breath whispered, through clenched teeth...

" Now listen, you little so-and-so, if you don't give me your name, I will take you to the head mistress, who will not be as tolerant with you as I have been."

Well, with the blunt end of her pencil almost through my chest, I decided to co-operate. There was no way I wanted to tackle Miss Beating, the head mistress, with a reputation that matched her name. I tearfully admitted who I was and where I was from and that I was just past my sixth birthday and had just started school now, 'because I had been evacuated to Stony Stratford'.

By this time the other children were coming into school and I was ushered into the hall with the rest of my class for morning assembly. I vividly remember singing 'All Things Bright And Beautiful' and Miss Beating conducting at the front with her arms flailing about, and her head bowing deeply with every 'The Lord God made them all.' She was your archetypal 1940's Head Mistress – steel grey hair tied back in a bun, spectacles, with lenses as thick as milk bottle bottoms, and a moustache that would have done any man proud. A 40+ bosom, strained at the cream silk blouse tucked into a below knee length skirt (which appeared to be made from a couple of very large sugar sacks) printed with a brown and green tartan-like pattern.

All of this was topped with an extra large navy blue cardigan, which covered almost everything and matched nothing. She was a perfect model for the Head Mistress of 'St. Trinnians', as portrayed in the films by the actor Alistair Sim.

She was so enthusiastic about the hymns and prayers, singing along with us and saying the prayers louder than anyone else.

"Now children: 'We thank You Lord for all Your Love'. This hymn is to say thank you to God for looking after us each day: for protecting us against all evil and for guiding us down the paths of righteousness. Now before we sing the hymn, anyone who knows what the 'paths of righteousness' means, please hold up your hands. Oh, not too many, so I had better explain.

The 'paths of righteousness' means, literally, the paths of rightness, or the right way to conduct our selves in society. How we treat each other. How we respect each other. How we love each other. They are all very important aspects of living together peacefully, and it is most important to realise that whatever paths we decide to take will affect us for the rest of our lives."

Everyone was silent; they seemed to be listening to Miss Beating so intently: whether they understood or not was another story. She ended by saying…

"Remember children, God loves everyone, good or bad and His Son came down from Heaven to persuade the good to help the bad to be better. So we must all try to follow His teaching.

Love thy neighbour as thyself, and if you take that path you will get love and respect in return.

Now we'll have, We Thank You Lord for all Your Love".

By this time my legs were aching from standing so long in one place. I was pleased to get back to the classroom to have a sit down. Morning assembly was more like morning marathon.

Miss Collins introduced me to the rest of the class.

"This is William Flannigan and he has just started school today."

She was very nice and I regretted being a pain earlier.

"Is there anyone in the class who knows William?" she asked.

Several children put their hands up but I only recognised Jimmy James, our coal man's son.

"Oh, you know James. Well he is in the top half of the class. So I'll sit you next to Stuart Gray and he will show you how we do 'add and subtract' cards".

Stuart showed me six cards, rather like large playing cards. Each one had a number of green hearts on one side and red hearts on the reverse. The green hearts had to be taken away from the red hearts and the answer had to be written on a slate. So if there were six green hearts on one side and eight red hearts on the other, the answer would be two.

I understand it now, just, but at six years old I couldn't get it into my head. I didn't want to ask for help and finally I burst into tears.

Miss Collins was so concerned as she squeezed herself onto the small bench seat beside me. She put her arm around my shoulder and talked me through the cards. I was so relieved when I finally grasped what was required. I had so much to learn, and so much catching up to do, having missed over twelve months of schooling.

This day had been charged with emotion.

It was the first day in my life when someone, other than my mother, had instructed me to do something. The first day in my life when I had to stay somewhere I didn't want to be.

Why did I have to know that 8 minus 6 left 2: what good

would that be to me if I were starving of hunger?

Why did I have to drink that whole bottle of milk?

I hated it.

Why was I here at all?

Chapter Two

"Biiillleee."

Oh no, not again, not twice in one week. How could I be so stupid?

She only shouts when I'm late, so I must be late.

The 9 o'clock buzzer summoning the night shift workers to their various factories had just sounded and while I was only ten seconds away from home I was also only ten seconds away from danger.

My friends and I had been playing 'stairs' (a game devised by my father's half brother) in the Armstrong's subway on Scotswood Road and we had lost track of time. None of us possessed a watch and when the buzzer sounded we were all taken by surprise. All of my pals were on the same curfew as me so we all made our way home, rapidly!

I raced up Edgeware Road and tentatively peeped around the corner of our street. Ma was standing at the front door with her arms folded across her chest. I had encountered this pose on several occasions and I knew it represented at least a clout. It was too risky to just walk straight past her, so I remained at arms length.

"Have you been shouting of me?" I said tentatively.

You would swear she had just been branded with a red-hot branding iron. Her arms unfolded in a flash, revealing a pair of metal curling tongs (which were heated and used for hair styling before perms and electric rollers). She aimed a blow at me in the same instant, but I was just a little too quick for her, and she missed. There was a loud 'clonk' as the tongs struck the cast iron drainpipe attached to the side of the house. It sounded like a large church bell with a crack in it. Our upstairs neighbour's bedroom window shot open, (the pipe went all the way up to the roof and was very close to her window).

"Eee, what was that noise, Mary?" she shouted down to my mother.

Mrs Hutchins was wearing a white night cap, which looked like a large tea cosy. A pair of black-rimmed spectacles were perched on the end of her nose and her white night dress was buttoned up to her chin. She was like some character from one of Dickens' novels.

Ma was standing at the edge of the pavement looking up at her.

"It's all right Jean, it was just our Billy knocking his bike against the drainpipe," she lied.

"Oh, thank goodness for that, I thought the Germans had landed or something," she muttered as she closed the window and drew the curtains.

I dodged the half-hearted swipe from my mother and was in the kitchen by the time she came in. I was standing on the other side of the room with the dining table in between her and myself. It was always wise to keep some distance between us, just in case she decided to launch an attack. It was a relief to me to see the smile on her face as she came through the door.

I'd had a bad experience with the curling tongs several weeks earlier when an 'officer of the law' called and informed my mother that someone had reported to the Police that I had been seen putting old coins on the tramlines. Not only was it illegal it was also very dangerous and I could be fined for 'reckless behaviour'. Also there was the question of defacing the effigy of the monarch, which was also illegal. When the policeman left, the likelihood of further action was distinctly possible; or so he said.

"Did you put things on the tramlines?"

Ma's attitude was very threatening. She was sitting on the fender curling her hair with the hot tongs.

"Yes but it was only two ha'pennies and they were Queen Victoria and she's dead." I replied, rather lamely.

She was still facing the fire when her left arm shot out with the tongs in her hand. I was struck squarely on the forehead with the hot metal, which burned the skin and one of my eyebrows. My injuries were only superficial but I didn't fancy that happening again so I made the table my first line of defence.

She looked at me and burst out laughing.

"Poor old 'Hutchy', she must have nearly died when I banged that drain pipe," she giggled.

"Did you hear what she said? She said she thought the Germans had landed!"

By this time Ma was crying with laughter and I felt it was safe enough to join in.

In the early 1940's most houses had outside toilets. The kitchen acted as the lounge or sitting room and the scullery was used as a dining room, washhouse and cookhouse. The 'front room' was where the best china cabinet was situated, along with the best furniture and an array of houseplants, usually geraniums.

Everyone who lived in Cannon Street seemed to be related in some way or another. Nanna and Granda Mills, and all of my aunts and uncle lived at No.14 (my mother's family). Granny Robson lived at No.22, with her second husband Nichol, and their two sons, Nichol and Ronnie. Christopher Flannigan (Dad's brother) and his wife Anne lived at No. 17, and we lived at No. 54. There were several cousins and distant relatives, also living close by. Granny Robson was originally married to my other grandad, Christopher Flannigan; so I was in quite a unique position for those times, I had three grandfathers.

Granda Mills joined the Army in 1914, when he was only seventeen years old. It didn't take him long to realise that the army wasn't the place for him, so he deserted. Although he was under age for the services, he obviously didn't realise that he could have been released quite legally. He was absent for several weeks and even had time to marry my Nanna. By the time the authorities finally caught up with him, he had reached his eighteenth birthday. It was too late to be released for being under age, so he was sent back to win the war with Germany.

'Home by Christmas', that was the slogan adopted in 1914 by politicians and soldiers alike. No one bothered to say which Christmas. It was true for some. They came home in there thousands, maimed, blinded and shell-shocked; the cannon fodder for the War Machine. My Granda was one of them! At least he did come home. There were thousands of other poor souls who never saw their homes again.

In July 1916 more than 60,000 German and Allied troops were killed on the first day of the Somme campaign.

The poem Flanders Fields by Canadian medical officer John McRae summed up the carnage with these immortal words:

In Flanders Fields the poppies blow
Between the crosses row on row
That mark our place and in the sky
The larks still bravely singing, fly
Scarce heard amid the guns below.

We are the Dead. Short days ago
We lived, felt dawn, saw sunset glow
Loved and were loved, and we lie
In Flanders fields.

Sadly he became on of the crosses.

Private Robert Mills was shipped to France shortly after being found guilty on the lesser charge of being AWOL
(absent without leave). Had he been eighteen before he deserted he probably would have been court marshalled and shot! Ironically, the Germans did just that shortly after he reached the front. He was shot in the left calf, not a life threatening injury, but the lack of proper medical care, and albeit unintentional neglect resulted in gangrene infecting the wound. The inevitable amputation swiftly followed.

I remember listening to my Granda's stories of his younger days. Witnessing illegal 'bare-knuckle' boxing matches, swimming in the river Tyne, riding on his cousins 'Moon Rocket' at the hoppings on the Town Moor, and how he became one of the twenty-odd thousand men and women who worked for Vickers Armstrong's on Scotswood Road. Never once did he mention the war, or his injury, or even if he had suffered much pain. It was just as though it had never happened. In 1953 he was admitted to Dunstan Hill Ex-Servicemen's Hospital, to have a piece of metal removed from his stump. It had been moving around slowly since 1914 and suddenly came to the surface. It required only minor surgery and Granda was in great spirits when I visited him after his operation.

"Ah bet that 'Jorman' who shot me never thought it would take nearly forty years for the bullet to gan through me leg. It doesn't say much for their guns mind, does it?"

That was the only time I heard him say anything about his injury, or the war.

Granda Robson (who was really my step-grandfather) worked for William Younger as a Drayman. He delivered the huge wooden barrels of beer to the local Public Houses, of which there were many. Twenty-seven in total along the three miles of Scotswood Road, and over three hundred in three square miles. He was a very big man, well over six feet tall, and he terrified me. If I was sent on an errand to my Granny Robson's at No. 22, I never walked straight into the house. I would knock first and pray that he wasn't in. Three knocks on the cast iron knocker, wait, and then the glass door in the passage would slowly open and there stood this huge mountain of a man, with his braces dangling at his sides.

"Wha di ye want?" he would roar.

I would blurt out my message, and sprint back to the sanctuary of No. 54.

Many years later, when he was terminally ill with cancer, he told me how much fun he used to get out of scaring me half to death.

"I could hardly keep from laughing," he said, "as you shot out of the front door."

I also learned that my father was part of the conspiracy, sending me on trivial errands to No. 22. I often wondered why I was sent so many times. Now I know!

Granda number three was Christopher Flannigan (or so he told us). There was speculation about whether his name was Flannigan or Escott. No one seemed to know for sure, and he refused to confirm or deny either.

I met him for the first time when he returned to Newcastle after living in Manchester for many years with his stepdaughter, my Aunt Kitty. He was over 85 years old and still tall and upright, but turning a little deaf. I liked him instantly, and our meeting was very emotional for me.

He married my Granny when he was 42 and she was just 17. They had five children, three boys and two girls. My father was the eldest son, and the only one of the five who was fully fit. His brothers Benny and Chris both suffered from severe epilepsy and the two girls had frequent bouts of depression. My father always maintained that the vast difference in age between his mother and father caused the illness genetically. Epilepsy had a bit of a social stigma attached to it at this time and to some degree this still persists today. The treatment was often more suitable for mentally ill patients than epileptics.

'Old Flannigan', as my father so irreverently called him, spent a lot of his early years in show business. He was known as Christopher Flannigan 'The Silver Voiced Tenor'. We never found out if Flannigan was his real name, or his stage name. My father always maintained he changed his name from Escott to avoid detection by either the law or another family he had deserted. George Formby Snr. The father of the popular 1940's comedian George Jnr. headed the group of performers that he toured with.

During one tour of the country Granda met the Irish songwriter James Lynam Molloy, who reputedly showed him the manuscript of his latest composition. He was very impressed with the song and offered to 'plug' it for him in an effort to get it published. This was a popular way of introducing new songs to the general public before the advent of sound recording. The success of any song or piece depended entirely on the sale of printed sheet music.

Having already written several successful songs, Molloy declined Granda's offer but was unaware that 'Old' Flannigan intended singing his song in public anyway, with or without his consent. He wasn't consulted about this and was furious when Granda became the first man in the world to sing 'Loves Old Sweet Song' (Also known as 'Just a Song at Twilight').

The song was eventually published in 1894 and with the help of the then famous ballad singer Antoinette Sterling; it became an all time classic.

No thanks to 'The Silver Voiced Tenor', he adopted it as his signature tune and Dad said he always sang it when he was maudlin or drunk.

The words were by Clifton Bingham and were often sung by the great Irish tenor 'John McCormack'…

Just a song at twilight when the lights are low
And the flickering shadows softly come and go
Though the heart be weary sad the day and long
Still to us at twilight comes loves old song
Comes loves old sweet song…

When his singing career came to an end Granda bought a Newsagent business in Perth, Scotland. This was followed by a Cobbling business, and a Billposting franchise. All three were quite successful, but he was drinking quite heavily, and it soon became apparent that this was to the detriment of the business. He moved back to Tyneside and settled in Gateshead, where he built up a very good cobbling business, which lasted for many years.

The demon drink finally ruined his business and his marriage. He left home in the 1930's, and never returned. The family lost touch with him completely, and only saw him again in 1951, shortly before he died.

My Nanna's brother Tommy Jackson was my Uncle Tommy for over fifty years, and we never lost touch. His three other sisters were Aunt Bella, Aunt Edna and Lizzie (who I never knew, she died very young). They were all sent to a children's home, after their parents died. It must have been a good character builder, because they all had special qualities.

My Nanna, Mary, was the youngest of the four sisters. She was a wonderful person, slim, dark and in her youth very beautiful. She was the apple of my eye, and I of hers. I adored my Nanna and couldn't wait to see her every day. Just to be with her was a joy. I used to help her to shake the mats in the back lane, and shovel the coal in, after the 'coal man' had delivered her weekly ration.

But Nanna was never very well, and in between good spells, there were long spells of illness. She was always very pale and looked much older than her 40 plus years.

Early one June morning in 1943, I woke up to find my mother's bed empty, and the hubbub of voices coming from the kitchen. It was a lovely day and the sun was streaming through the bedroom window. I remember it as though it was yesterday. I got out of bed to find the whole family in deep distress. I started to cry before anyone said anything. I didn't know what was wrong, but I knew it was serious. Then came the bombshell. My mother managed, in between sobs, to tell me my beloved Nanna had died during the night. I was sitting on the arm of one of our chairs at the table under the window. I looked down at the blue and yellow 'lino' tablecloth and remember saying…

"But why? She was only bad, she wasn't really ill."

I was inconsolable. I cradled my face in my arms and just sobbed and sobbed.

My mother said I was not to be so sad, as my Nanna would still be able to see me from up in heaven, and it would make her very unhappy if she saw me like this.

When I saw her for the last time, she was more beautiful than I had ever imagined. She was dressed all in white like a bride, lying so peacefully, in the front room. I could smell the geraniums on the windowsill, and to this day they still remind me of her. I tended her last resting-place with my mother for many years and I still have the cemetery gardener's plant new flowers for her.

I will end up with her again when my time comes. That will be one good thing that comes out of leaving this life. I still have dreams about her that are very real, and I'm sure she still thinks of me.

Chapter Three

April 11th 1941: I was five years old, and today was my birthday. I waited anxiously for the postman to arrive. My mother and I were living in a boarding house in Stony Stratford, near Banbury. I suspected there had been some trouble between my parents, as Dad was in the army and Ma was alone. I don't think they trusted each other, and I learned years later that this was in fact the case. Their marriage went through a very difficult time, as did many others during the war years. Dad was stationed only a cycle's ride away, so he was able to visit us whenever he was off duty. Being together again seemed to help my parents in their relationship, and we stayed there for about a year.

Marion and Harry Charlton owned the house we lived in. American servicemen rented several of the rooms; they were very friendly and really kind. I was never short of sweets or chocolate, which were in very short supply during the 1940's.

Marion was quite a nice person, but very strict. The house was always being cleaned, and poor 'henpecked' Harry, did most of the work. He would often slip away with his newspaper, and I would find him sitting on the stone staircase leading down to the cellar, smoking a Woodbine and reading the newspaper. A stream ran through the cellar and I used to have many adventures down there. Sailing paper boats till they were out of sight. Catching frogs and playing all the usual children's fantasy games.

Harry was a rather eccentric character, who seemed to live in his own little world. There was a large garden at the back of the house, with a very large wooden shed full of junk. It was an Aladdin's cave for a five-year-old. The outside toilet was also made of wood, and was another one of Harry's favourite reading rooms. Often after playing in the shed I would make my way into the house past the wooden loo. Harry would be sitting there reading his paper, with his trousers 'round his ankles and the door wide open, cigarette smoke spiralled up from the Woodbine on the wooden seat next to him. He didn't even realise anyone was there, or if he did, he didn't care.

Marion seemed to resent her husband having any free time. He was her general dog's body; he peeled the potatoes, washed the dishes, cleaned the fireplaces and anything else she could think of, for him to do. He complained loudly, all of the time, to the two Persian cats, to the frogs in the cellar, and to Marion, but only when she wasn't there!

For a while Dad worked as a cook in the Officers Mess. Being in charge of all of the stores placed him in a position to supplement our rations with little tit bits. For example, real eggs, jam that didn't taste of turnips, tinned cheese, sugar and much more. He called it constructive management, or in plain English, stealing. He would bring white flour for making bread; this was not just scarce; it was totally unobtainable by the general public. Most of our flour was imported from America, and then mixed with bran and other products introduced by the Ministry of Food, in order to stretch the supplies. The result was very dark bread, not brown, more like a dirty grey. My mother used to sift the flour through an old silk stocking in an effort to remove the bran and other impurities. The amount of black and grey particles that she separated from the flour was quite considerable: sometimes as much as a third of a three-pound bag. This practice was illegal and anyone found guilty of sifting flour could be fined up to £1,000 or 12 months in prison. Since it would take about five years to earn £1,000, the prospect of spending 12 months in prison, with free meals and accommodation was more of an incentive than a deterrent.

Sunday lunch (Sunday dinner to Northeners) was always more of a ritual than just another meal. There was always meat of some kind, Yorkshire pudding, two kinds of potatoes, mash and roasted, and thick brown gravy with bits of onion floating on the surface.

Dad had managed to snare a rabbit one Sunday, and we all waited in anticipation as Marion prepared the meal.

The smell from the scullery was mouth watering. The pans were rattling on the hob and the windows were all fogged up with steam. Harry put my plate down in front of me and being ignorant of the social graces, I started immediately. The food was superb, the Yorkshire pudding, which Dad had prepared, was about an inch thick, saturated in brown gravy, with crispy corners. The rabbit meat just fell off the bone and seemed to melt in your mouth. I was happily wading through this banquet when Dad uttered a loud

"Aarrgh!"

His head shot forward and he spat out a mouthful of food. I thought he had burned his mouth on a roast potato.

"Stop eating everybody. Marion!"

She was still in the scullery.

"Did you not gut that bloody rabbit before you cooked it?"

"Eee Bill, I thought you had done it at the camp."

Dad had skinned the rabbit and removed its head and feet, so Marion had thought it was ready for the pot. She had cooked it with all its entrails still intact. Dad had almost consumed a mouthful of rabbit droppings and Marion's tearful apology did nothing to pacify him. The dinner was over, or more accurately, abandoned. Dad and Harry peeled some more potatoes and we all had chip sandwiches, followed by rice pudding and sultanas. The rabbit affair became a family joke after a while, but Dad never seemed to see the funny side of it. Rabbit meat was eaten very infrequently in the Flannigan household, thereafter.

The postman finally arrived with my birthday cards: one from my Nanna, and one from my Aunts. Grace had written one card out, even at that early age I could recognise her left handed writing. The other card had five rabbits on the front, one for each year, and the message read 'Lots of love to our nephew Billy on your 5th birthday' there were lots of kisses. I missed our Rob and the girls very much, and my Nanna most of all.

I longed to be home.

For a birthday treat Harry took me to the local park. There was a small roundabout called a 'tea pot lid,' a see saw and a banana slide. There were lots of other children in the park that day and I was having a great time. Up the ladder, down the slide: running and jumping onto the 'tea pot lid' while it was still going 'round, all exciting stuff. Harry was totally oblivious to all of this. Sitting on one of the park benches reading his paper, with the ubiquitous Woodbine dangling from his lips. We must have been there some time when my Mother appeared in the distance. I waved to her and I thought I would show her how clever I was on my fifth birthday. I climbed to the top of the banana slide and turned to wave again. The next thing I remembered was landing with a thud on the concrete base. There were no soft landing tiles in those days. Although it wasn't very high and I didn't hurt myself too much, I still had all of the wind knocked out of me.

Poor old Harry, I thought my Mother was going to kill him.

"He's alright, he's alright" Harry said slowly, wondering if I really was all right.

"He's not alright, he's just fell off the top of there you bloody idiot, how can he be alright?"

Ma's voice was raised now and all of the kids were looking at her and Harry.

"You can't even look after one child for a few minutes, God help you if you ever have kids of your own."

Poor man; he adjusted his trilby hat, put his newspaper into the pocket of his brown overcoat and just walked away.

The two other lodgers in the house were both lorry drivers. They were working on a new aerodrome for the RAF, transporting 'quarry waste' for the foundations of the main runway. When Ma and I got back to Marion's, Jim the younger of the two had just come in from work.

"Good gracious what's all the tears about, and on your birthday as well" he said as he lifted me onto his knee.

Ma told him about my nosedive from the top of the banana slide and about the 'useless sod' who was supposed to be looking after me.

"Well now I'll tell you what we're going to do." He said.

"Seeing as how you've had a disastrous birthday, I think, if it's all right with your mum, you should come to work with me tomorrow in my lorry; that is if you want to."

If I wanted to: I couldn't wait for tomorrow to come. I had been for several walks with Jim in the past but this was to be my first time in his lorry.

Next morning I was up before anyone else in the house. I had my sandwiches wrapped in a tea towel and my bottle of lemonade. Jim and I had breakfast together, and then off we went to work!

I had a fantastic day. The new airfield was enormous. We went to the quarry several times where a huge crane filled our truck with sand-coloured rocks. I very foolishly poked my head out of the window while we were being loaded up and received a large bump from a stray stone.

On the way home Jim said…

"Well what did you think of that? Now you can tell all your friends back in Newcastle how you helped us to win the war, working for a whole day on the new aerodrome."

※

The War seemed to be going badly for us. We were right in the middle of the 'Battle of Britain', and the Germans were trying their best to demoralise the whole nation. Every railway station we passed through on our way back to Newcastle had either been bombed or machine-gunned by the Luftwaffer. Not one pane of glass remained intact in the vast roofs over the station platforms. Lord 'Haw-Haw,' the British traitor William Joyce; was broadcasting a lot of Nazi propaganda from Germany, trying to persuade our soldiers to surrender. Telling the populace how bad the war was going for Britain and the Allies, and how well we would be treated when Hitler was running our country. I don't think he was very popular, if my father's comments were anything to go by.

Most of the people, who were on the train, were either in uniform, or in civilian clothes, carrying large kit bags. In our carriage we had a sailor and two ATS girls. They were very nice to me and I had plenty of attention during the journey. The sailor told me to lie down on the seat opposite him with my head on my mother's lap, while he covered me with his heavy overcoat. When the two girls left the train at Doncaster, they gave me two bars of chocolate, both Cadbury's, one in a blue wrapper, and the other in red. I ate the one in the blue paper, but the red one I kept. It was Cadbury's Bournville, a very dark chocolate that I was even more delighted to get, because I knew it was my Nanna's favourite.

It was quite sad leaving Marion and Harry, knowing that we would probably never see them again. I often wondered what they were doing as I grew older. All I had to remind myself of them were the two kittens we brought home, from their white Persian cat's litter. Their address has always stayed in my memory, 63 Woolverton Road, Stony Stratford.

As far as I remember at this time Grace had left her job at the Lowther Hotel in Newcastle and had joined the ATS. Jenny was working in 29 shop for Armstrong's and Dot and Liz had been evacuated to a farm in Carlisle. It was very strange with the girls being away from home, but my mother promised me we could go and visit the two on the farm in the not too distant future. In the mean time I had my Uncle Robert's undivided attention.

He took me to school every morning but it wasn't the same. He had his own mates now, older than me, so I felt a little bit out of it. I decided I needed to do something to impress him. Something to gain his attention once more, to show him I was as good as his mates.

School was at the top of James Street, which at that time was a very select part of Elswick. The people who lived in these terraced flats were quite well off. Most of them had stair carpet, which we thought only the King could afford!

Every morning I walked past all of these light oak grained doors with black knockers, and numbers to match. Doorsteps all yellow ochred and two empty milk bottles, sparkling clean, with two milk coupons; one blue, one green in the bottom of one of them. The idea of the tokens was mainly to prevent anyone from stealing money left out for the milkman, being of little use to the individual, except to purchase milk. The coupons were blue, green, and pink. Pink being for families with a new baby, these were a little cheaper than the others were. The Co-op, who also owned the dairy, issued all of the coupons. As I surveyed the scene I hatched a little plan. I decided that today, no one in James Street would get any milk.

Rob was three or four yards ahead of me, larking about with his friends, so I just removed the milk tokens from each step as I walked past. It was so easy. I felt very clever and wondered why I hadn't thought of it before now. By the time we reached the top of the street my pockets were bulging with green, pink, and blue coupons, so I put them into my cap and ran back down and started on the other side. We were always early for school so I had plenty of time before the bell for assembly. I hid the booty in the big air raid shelter in the school playground. Retaining a few to show off to the kids in my class.

I really felt proud of myself. No feeling of guilt or remorse. No fear of being found out or punished for this 'criminal act'. Nothing, just total elation, until later…

After morning 'playtime' we all filed back into our classroom. Miss Beating was standing at the door smiling and nodding: she seemed to be in a really good mood as she waited for us to settle back into our seats.

"Sit up straight everyone, hands behind backs."

She always said that, even if your hands were already behind your back.

"Now children," she started, "we seem to have a problem of some missing milk tokens. I am confident that it has nothing to do with any of our children, but I have been asked by Mr. Brown, the Head of the senior school, to see if any of you have heard of anyone possessing any of the aforementioned tokens."

My complexion changed as quickly as a startled chameleon. One minute I was my usual pasty-faced self, the next I was like Hiawather after a ten-mile run. But she didn't notice and I breathed a sigh of relief as she left the room. I realised I had to get rid of the damning evidence secreted in the school air raid shelter, so I decided in my infinite wisdom, to give them away. Not to throw them away like some intelligent person may have done: but to actually give them away.

My desk partner (we sat two to a desk on bench seats with lift up desktops) was a boy named Stuart Gray, a very tall posh kid who I didn't like very much. I could never understand why parents gave their offspring names like Stuart, Garry, Cedric, and Graham, what was wrong with all the traditional names like Geordie, Tommy, Billy, John etc.

Stuart's mother walked him the fifty yards up to school every day. He was just past his seventh birthday and I was six and a half going on fifteen. I moved a little closer along the bench.

"Stuart, I've got some of the lost milk tokens, I found them in the toilets, you can have them because you live in James Street and your mother must have had hers stolen," or pinched, I think I said, as I showed him the half dozen tokens.

I had recently moved up a class from Miss Collins, more because of my age than my ability. My new teacher was Miss Stevens. I remember seeing her, or someone just like her, in the film 'The Wizard of Oz' a few years later; only she left her tall black hat and broomstick at home when she came to school! She looked at Stuart, then at me with her hawk like expression, pointed a boney finger in our direction, and demanded...

"What are you two talking about?"

Well, me being a natural born liar, I could have brazened it out with some 'cock and bull' story, but my idiot friend, turned bright purple and blurted out.

"Please Miss, he's got some milk coupons."

I could have punched him, as I had done on many occasions. This was it; this was how he was going to get even with me. He knew he couldn't 'fight' me, so he stooped to treachery. I tried desperately to convince Miss Stevens that the coupons were in fact his and he was trying to give them to me, but that didn't work. She knew he hated me and wouldn't give me anything, stolen or otherwise. As soon as I realised that I was in it up to my neck, my brain started to work overtime. I needed to come up with something to get myself out of this predicament. When I think back, I am amazed at the ingenuity of a six and a half-year-old, with senses, razor sharp, and a deviousness as mature as any adult.

As I was frog marched to Miss Beating's office I toyed with the idea of making a run for it, or maybe I could throw some water over her and make her disappear; but the firm grip on my shirt told me that wouldn't work. There was only one thing to do. Convince them that I had nothing to do with the theft: but how? The possession of the half dozen tokens was a little damning… The only thing that was diverting my attention away from my perilous plight was, how I could get Stuart Gray away from his mother long enough to give him a good thumping.

Miss Beating couldn't have been more charming. She sat me down on the only chair in her office, which was more like a large cupboard, and smiled as she said…

"Come along now William, we have to know where these tokens have come from."

'Oh William' I thought. My full title was Arthur William Flannigan but I usually got only Flannigan, or on the odd occasion Arthur. I was called Billy by all of my friends and family, but William; I was quite impressed.

I looked down at my hands clasped in my lap, what could I say?

"Did you find them or did someone give them to you?"

I thought, 'saved'!

"Yes Miss, a big lad gave them to me." I sighed, with more than a hint of resignation in my voice.

She smiled at Miss Stevens as she straightened up to her full height.

"I knew it," she said triumphantly.

"I knew it all along, those seniors are always up to no good."

The fact that I had only six tokens tipped the scales in my favour. If I had stolen the thirty odd that were missing, surely I would have had them all in my possession!

Miss Beating took me by the hand and we made our way to see Mr. Brown the senior head.

On hearing the evidence he decided that there was a very simple way of identifying the culprit. I was to be taken round each class in the senior and junior school in an effort to pick out the 'phantom milk coupon thief'.

It came as no surprise to me when I failed to point out the mysterious 'big lad' who had given me the tokens.

The investigation went on for over a week until it was finally decided that the person we were looking for was not from Elswick Road School at all. It must have been one of the older boys from the Catholic school further up the hill. I was completely exonerated and Stuart Gray was suitably sorted out. Our Robert threatened to kill me because he knew I had taken the coupons, but I was soon back in his favour when I handed them over to him. He sold them for three shillings, and I was well pleased with my 'treat' to the pictures on Saturday morning. He even bought me a toffee apple.

After such a close encounter with authority I decided I had had enough of school for a while. I persuaded Rob to let me go (or not go) to school on my own. I say persuaded, but I think blackmailed would be more appropriate. Under the threat of my Granda being told that he had sold the stolen milk tokens, he capitulated.

"If you 'play the wag', I'll deny that I know anything about it, but I won't tell on you".

The weekend came and went along with my enthusiasm for school. The first lesson on Monday morning was 'reading' and I didn't like that very much. During my first few weeks in Miss Collins' class I had been selected with five other children to read aloud, from our current book, in front of the whole class. Three boys and three girls and each had to read a paragraph from 'Billy Bun', book number three in the reading programme. The girls read their pieces with no trouble at all and I followed the story as they completed each paragraph. I even forged ahead to where I thought I would have to start.

The 'word' hit me right between the eyes. It looked more like Greek than English. I had never come across it before in any of the previous books. How was it pronounced? No matter how many times I spelled it out I just could not make it into a word. It must be a mistake! Not only was it a mistake, but also a double mistake, the word was repeated after just a comma and nothing else. The first boy read his paragraph and the second boy started his. He was a good friend of mine and we lived only three doors away from each other in Cannon Street. In fact his grandparents owned most of the houses in the street along with the local corner shop and coal business. Jimmy James was very bright, and a good reader. He raced through the first sentence, the paragraph, then straight on to my piece.

"Enough, enough, cried Billy Bun."

So that was it, eenuff. My sigh of relief could be heard right at the back of the class. 'Eenuff', why couldn't they print it like that, who in his right mind would believe that ENOUGH would be pronounced EENUFF? Jimmy had saved my life, which I was to reciprocate under slightly more serious circumstances many years later. I had worked the pronunciation out as near enough, eenogg, but I didn't have a clue as to what it meant, or if it meant anything at all. As we turned the page with Jamesy still reading, I saw the two most welcome words, in slightly bolder type, at the bottom of the page – The End.

Miss Collins stopped him at the end of the sentence and I carried on to complete the last few lines, which incidentally contained another 'eenogg'.

We all received a boiled sweet for our efforts, the kind of sweet that would be regarded as a lethal weapon today. The teachers would probably end up in the European Court of Human Rights for attempted genocide if they gave them to five and six year olds today. But we liked them, and they usually broke before our jaws did.

As we approached the red brick 'pain factory' my mind was made up. How could they possibly miss one boy out of all the others attending school? It would take them a week to find who it was and I would be back by then. The thinking was a little naïve maybe, no, more stupid than naïve.

I looked at Rob, as I turned left, away from the school gate. He just shook his head and looked away as I made my way back to Elswick cemetery.

I climbed over the grey sandstone wall using the little stumps of iron railings left by the council workers, when they cut them down for scrap for the war effort. I walked across the grass and in amongst the gravestones. No one would ever find me in here; I knew the place as well as I knew my own front room. Most of the headstones were either grey marble or red granite, all very large and ornate. Some had whole families in one grave. On one it read, 'Richard Townsend

1849–1904, husband of Rose, father of Richard and Angela, R.I.P. (R.I.P.–Rest in Peace is usually put on Catholic headstones)'. How old was he when he died? I didn't have enough fingers to work it out; I was still having difficulty taking seven away from ten and ending up with three. I settled for about ten times older than me, which wasn't correct but close enough.

'How do you live to sixty? It must take years' I thought, I hope I don't live that long. I think thirty would be long enough for most people. Imagine having to work down the mines for fifty years, or in the Tanyard, amongst the evil smelling animal hides, or even worse, as a teacher at Elswick Road School; no thanks not for me. Thirty would do nicely.

I congratulated myself on my choice of days not to attend school. It was nice and warm and I was sitting on a cool gravestone of red granite, inside the biggest mausoleum in the cemetery. It was almost as big as the chapel where the services were held. The grey sandstone spires were blackened from pollution created by factories, old steam trains and coal burning domestic fires. The door to the crypt was solid steel and I had no success trying to open it. It would have made a great gang hut, or even my own personal 'smeck'. Maybe I could try later with the help of some friends.

Hunger was something often endured during wartime but I'm afraid I wasn't very good at enduring. I was hungry, and that was the most important thing in my life at that moment. I needed something to eat. I had missed my bottle of free milk, which I was quite pleased about, but now I realised it was the milk that stopped the hunger pangs every day as dinnertime approached. I had no idea what time it was but it seemed as though I had been in the cemetery for days. Then suddenly the long drawn out wail of the 'twelve o'clock buzzer' droned out, signalling the start of the lunch break for the factory workers. It was in a slightly different key to the air raid siren, so to the trained 1940's ear it presented neither fear nor panic. No dash for the nearest air raid shelter or the cupboard under the stairs, and it was safe to leave your gas mask in its little brown cardboard box.

Over 20,000 people poured out of the various exits along the three miles of Scotswood Road. From a birds eye view it must have looked like a giant anthill disgorging its entire population of blue overalled ants. The noise from the multitude of boots, studded from heel to toe with 'hob' nails, could be heard long before they came into view: each owner bending forward to compensate for the steep incline that was Glue House Lane. Everyone was wearing some kind of jacket from an old lounge suit over a blue bib and brace overall, with an oil stained cap perched jauntily on one side of the head. They all seemed to be at least 60 years old, with the exception of one or two fresh-faced apprentices. The absence of young men from 18 upward was painfully obvious. They had all vanished overnight when the government introduced conscription.

The definition of conscription in the Oxford English Dictionary is, 'compulsory enlistment for state service, especially military service', from the Latin, conscriptio, meaning enrolling.

What the dictionary fails to define is the army version of conscription, which is the complete stripping of your human rights. Your dignity is flushed down the toilet with several sheets of Izal glass faced toilet paper. You are transformed into a thing, which can only be identified by a number. Your hair is shaved off; a scrawny old bloke in a white coat squeezes your testicles, but you're not allowed to scream in agony, oh no! You're only allowed to cough!

Everyone in the army is deaf! They all shout questions at you at the top of their voices and you have to reply at the same volume. You know you had parents when you were called up, but somehow once every conscript gets into uniform he becomes a 'useless bastard' who'll never be any good for anything. That's the army version of conscription, that and all of the other indignities endured by the young men who were forced to go to war and die for their country.

The Mines, the Steel works, the Merchant Navy, the Fishing fleet were all so much more attractive after a few weeks in the army. But sadly a lot of them never returned to find out.

I raced down from the cemetery and took my place on the step in front of Annie James' shop. The step was over ten inches high at one end and only an inch at the other due to the entrance being on the bank. Standing on the high part I was almost as tall as the men hurrying past me.

"Ha yi got any spare bait mister?" No response.

"Ha yi got any spare bait mister?" I repeated.

It always took a little time for something to happen but I didn't despair. I'd had plenty of experience at this. Soon I had several little parcels of food left over from the morning ten o'clock break. When the stream of workers started to thin out I opened the half dozen parcels of 'spare bait' that had been handed to me, all neatly wrapped in newspaper.

Two palony sandwiches, one cheese and onion, four Jacobs cream crackers, a stotty sandwich (home- made bread) with brown sauce running down the edges and two digestive biscuits. The stotty sandwich turned out to be a brown sauce sandwich, which I left for the birds. I made my way to the old derelict buildings in Back Cannon Street and laid my dinner out on the windowsill of one of the empty houses. After consuming all of the food I had begged, I needed something to drink. I had never been able to eat anything without a drink, a problem that persisted through to adulthood.

The safest place would be my Nanna's house. The door was never locked and even if she caught me I could easily make up a story about school to cover my truancy.

I was anxious not to be seen by anyone who knew me and peered cautiously around each corner to see if the way was clear. Back up Glue House Lane to Annie James' corner shop, which was only thirty yards from my goal. I stood on the low end of the step and glanced 'round the wooden doorway. I found I was looking straight into the eyes of my Nanna's upstairs neighbour, Mrs. Morgan She looked at me with that same accusing stare that I had seen several times before. A couple of days earlier she had caught me in her back yard retrieving my ball and I had given her some cheek, so she was delighted to see me acting suspiciously.

"Ah seen yi, ya waggin" she squawked.

"Ah'll tell ya mother", and off she shot.

Well she certainly kept her word. She told my mother, my Nanna, her daughter Janie, the neighbours, and if my memory serves me correctly 'The Pope!'

My mother appeared only seconds later; I thought it was an aberration. How in Heaven's name did she get there so quickly?

The 'aberration' grabbed me by the scruff of the neck whilst muttering some strange foreign words through her clenched teeth.

31

'Friggin' was a very popular part of Ma's vocabulary along with 'Kill' and 'For Two Pins'. If anyone had ever given her those two vital pins when she asked for them I would never have reached my sixth birthday. She held me by the back of my coat and rained blows down from the back of my head to my shoulder blades. It was always the same, blows first, questions later.

I was shouting…

"What's wrong? Ah haven't done anything. Whad are yih hittin' is for?"

She hesitated for a second and then shoved me into my Nanna's. So that's how she appeared so quickly, she was in my Nanna's house when Mrs Morgan raised the alarm.

"Your Billy's playing the wag", was all my mother heard, plus the directions to my hiding place (wag is a local slang expression for truancy).

Fancy taking her word for it, fancy punching me on her say-so without giving me the opportunity to lie my way out of it. It was more than flesh and blood could stand.

I ran to my Nanna's protective embrace and pressed my face into her 'pinny' sobbing my innocence. She listened as she always did. She admonished my mother for 'jumping to conclusions', and her 'bad temper', and then proceeded to condemn Mrs. Morgan's story of my playing truant.

"She can't mind her own business, for minding other peoples". She said angrily.

That was sweet music to my ears. I wasn't all that badly hurt, but I always made it sound as though I was being beaten to death. This was a very tactical ploy on my behalf. I had discovered that the louder you screamed the lighter the blows became and, strangely enough, less frequent.

Now it was my turn. I was asked to explain why I was hiding in the back lane, why I was playing truant and for what was I protesting my innocence (once again). I thought, 'if my mother takes me to school tomorrow, the whole milk coupon saga would surely come out. As I had not confided in her about the affair it would be safe to assume that I would have some serious questions to find answers to. So it was confession time. The full story of the 'big lad', who had thrust the stolen milk tokens into my hand and then proceeded to disappear from the face of the earth. How I thought everyone was still blaming me for the theft, and I had 'played the wag' because I was scared to go to school. In case someone like Stuart Gray's mother accused me of punching her son for telling the teacher that I had milk tokens, 'when he knew it would get me into trouble!' It came out just like that, without commas or full stops, or anything else resembling punctuation, just one long sentence accompanied by a few tearful sighs. I didn't think much of the story at the time, but my Nanna was impressed.

"He couldn't of made all that up our Mary at his age, he's still only a bairn!"

So Ma took me back to school the next day. Miss Beating assured her that the milk token incident was closed, and what a silly little boy I was to think that anyone was accusing me of anything.

"We all knew it was someone from the Catholic School all the time," she said without even a hint of religious intolerance.

Fortunately she didn't mention Stuart Gray's 'accident', or anything else that may have incriminated me further. I breathed a sigh of relief when my mother said she was going. She left the school without a backward glance. The look on her face told me never to push my luck this far ever again. She didn't actually call me a liar and she accepted that I was innocent as far as the school was concerned, but the look remained and that spoke volumes. If she ever found out what really happened I didn't need to speculate on what the outcome would be.

After the dust settled, Miss Beating seemed to take a liking to me and I often acted as her 'runner', or message boy whenever she asked for a volunteer, it was much better than 'eight minus six' or 'eenog, eenog'!

Winter arrived with a vengeance in 1942 and seemed as though it would never end. Ma had put my name down for Elswick Road School but fortunately, for me; I was not allowed to start until after the Easter holidays.

As late as March the snow was still drifting to over six feet deep in places. One of those places was our front door. It was even up to the glass panel, which for some unknown reason was called the fanlight. The door seemed to be stuck when my mother tried to open it. She pulled until there was a crack as it broke away from the frozen snow. It was sensational, just a huge block of pure whiteness with the imprint of our front door perfectly formed on its surface.

Deathly silence. Not a sound of trains, trams or people. It was like being on the moon. I thought it was great and couldn't wait to get out with my little sledge that my Granda Mills had made for me. How to get out was the problem. Ma decided we should wait awhile to see if the council workers would come 'round to clear the street.' It was imperative that they cleared our street very quickly as it happened to be one of the main thoroughfares to Armstrong's factories, and the wheels of the war machine had to be kept turning.

The men who emptied our rubbish bins were generally known as 'The Ash Men', not in any derogatory way, it was just that they emptied our bins and all they contained was ash! There were no smokeless zones, no greenhouse effect problems and the ozone layer was something that was too far up in the air and too far over our heads to even think about, let alone worry about. Everyone burned coal on open fires. The fire boiled the kettle, heated the oven and the house. Anything that would burn was used as fuel, with no recycling. Even old jam jars and milk bottles would keep the fire going for an hour or two.

Eventually the sound of men's voices, shouting and laughing could be heard coming from the street. The 'Ash Men' had finally arrived. They were shovelling snow up and loading it onto the back of a tipper lorry. The same lorry I had let the tyres down on, on several occasions, and the registration number just stuck in my mind JTN 164. When it was fully loaded the driver reversed back along the path his colleagues had cleared for him and tipped the snow onto the old building site at the end of the street.

The fall of snow had been really heavy but drifting had caused most of the problems. Everyone was out digging paths through the snow so that the factory workers could get to Armstrong's Elswick factory. They helped the 'Ash Men' to fill the lorry several times and everyone cheered as he emptied his white cargo onto the derelict land, which was rapidly turning into a snow mountain.

My Granda's brother Jim shouted to us through the hole he had made in the snow piled up against our front door.

"C'mon you two, it's clear enough to get right along the street, ya muther's got some broth made."

That sounded very inviting. A basin of Nanna's broth would go down very well on this cold morning.

Uncle Jim was Granda Mills' younger brother; he was Station Officer at the local Fire Station. There were five brothers and sisters in the family, three girls, Jenny, Florence and Elsie, and two boys, Granda Robert and James. Great Grandma Mills was a tiny little woman but ruled with a 'rod of iron'. She always wore long black dresses down to her feet, and her hair pulled tightly back in a silver grey bun. I can remember her scolding my Granda on several occasions and marvelling at his reaction. He never once answered her back, he just sat there looking down at his hands and muttering the odd 'Aye Ma'.

'Uncle Jim' dragged me through the hole in the snow and tucked me under his arm. He carried me along to my Nanna's, and it was the most painful journey I had ever experienced. My ribs were crushed up against his hip and I could hardly breathe. He didn't have any children of his own and it was painfully obvious that he had little or no experience in handling anyone else's. The silver buttons on the sleeve of his uniform made bright red marks on my skin. The more I squirmed the tighter he gripped. I was never so relieved to be hoisted up onto my feet and bundled into Nanna's doorway.

All of this happened in early March of that year, but the snow remained in evidence until nearly the end of April.

I was able to try my little wooden sledge on the mountain of snow at the end of the street. Usually I just used a shovel to sit on and slide down one of the hills, but this winter was different. Granda Mills had made two sledges, a small one for me and a bigger one for Robert. I was happily sliding down the mountain of snow left by the council workers when one of the local bullies decided he would like to try my sledge. He didn't bother to ask if he could borrow it, he just snatched the string out of my hand and ran to the top of the 'slide'. When he reached the bottom I ran to retrieve my sledge, but he just pushed me away and made his way back up the hill. By this time I was crying and begging him to return what was mine, but he just laughed. The next time he reached the bottom I was waiting for him. I had been to our house, which was only 25 yards away, and found myself a weapon. As he rolled off the sledge into the soft snow I ran forward to grab the towrope and pull my sledge away from him. He laughed again, a sickly cruel laugh and pushed me into the snow. I leapt back at him and lashed out with the jack knife my father had left on his last 'leave'. He cried out in amazement as the 'pig sticker' on the back of the knife tore a hole in his jacket.

"Did you see that? That little bastard tried to stab me."

I ran at him again slashing left and right with the knife, but failing to make any contact. He was much older than me but I really scared him. He took my sledge and threw it up into the air and scurried away as I went after him again. It's a pity I wasn't able to get close enough to inflict some damage on him. It may have saved the life of the poor woman he shot and killed a few years later.

Winters in the North East of England are slightly harsher than other areas of the country. The wind chill from the North Sea can reduce the temperature by as much as 10°F below normal. Trying to stay warm without the benefit of double-glazing or central heating and very little coal, magnified the problem ten-fold in the early 1940's. There was no shortage of gas, but that had to be paid for in advance, which restricted its' use much more effectively than rationing. Quarterly accounts were almost unheard of and were mainly for upper or middle class households in Gosforth or Jesmond, not for the likes of us. A penny in the slot meter was all we could afford.

My mother baked every Sunday. By baked, I mean she performed miracles with the meagre rations we had to sustain us in this austere climate. She made cheese scones from sifted flour and tinned cheese from army combat rations, jam tarts with home made jam, cheese and potato pies and occasionally date square, depending mainly on the parcel of 'laundry' which arrived weekly from my father. We had enough to eat, but money was very short. To save a few pennies we used to disconnect the incoming gas pipe: tie an old bicycle inner tube over the end; by-pass the meter and connect the other end to the outgoing pipe; Hey presto, free gas. Ma could cook the Sunday dinner; bake all the treats for Sunday tea and it never cost a penny.

We only did this on Sunday's, as this was the most expensive day of the week. Also there was little or no chance of anyone turning up from the Gas Corporation to catch us stealing their gas.

These were very hard times and a lot of thought went into the day-to-day running of the household. Dangerous and dishonest acts were commonplace, but no one ever stole from a neighbour. No one ever locked their doors. We all had the same, nothing, so nobody coveted their neighbour's possessions.

There was a strong smell of gas when I opened the kitchen door.

"It's always the same when we put the pipe on", my mother explained.

I ignored it for a while, but it seemed to be getting stronger.

"You're right," agreed Ma.

"It does seem to be stronger than before".

The kettle was on the top of the cooker with the gas turned up high and all of the other gas taps were in the 'off' position. There was no sign of damage to the lead supply pipe, but the smell was very strong beside the cooker. The oven was heating up in preparation for the baking to be done that day, so I just opened the door to check that all the jets were lit.

There was an almighty bang. I was thrown backwards by what appeared to be a giant blue hand, which propelled me out of the back door and into the yard. The whole house shook and I screamed in terror, everything went black. I could hear my mother shouting.

"Open your eyes, open your eyes".

But they seemed to be glued together; I couldn't open them!

I was completely stunned and staggered about the yard like my Granda Mills on his way home from the pub on a Saturday night. The hens were running up and down the yard clucking and squawking, and peering very curiously at the back door, as though they were waiting for the next explosion or the siren for the 'all clear'.

Ma sat me on a chair in the scullery and gently bathed my eyes with warm water. I was much calmer now, once I realised that I wasn't dead or even badly injured. Gradually I was able to prise my eyes open and it was such a relief to see the light streaming through the window. My eyebrows had gone completely and the front of my hair was all tiny little tight curls, smelling like cinder toffee. My eyelashes seemed to have melted rather than burned and my eyes were just enormous red rings. The usual pale face had been transformed into a bright red North American Indian complexion, but none of the skin was broken. It was more like a bad case of sunburn and it didn't feel too bad as my mother dabbed a little calamine lotion on the worst affected areas.

The oven had been warming up prior to being 'disconnected' and was not re-lit when the free supply was put into operation. The consequence of this was a build up of gas in the un–lit oven. Although the gas ring on the hob was merrily burning away, the oven was rapidly turning into a time bomb. Had it been any longer before we smelled the gas the consequences could have been very serious indeed. It certainly taught us a lesson and free gas was never an option from that day.

Shortage of money was a constant dilemma affecting most families in the early 1940's. The family provider had been conscripted into HM Forces, leaving the women and older men to take their place. Pocket money and treats were very rare and children became very adept at earning a few 'coppers' for themselves. Running errands for old or infirm neighbours, selling sticks for fire lighting, clearing footpaths in winter and many other things. I had devised my own ways of raising revenue, not always strictly legal but quite effective. A favourite of mine was to stand at the local tram stop rummaging through my pockets. Once someone noticed, I would tell them I had lost my penny tram fare and if they could loan me the penny I would give it back when I reached my destination. It always worked, although sometimes it would take a while, but it always worked. Some kind old lady would always fall for it and hand over her precious coins to this seven-year-old con man. I often had to take a tram ride with the odd person who insisted on paying the conductor the fare rather than handing over the money to me. This worked out even better as I could then ask people who knew me, for help as they made their way home. They usually paid my fare along with theirs and gave me the odd pennies change.

On most days I could earn about a shilling or so but on one occasion during Race Week, when I really did lose my fare home, by way of a 'one arm bandit', I made a lot more. There were two of us, Tomma Brown and me. He sat on the wall at the bottom of Leazes' Park and asked passers by, coming from the 'hoppings', for help towards our bus fares. It was a bonanza, no one refused, we just kept on asking and they kept on giving. When we decided it was time to go home we had over four shillings between us. With me being the eldest I did the sharing out. Thirty pennies for me and over thirty halfpennies for him. He didn't argue about the share out and being so 'young and innocent' I thought it only fair that my share was slightly more than his. After all I did pay his bus fare to the Town Moor and for his ride on the 'Mauritania'. I must be one of the few people to have come back from a day at the 'hoppings' with more money than they took.

Collecting empty bottles was quite a lucrative source of income but it had to be properly organised. There was little point in taking one or two 'pop' bottles at a time; it was much better to have a bag full. It was also very important that the 'empties' were clean.

I was able to collect some bottles from my immediate family who allowed me to keep the deposit on returning them to the local shops. If any were too grubby I washed them in the wooden 'poss tub' in the soapy water left over from the Monday washday, making sure that the labels didn't come off. The next step was to climb over the wall of the local pub and 'retrieve' a few empties from the crates stacked in the yard. It was a simple task to open the back door, stand a few bottles on the pavement, lock the door and climb back over the wall. I took only one or two from each crate not wishing to alert the manager by taking too many. This was not a get-rich-quick operation; this was regular income, not to be spoiled by greed, or overkill. It was always better to have a mixture of beer and soft drinks bottles just to allay any suspicious thoughts the shopkeeper may have.

The older boys had different methods of supplementing their

income and one of these was a very early version of 're-cycling'! They would send us youngsters off around the streets to pick up cigarette ends, or 'dog-ends', as they called them. We were paid a penny for every matchbox we filled. We could also earn more money by helping to manufacture the end product. This entailed cutting all of the burnt ends off the 'dumps', breaking them open and extracting the unused tobacco and piling it up into the middle of the table. Then we added potato peelings, covered it with newspaper and left it over night. The peelings were used to introduce moisture into the mixture, for reasons unknown to me.

Next morning armed with several Rizla cigarette-making machines we rolled the tobacco into new cigarettes. There was no lack of customers as there was a shortage of regular cigarettes due to rationing, but packaging was much more of a problem. Clean, empty packets were quite scarce and were very saleable. One of the best places to find them was in the Cinema. I spent many a night crawling about under the seats in the local picture house collecting, Players Senior Service, Craven A and Woodbine packets, which were the most popular. But any kind would suffice as long as they weren't Pasha, a foreign brand that smelled like tomcats.

All of these little enterprises helped to pass the time in a very constructive way. I'm sure it helped to mould some of the participants into their various careers and occupations. There is no doubt in my mind that my experiences encountered in those early years helped me to survive in business through three deep depressions.

Several other means of making extra money came along at irregular intervals but not allowing anyone to make a living from them. Nevertheless they created a little extra income for us youngsters, while they lasted.

Picking coal meant spending hours on the local pit heap (or slagheap) selecting the bits of coal that had slipped through the sorting belt underground. It could take several hours to collect a saleable amount. A pram or bogey was essential to hawk it 'round the houses and you could reckon on a whole day to complete the sale: very hard work!

Then there were the telephone boxes, very few around but they usually dispensed a small amount of cash. The idea was to start on

Scotswood Road and walk to Marlborough Crescent checking each box along the way. Pressing button 'B' to see if anyone had left any money in the meter. It cost tuppence to make a local phone call and when you were connected to your number you had to press button 'A' on the meter. If you were not connected you simply pressed button 'B' and retrieved your money. This technology was far too advanced for our generation and most people were terrified of the telephone anyway, so they often left the box without pressing button 'B', leaving their money for us scavengers. Sometimes the meter required a little persuasion, but they were never vandalised and were almost always in working order.

Last, but certainly not least, there was the 'Fever Grate', fondly named by our parents in an effort to scare us away from them, on the pretext of catching something nasty. It was only the local street drain, which took away any surface water whether it be rain, melting snow or residual water from swilling the pavements, a regular household chore. The soot from coal fires, steam trains and factory chimneys also went into the drain and settled to form a thick layer of black mud in the sump of each grate. This was where the treasure was hidden. The trick was to scoop out the entire contents of each sump and gently pour water over it until it revealed the little shiny objects we were searching for. This had to be done before the Corporation sewage tanker came and sucked it all out, treasure and all, an operation that took place about once a month. Emptying the sump was the worst part of the job and had to be done by hand. The sludge stank to the high heavens but that didn't deter us in any way. The metal grate covering the drain was made of cast iron and weighed in excess of sixty pounds. Fortunately it was hinged at the kerbstone end allowing us to swivel it open into the upright position. If it had of fallen on anyone I think an amputation would have been inevitable.

It was quite exciting sifting through the black mud and we often made it into a game, pretending to be gold prospectors 'panning' for the yellow metal that would make us all rich. We didn't get rich but we often found things of value to us. Marbles, keys, military buttons, coins and even a cigarette lighter were just some of the things that came up to the surface, and of course the odd eel would appear wriggling around, anxious to be on its way to the Sargasso Sea.

One day my friends and I were doing the 'Fever Grates' when we heard several women shouting.

"Somebody pull him out! He's been down there for ages."

They were looking down a hole beside the lamppost outside of Annie James' shop. The man in the hole was repairing a gas leak and had obviously been overcome by the fumes. Two local men passing by dragged the unfortunate individual out of the hole and laid him on the pavement. Mrs Buckton, who lived opposite to the shop, put a cushion under his head and Geordie Flynn, one of the men, started to apply artificial respiration.

The man appeared to be totally lifeless, there was no response at all from his limp body and his head rolled off the cushion and thudded on the pavement. The two men took turns applying the first aid and they seemed quite exhausted by the time the ambulance arrived. I'm happy to say that the 'gas man' recovered fully, due largely to the efforts of the two men who just happened to be in the right place at the right time.

I hated Saturdays! My friends played football or cricket or just walked down to the slaughterhouse at Marlborough Crescent to watch the beasts being transformed from living things into food. But none of this was for me. I had this ball and chain round my leg called 'messages'!

Saturday was definitely the worst day of the week.

The pleasant feeling of not having to go to school was completely overshadowed by the realisation
that it was message day. First stop was the butchers. I had to be there early in the morning to ensure we got a decent cut of meat. The later you were the less likely you were to get what you wanted. It was more than a two-mile round trip, which was nothing exceptional but I had to pass my other two destinations on the way. Ma would not let me do all three in one go. She insisted I did them individually. Her reasoning was, if she spotted an error in the change or any discrepancy in the purchases I could take it up with the culprit on my next trip. I never seemed to be able to work that one out!

The queue at the butchers was right outside of the shop and by the time I got inside I was wishing that I was anywhere else on earth but there. I was kicking the sawdust around the floor when 'Bob the

Butcher' said.

"Right bonny lad, what can I get for you?"

I handed him my note and waited anxiously as he and his sister discussed it. I had no money, so it was obvious that my mother was asking for 'tick' for this week's meat before paying for last week's. I turned bright red with embarrassment when Bob's sister took me into the back shop and proceeded to tell me that this was not the way she ran her business and what did my mother think they were, a charity? I couldn't think of anything to say and 'sorry' at that time was not part of my vocabulary. I just hung my head and sniffed a few times while I 'fiddled' with the blue Ration Book in my hand. I was thinking, 'if I go home with no meat, I may as well join the Foreign Legion or emigrate or something. It might even be a good time to book my place in Elswick Cemetery, because my mother would kill me. Bob's sister took the Ration Book from my hand, opened it on the wooden chopping block and took a rubber stamp out of her blue overall pocket. She breathed on the end of the stamp and pressed it onto a purple pad housed in a brass coloured tin box on her bench. Three little circles the colour of Gentian Violet was stamped into the space marked 'week 22 meats'.

Bob's baldhead appeared around the doorway followed by his left hand holding a large parcel neatly wrapped in newspaper. I took it from him, not taking my eyes off the big red blood stained bandage on his forefinger. He always seemed to have at least one finger bandaged every week. The 'tick' wasn't mentioned again, but I was given a note to take back to my mother. I didn't care about the note. I had the meat and the sausage and felt pretty relieved.

When I got home my second excursion was well prepared for me. It was going to be a little more risky than the butcher's trip, so 'Agent Ma' briefed me like some spy who was about to be parachuted into enemy territory. She opened the green Ration Book at the page headed 'FATS'. I was immediately on my guard, I knew we had had our weeks ration of fats at the local corner shop so what was she up to? Ma had been trying various potions on an old Ration Book to see if she could bleach out the purple dye and re-use the book to get another ration of butter or margarine etc. She had tried white spirit, meths, liquid flux and several other concoctions from my Granda

Mills' French polishing cupboard. This time she had it right. Milton, a well-known cleaning fluid had done the trick. The page marked FATS was as clean as a whistle, slightly paler than the other pages but clean, and not a trace of purple. I felt really proud of her and couldn't wait to go to the Co-op to try it out.

The old gentleman serving on the butter counter opened the Ration Book and looked knowingly at me over the top of his half spectacles. I just stared back. I was convinced that the page was OK so why shouldn't he be?

"What do you want?" he asked gruffly.

"Can I have all butter please, two weeks, this weeks and last weeks?" I replied.

He looked at the book again then marked the page with the purple stamp, and threw it in my direction.

An elderly lady standing behind me remarked,

"Mind he's in a right fettle with eesell the day, that's twice he's flung a ration book like that. What's the marrer, did Hitler distorb ya sleep last night?"

He ignored the comments as he cut a large wedge of butter from the big block standing on the marble slab at the back of the counter. He threw it onto a piece of greaseproof paper, weighed it, cut a small piece off, then he wrapped it up in more greaseproof paper.

"One an' tuppence" he said with a sneer.

It was a lot to pay for just butter, but it was a huge piece. The old man was furious, he knew there was something amiss with our Ration Book but the element of doubt in his mind prevented him from taking it any further. It didn't bother me what he thought, I had my butter and that was all that mattered. What difference did it make to him if we managed to beat the system to get a few more ounces of butter? We still had to pay for it; it wasn't free. I think some of the older men left out of the war thought they were 'doing their bit' for the 'war effort' by trying to catch out people who 'fiddled' the system. I think it was loyalty misplaced; the survivors of this war were as important, if not more important, than those taking part.

We played the 'Milton' game for many years after the war until rationing finally ended. We didn't lose the war because of anything we did during it, so what harm did we do? None at all, I suspect.

Next stop on this sunny Saturday was to Mary Baxter's our fruit and veg. shop. The queue outside, as usual, went right along past Isaac Bendon's newsagent's shop. Another long wait was in prospect, so a visit to Isaac's for a comic to read in the queue was in order.

Mr Bendon was a very nice Jewish gentleman but his shop was absolutely chaotic. Newspapers were piled high, comics, boy's books, magazines, sweets, cigarette cards all strewn everywhere, not a semblance of order. How he ever found anything is a mystery to me.

"Film Fun please Isaac".

His hand reached out without him turning his head as he carried on a conversation with his ninety-year-old mother and the comic landed mysteriously on the box of liquorice comforts in front of me.

"That's last weeks Isaac," I said.

"Have you read it?" he replied.

"No" I answered, slightly confused.

"Then what difference does it make?"

I could see the logic in his statement, but I thought, 'I'm not paying thruppence for last week's comic'.

"I'll give you tuppence for it".

"Alright" said Isaac, "tuppence it is".

I took my place in the queue and opened the comic. Laurel and Hardy on the front and Old Mother Riley and her daughter Kitty inside. These two were played by Arthur Lucan as Mother Riley and Kitty McShane, 'his wife', as Kitty Riley, 'her' daughter! Frank Randal's toothless grin, gormless Enoch and overweight Harry Korris made up the hilarious Hippodrome Gang. Tommy Trinder, Vic Oliver, Abbot and Costello and many more, all from the good old days of 'Variety' and all very funny people. There were very few lady 'comics' in those days but I can remember Elsie and Doris Waters, Dorothy Summers as Mrs Mopp from 'Itma', Joyce Grenfell and the Lancashire soprano Gracie Fields. They all did quite well in 'Radio' and several of them very successfully made the rather difficult transition to films and television.

I had just finished the last page of my comic when Mary Baxter shouted.

"Next".

I gave her my shopping list and she disappeared behind the tall counter. When the order was complete she packed it into my shopping bag shouting out the price of each item as she reckoned up the bill.

"That's one and three for your potatoes, your cabbage is fourpence so that's one and seven, your peas are sixpence that takes it to two and a penny."

And on she went until she reached the final total. I always dreaded this moment wondering if I had enough money. My mother never gave me more than she thought I would need.

Mary said…

"That'll be six and ninepence all told" as she popped the final paper bag of tomatoes into my shopping bag.

Her red face appeared over the top of the counter.

"Are you carrying all this on your own pet? Mind it's very heavy."

"Aye, al manage, al haf to there's only me here."

I handed the three halfcrowns over and waited for my change.

"There y'ar pet, ninepence change, Next!"

This was my third trip along Beaumont Street so I was nearly up to six miles of humping heavy shopping bags. The butchers was first then the Co-op and now the green grocers. I staggered down Glue House Lane and stopped at Chipside's shop for a breather.

Tommy Chipside had a little lending library of old comics and boys books, so I thought I would have a look at what he had while I was resting. I picked out a copy of the 'Adventure' with 'Strang The Terrible' on the front cover. Tommy said it would cost 'tuppence' to borrow it and I would get a penny back if I returned it in good condition. He also agreed to buy my brand new last weeks Film Fun for 'tuppence' so I thought that was a reasonable bit of dealing.

Ma reckoned up the bill for the veg etc. and to my dismay she cried…

"She's overcharged you."

Oh no! Surely I wouldn't have to go all that way back again.

"How's that". I responded.

"I got everything you wanted and you reckoned it would be

over seven shilling."

But as usual she was right and back I went with a note of what we had received and what we had been charged. When it was all sorted out I was given eleven pence back, but my mother had worked it out as only sevenpence, so at least I was fourpence into pocket and I made sure I spent it before I got back home.

I was quite elated as I skipped down Glue House Lane reciting one of my favourite rhymes dedicated to that very popular Jewish gentleman, Isaac Bendon:-

Isaac Bendon king of the Jews
Bought his wife a pair of shoes
When the shoes began to wear
Isaac Bendon began to swear
When the swearing began to stop
Isaac Bendon bought a shop
When the shop began to sell
Isaac Bendon went to hell.

It was very popular for many years and the girls even skipped or played ball games to its refrain; fame indeed for a very nice man who would try to sell you last weeks comic but wouldn't mind haggling over the price.

On Sunday afternoon Granda Mills would read me the latest episode of the 'Bare Knuckle Breed' from one of the Sunday papers. They told stories of the fistfights that took place all over the world in the eighteenth and nineteenth centuries. Granda had witnessed several illegal matches that were still taking place in the early twentieth century. After reading the current episode he would tell me about the fights he had seen. He remembered old champions who fought under the London Prise Ring rules and who fought for twenty, thirty or even fifty rounds, sometimes taking over three hours. One round lasted for as long as it took for one or the other of the contestants to be knocked to the ground.

John L. Sullivan was the last world champion under these rules. He lost his 'title' to 'Gentleman' James J. Corbett under the new rules, wearing boxing gloves. Then there was Bob Fitzsimmons the Cornishman who became world champion at Middleweight, Light Heavyweight and Heavyweight, the only man to achieve three world titles at these weights and the only Englishman to win the Heavyweight title in the last century. I loved the stories but missed my Nanna so much. I couldn't get used to her not being there and gradually my visits became less and less frequent.

I started to go fishing on the Tyne at Wylam. I only had a hand line so I didn't need a license, not that the lack of a license would have prevented me from using a rod if I had possessed one. We caught eels mainly, which were much nicer to eat than they looked. They almost jumped out of the frying pan when you cooked them, even without heads or skin they still jumped about. Potatoes roasted on a wood fire till the skins turned black, fried eels and a bottle of homemade ginger beer, this was living, champagne and caviar didn't have a look in!

My aunts had all worked together and made a fantastic tent for me as good as anything I had ever seen. So if the weather was kind, and permission had been granted by the various parents, we often stayed overnight.

All of our money was pooled to buy a loaf of bread at the local grocers; the rest of our diet lay in the lap of the Gods. Fortunately there were several allotments in Wylam so nightfall meant a visit to one or two of them to see what they were growing. Raspberries, strawberries, apples and rhubarb, together with potatoes and turnips and a bottle of milk from some unfortunate's front step meant we wouldn't starve. If we had been able to afford sugar for the rhubarb we would have settled there forever.

One Sunday morning we congregated at Elswick Railway Station at ten o'clock. Four of us paid at the ticket office while the other four bent low enough to slip underneath the glass panel out of sight of the Porter and straight into the gent's toilets at the other end of the platform (a regular hiding place) until the train arrived. We paid fourpence each, which was the correct fare to Ryton Willis but we always stayed on to Wylam, which was another two pence (2d). The Station Master usually let us through after a little argument about the train not stopping long enough to let us all off or how we had all fallen asleep (at the same time) and missed our stop.

While this was going on the four stowaways slipped away and into the gent's toilets again, making their escape when the official went back to his office.

It was no big deal 'dodging your fare'; it was just a game. Why pay more than you needed to? We did it all the time, on the trams, at the cinema, on the hoppings at Race Week; the occasional clout was the most you had to endure, so it was well worth it.

We walked along the riverbank to our usual 'campsite', a huge oak tree that must have been cut down about fifty years earlier but was now our 'castle'. The two main branches were in the form of a 'Y', which was perfect seating for eight scruffy kids from Elswick. The fork of the 'Y' was where we had our campfire. Sheltered from the wind and with a large circle of pebbles collected from the banks of the Tyne, it formed a perfect cooking range. Whenever I saw that tree in the distance it always gave me a thrill. Like the thrill you get when you've been away from home for a long time and you turn the corner, to find your house and all of the familiar things that go with it are still there unchanged. There was strictly no camping in Wylam, which we ignored completely. What could they do to us, send us packing, chuck us in the Tyne, or give us another clout 'round the ear? All of these we could cope with so Wylam was our camping ground. It was very exclusive; no one ever camped beside us. Maybe the glossy black sign just outside of the station saying, 'Camping in North or South Wylam is Strictly Forbidden', in metallic gold lettering, put them off. It never bothered us; in fact none of us could read anyway, if anyone ever asked!

George Stephenson lived in Wylam for many years and his cottage was just a couple of minute's walk from our tree. Through the bushes, over the railway line and there it was, the home of the man who invented 'The Rocket', the first steam passenger railway engine. I knew all of this but not from school lessons. My Granda Mills was a walking encyclopaedia on local history and took great delight in passing it on to me.

It was normal practice to visit the house several times during our stay, but it wasn't some sort of shrine for us. We knew who had lived there and how important his inventions had been to industry, but the cottage had one very important feature; an outside water supply. We could fill our bottles and pans and be back to our campsite in two minutes. Bless George Stephenson and his outside tap!

Once while we were picking wild raspberries, a tall pale-faced stranger suddenly appeared. He was smartly dressed in a light grey suit, white shirt and 'dickie bow' tie. The bicycle clips made it obvious to us that he had a bike parked somewhere.

"What are you up to lads? He asked, very cheerily.

We told him we were picking raspberries and he seemed very impressed.

"I've been cycling up and down these paths for over three years and never knew there were any raspberries around here. Do you mind if I join you?"

A stranger in our private orchard was not very desirable but he seemed very friendly so we consented without actually saying anything. He didn't have a container for the fruit and when he had picked a handful he put them into one of our tins, seemingly not interested in having any for himself, which made us feel a little better about him being in our domain. He stayed with us all day, praising us for being so self-sufficient, as he called it, and saying how refreshing it was to see a bunch of young boy's living off the land and not being a burden to anyone. He just went on and on. I thought he was a schoolteacher or a professor or something, since he seemed to be very intelligent and so interested in everything we were doing. We played football and he joined in. He let us ride his bike up to the village and back, sometimes with three of us on board. We had our dinner together and he even drank some of our smoke-flavoured tea. He even seemed to enjoy it. We all felt as though we had found a new friend.

During one of our mass wrestling matches the eight of us were rolling about shouting and screaming, when we rolled over our newfound friend who was laughing and shouting as much as we were. He gasped as we fell on top of him then laughed even louder as he joined in the melee. He was very slightly built but being much older and maturer than we were, was considerably stronger. He pinned down one of the lads, Tony, with both hands so two of us dived on him to help our friend but he didn't let go. He straddled himself over Tony and laughed a more breathless, sinister laugh. His long fair hair was all over his face and he was sweating rather heavily. We managed to pull him away but he was determined to maintain his hold. It was still all friendly and we were all laughing and carrying on when I noticed the strangers fly buttons were all undone. It must have happened during the wrestling I thought but he didn't make any attempt to fasten them up.

"Peter", he had told us to call him Peter.

"Peter your flies are all undone".

"So what?" He smiled "we've all got the same", and he proceeded to undo the rest of the buttons. He moved to the bush nearest to him and relieved himself making sure that we could all see what he was doing. When he turned back towards us he continued to leave himself fully exposed, not making any attempt to cover himself and in fact fondling himself quite vigorously on the pretext of removing any surplus water.

Everything went deathly quiet. We all looked at each other then down at the ground, a horrible sickly feeling shot through my system as I realised we had a problem.

'Paedophile' wasn't a word that I had heard. In fact it wasn't a word that you could find in any school dictionary and if anyone had of mentioned the word to me I would probably have thought it was some kind of Dinosaur. We had a name for this kind of person, a four-letter word usually preceded by a seven-lettered word. The four-letter word was puff. Our tall well-dressed new friend was a f......g puff.

He continued to smile.

"Come on lads, we're all friends, it wont do you any harm".

He went on to tell us how healthy it was for young boy's to get rid of the feeling of frustration often felt during puberty, none of us had any idea about what he was talking about. We hadn't even heard some of the words he was using, they sounded like something out of a Boris Karloff film.

"Come on lads, our Robert and his mates should be coming on the next train, let's all go down to the station and meet them" I said.

Everyone looked at me as though I had just lost my marbles.

"Robert and his mates, who said they were coming to Wylam?"

Then the penny dropped.

"Yeah our kid will be coming as well, I hope he brings his air pistol"

Billy Thorburn followed suit.

"Wore Dohdi said he might come an al and he's a boxer."

Peter wasn't impressed and scoffed at our feeble attempts to intimidate him. Suddenly he became very hostile. The change was quite frightening; he said that if we didn't do as he said, he would beat us up one at a time.

That did it; being threatened by this pervert brought the best out of everyone. We turned on him as one and pointed out that there were eight of us and we had several weapons, such as pans etc. and if he started anything we wouldn't hesitate to use them. We spoke very loudly and punctuated our threats with every four-letter word that we had ever heard plus a few of our own. He was quite shocked at how aggressive we had become and it took the wind completely out of his sails. He reverted back to being the friendly pale faced stranger again. He said he was only joking, but the damage had been done. Now he was the enemy and we wanted rid of him.

Not having any return tickets for the train back to Elswick we decided to walk back to Ryton Willis, then beg some tram fare home. We had done this on several occasions and it always worked out fine. Peter decided he would accompany us on his bike, saying that he lived near Ryton so it was on his way home anyway. He chatted in his very friendly way trying to reassure us that anything he had said earlier was only a joke. He seemed to have accepted that we wouldn't indulge in his perversions. When we reached the part of the path that was shrouded in dense trees and bushes Peter dismounted from his bike and asked me to push it for him. I was happy to do this as it meant I would be well away from him. Then he put his arm around 'Eddie's' shoulder and the other hand down to the front of his trousers. Ed was too scared to say anything so when I realised what he was up to I took his bike and threw it from the top of the riverbank into the Tyne.

"Run everybody the bastard's at it again." I shouted.

We all took off as fast as we could go, trying to put as much distance between the luckless Peter and us as we possibly could.

I'll never know if he retrieved his machine from the Tyne, we never saw him again. Perhaps because there were more people about as we neared Ryton Willis, or maybe he just had to sit and wait for the tide to go out before he could reach the submerged bicycle. I remember the shouts and curses as he plunged through the undergrowth to the riverside. I felt sorry for his bike but not for him.

Ryton Willis had one of the few toll bridges left in our area and having to pay just to walk across a bridge was needless to say a bone of contention. A little fat bloke sat behind the window of the tollbooth and let us through the turnstile one-at-a-time, as we handed over our money. This was another hurdle we had to overcome on our way home. We had tuppence between eight of us and you don't have to be a mathematician to work out that eight into two doesn't quite go. We had to rely on our wits once more. First one went through, paid his money, turnstile opened, then clanked shut again waiting for the second penny to be handed over.

"Me brothers got mine."

It worked, the turnstile opened.

"Next."

"Me brothers got mine as well."

That was three through and only one had paid, then four, five, six and seven, one to go.

"Next."

The penny was handed over; the turnstile opened and John Hodson was through before the collector could blink.

"Hoi, you, you're supposed to be paying for the others," he shouted.

"Not me mate, I don't even know who they are."

The little fat man had no chance of catching any of us and anyway he couldn't leave the tollbooth so he consoled himself with curses and threats. According to him none of us had any parents and he would remember us next time he saw us!

We walked from the bridge to Newburn tram terminus. We were all starving of hunger by now so we decided to try our luck at the 'drink of water' ploy.   One of us had to knock on a selected door and ask the lady of the house if we could have a drink of water. It was rarely refused, and while she was filling the cup or glass we would casually mention that we had just walked from Wylam as we had lost our train fare home and would probably have to walk all the way to Elswick, and we'd had nothing to eat all day. Talk about pulling at the heartstrings. We ended up with a drink of water for everyone and eight slices of bread and lemon curd. This particular angel of mercy filled two lemonade bottles with water and gave us sixpence towards our fare home. We emptied the water out of the bottles and took them back to the local General Dealers but he would only give us a penny for each because they had no labels. He said it had something to do with not being able to identify whether they were his or not. That wasn't right and we knew it so we felt justified in stealing the six large potatoes we had helped ourselves to on the way out of the shop. We could make enough chips for all of us later.

The whole day had cost about one and tuppence between eight of us, not bad when you think how far eight people would get on less than six pence today. We had visited the home of George Stephenson; we had eaten eels washed down with smoky tea and wild raspberries for sweet (dessert). We had despatched a pervert without succumbing to any of his demands and we were all safely on our way home savouring the taste of lemon curd that still lingered in our mouths.

As we passed the old chain bridge at Scotswood someone mentioned the 'Sand Hills'. We hadn't been there for ages so our next adventure was already in the planning stages. We would spend a full day picking blackberries at the Sand Hills; it sounded like a great idea.

The Sand Hills were just that, hills of sand. They were outcrops of very dry clay thousands of years old. The face of the hills was dotted with hundreds of Sand Martins' nest holes, out of reach of predators and human nest raiders. At the base of the hills the soil was very fertile and supported tough wild fruit bushes such as blackberries and raspberries. We all carried some form of container and several of us with young siblings sported our 'National Food' tins. The tram dropped us off at Scotswood Bridge. The rest of the way was on foot, towards Blaydon. Then it was a left turn over the five bar gate, trespassing on railway property as we went. The signs read, 'Private Property, Trespassers will be Prosecuted, Penalty 40/-, see byelaws'. The usual ribald remarks greeted the sight of these.

"Two quid for a penalty, crikey who could miss at that price?"

"Well a'm okay anyway a'm not a trespasser, a'm Chorch of England!"

The Railway Police patrolled the line at regular intervals but they were usually fat old ex-constables who had retired from the police force and posed very little threat to us. We could outrun them most of the time but if they caught us by surprise they only gave us a good telling off or a 'thick ear'. On one occasion we were chased by a rather portly gentleman wielding a very lethal looking walking stick. He popped out of the bushes almost on top of us and made a grab for two of my friends. They managed to pull themselves clear from his clutches but in the process one of them had to leave his coat behind.

The constable shouted...

"Stop! You're all trespassing, I'm the police."

He may as well of shouted...

"Run for your lives I'm Sandshoe Dick."

We were very familiar with this area and when we reached our favourite bushes we were more than surprised to see that they had been stripped of fruit. This was rather disappointing, but not the end of the world. There were lots of other bushes around so we decided to go deeper into the woods than we had been previously. After a while we emerged from the woods, and beyond another fence there was quite a busy road. On the other side of the road there was another wood completely new to us. We approached this new area with some caution; we always liked to check the land for 'No Entry' or 'Private Property' signs, just in case there was a gamekeeper or estate warden in residence. Everything appeared to be okay, no signs, poor fencing, rusting barbed wire; it was obviously just a very old wood with easy access and good escape routes!

We all slipped through the wooden fence where the barbed wire had disintegrated and wandered around looking for signs of blackberries or anything else worth having, when we stumbled onto another barbed wire fence, very rusty and full of gaps. There were several metal angled posts about six feet high with the wire still attached to them, but they were all in a bad state of repair. On the other side of this fence the trees took on a more orderly appearance, they were spaced at regular distances apart and all seemed about the same size, looking very old and very tall. There were lots of thick bushes that turned out to be blackberries, so big they looked like plums. I had never seen blackberries so large they were enormous. We filled our tins and containers in a matter of minutes, eating almost as many in the process. Looking back at the bushes, there seemed to be as many berries left on the branches as we had picked. Nobody must have touched these bushes for hundreds of years. One of the other lads had climbed a tall oak like tree and shouted.

"Look at these, they're bloody pears."

We all hurried over to the tree and sure enough they were pears. Then someone else shouted.

"Hi, a've got apples up this one!"

Apples, pears, extra large blackberries indicated only one thing; we were in a private orchard. Being in an orchard wasn't unusual for us but it required a somewhat different approach, and shouting 'A've got apples up this one', was not the way; caution was what was required and a sharp look out.

Everyone was busy collecting (or stealing) as much fruit as they could. Jerseys were tucked into trouser tops and filled with apples or pears until the owners looked like giant hamsters with their cheeks bulging with food.

The feeling of euphoria was unceremoniously transported back to reality when someone shouted.

"Gadgy".

'Gadgy' was a word we used to describe, in an instant, someone of authority, such as a watchman or gamekeeper or even the owner of the orchard. It also meant it was time to vacate wherever you were not supposed to be, with all the haste you could muster. To us 'Gadgy' meant run, don't look back, head for the nearest exit. It was a very strange word possibly originating from somewhere between Gardai (pronounced Gardee), 'a member of the Irish Republic Police force', and the second literal translation of Gadfly, 'an irritating person'. Wherever it originated it was accepted on Tyneside as readily as the air raid siren, and even more so if it was preceded by 'Nit, nit!'

I picked up my food tin and headed for the gap in the fence. Everyone was doing his best to get there first; it was like the 'Charge of the Light Brigade'. The 'pastoralism' of the older boys shone through as they flung each youngster to one side in an effort to reach the escape point before them. Two of my friends were just ahead of me but I was gaining on them rapidly when suddenly there was a loud bang in my head and I ended up on all fours. My head was spinning as I scrambled back to my feet and continued to run forward. My legs felt like rubber as I desperately tried to catch the others, but they were simply running away from me. I felt as though I was carrying two other people on my back so I shouted.

"Wait for me."

But it sounded as though I was shouting up the bell end of a euphonium. The gap in the fence was straight ahead but no one seemed to be making for it but me. I tried to run a bit faster thinking that my friends hadn't seen the opening but my legs weren't working properly. I staggered through what I perceived to be the way out and ran into five strands of rusty barbed wire. The barbs tore at my face and I was catapulted backwards like a rag doll. I thought I was having a nightmare, my face was bleeding, my head was 'thumping' and I didn't seem to have control of my legs. I followed the last of our band as he ran through the fence between two of the metal posts (with no barbed wire) and climbed over the low stone wall and onto the road.

I was the last man out and no one had bothered to wait for me. My head was beginning to clear but I still couldn't fathom out what had happened. However everyone who saw it was happy to fill in the details.

"Ave never seen owt like that in my life.

Followed by peels of hysterical laughter.

"Me neether, it was bloody unbelievable, what's ya heed like?"

My father's half-brother Nichol was almost crying with laughter as he tried to tell me what had happened. When the cry of 'Gadgy' went up, Jim Philips was several feet up a large pear tree. In his haste to escape from the orchard he swung himself onto an overhanging branch and without looking, dropped to the ground. At least that was what he tried to do, in effect, what really happened was, he let go of the branch just as I was passing beneath him and landed with both feet on top of my head. I was completely stunned. 'So that was what the bang was'. No wonder I couldn't find the hole in the fence. I was lucky my neck wasn't broken. The two large bumps on the top of my head were very tender by now but my headache was getting better. The barbed wire had done very little damage to my face but someone had to prise a piece of rusty metal out of one of the wounds.

No one was able to describe what the 'Gadgy' looked like, he was only seen from a distance and he was reputedly carrying a 12-bore shotgun. I had my doubts about that. First of all they didn't usually carry weapons, maybe a crook or heavy walking stick, and secondly how could anyone have identified a 12-bore shotgun when they couldn't even make out what the man looked like. I think the whole episode was a figment of someone's imagination followed by sheep like panic.

On our way back to the tram terminus we called at a small general dealers to buy a bottle of lemonade. We all crowded into the tiny shop, which was run by a rather elderly lady. We asked her all of the usual questions.

"How much are your tuppenny cakes?"

"Ha yi got any milk left?"

"Yes"

"Well yi shouldn't iv ordered see much!"

The old dear was ever so patient and laughed at our stupid wisecracks.

"Come on now boys, what can I get for you?"

"Well me mother got ten bob for me from the people next door but they gave her two quid to take me back after just a week!"

We purchased our bottle of pop and filed out with the usual 'tirrars'.

When we were well clear of the premises we surveyed our spoils: four bottles of Tizer, numerous raw potatoes, a small brown loaf and two packets of Oxydol washing powder.

"Could nee body pinch any butter for the bread?"

"Why aye, ah could ih got some easy, but ah think she might ih noticed me climbing ower the coonta like!"

"Who got bloody soap poodah anyway? What's the use ih that?"

"It's dead handy when you want to wash ya clays."

"Aye true, but it's not much bloody good for puttin' on bread!"

We all had a good laugh about the 'Oxydol'. It was the popular soap powder of the day along with 'Persil' and 'Sylvan Soap Flakes'. The distinct orange and black box looked a bit like the rising sun design on the Japanese flag and could be seen everywhere. On the large advertising hoardings, in the Picture Post and Illustrated glossy magazines, on the Pearl and Dean advertisements shown between films at the cinema and of course the famous 'Oxydol' jingle played continually on Radio Luxembourg, the commercial radio station.

O–X–Y–D–O–L
Makes whites whiter than white
Makes colours' shining bright
White without bleaching
That's what we are preaching
There's nothing like Oxydol!"

It was a catchy little tune and most of the kids knew the words so it was obviously a successful bit of advertising. At around the same time there was another washing product which always impressed me, 'Floating Soap', soap that didn't disappear in the bath. Soap that was always there floating on the surface. No more groping around under the water trying to locate that elusive tablet, which always vanished, only to re-appear over the plughole after all the water had run out! I have no idea how the manufacturers produced soap that didn't sink but I'm convinced that it could make a spectacular comeback in this technological age, along with several other products supposedly out of date.

'Derbac' soap was used extensively in my childhood to combat the ever-persistent head lice or 'dickies' as we knew them. This soap was very effective and was used in conjunction with a very fine comb manufactured by the same company. After the once a week bath in front of the open fire came the hair ritual. Your hair was washed in the bath water with you kneeling with your head over the side. You couldn't wash your hair while you were in the bath because of the very strong medical odour from the soap; you would smell like strong alcohol for days. When the hair was washed and rinsed with clean hot water Ma used to produce a small flat tin with 'Derbac' embossed on the lid. In the box was a wafer thin comb known as a 'small toothed comb'. This was a precision made instrument manufactured to the highest standards and measuring 60mm x 40mm. Made of the finest steel; the device was indispensable in the constant battle against head lice. The small 'teeth' were so fine that the manufacturers provided a special cleaning plate thin enough to fit between the minute spaces to enable any obstruction to be removed. It was virtually impossible to use the comb when your hair was dry so the 'ritual' took place immediately after washing while the hair was still slightly lubricated.

First of all you combed your hair with an ordinary comb to eliminate any small 'knots' or 'tats', then you slowly pushed the Derbac comb forward through from the back to front of the head whilst leaning over a sheet of newspaper. As almost everyone had head lice to some degree, there was no shock or horror at the tiny little life forms as they dropped onto the paper. In fact it was quite a novel event. 'Nits' were the lice eggs, tiny little white specks that were more difficult to remove. Their parents could be washed away with the help of the strong soap but the eggs had to be combed out. After hopefully removing all of the parasites the newspaper was rolled up and thrown into the open fire. The burning of the paper was always accompanied by the rapid cracks of the exploding eggs and lice; they made quite loud reports for such small creatures.

The day at the Sand Hills had been quite an adventure but two of my pals had confided in me about another little adventure they were planning.

Eddie Schofield lived in a flat with his parents above Benny's the Bakers on Scotswood Road. The aroma of cakes, pies, scones, freshly baked bread etc., coming from the ovens downstairs was sometimes overpowering. As none of us could afford to buy any of the baker's produce Eddie had decided we should have some, one way or another.

This was the plan:

The three of us would pretend to be repairing an old 'boneshaker', making a lot of noise in the process.

One of us would prise open the window at the back of the bakery under the smokescreen of the noise and gain entry to the area where all of the baking took place.

The bakery closed on Saturday afternoon so that would be an ideal time to hatch the plot. No one would question our right to be in the yard as both upstairs flats shared the entrance and the outside toilets with the baker.

It sounded like a master plan.

We could even lock the back door from the inside so that no one could get in from the back lane to surprise us; it seemed to be fool proof!

Eddie's dad shouted down from the back window above the yard.

"Stop that bloody racket you noisy sods, ah cannit hear mesell speak, anybody would think you were building a bloody battleship never mind mending a bike."

Old Henry was well over sixty. Eddie had been conceived very late in life and at twelve years of age showed little or no respect for his four foot ten inch father.

"Stop you're bloody moaning and shut the window will yih, you're making as much noise as us wi' yah whingeing," he replied with some alacrity.

The screeching of the sash window being forced down indicated that the diminutive patriarch had heard the retort from his son and obviously didn't intend to pursue the matter any further. I thought to myself 'what would have happened to me if I had of said that to my father, or even worse, to my mother, joking or not?'

The bakery window was finally opened, not by force, but by careful manipulation and a very thin bicycle spanner known as a cone-key. We climbed through, just two of us, John and myself. Eddie would keep a look out and if necessary close the window if anyone needed to be in the yard.

Everything was covered in a fine layer of flour. Even the floor was white. The footprints made by the staff were clearly visible from the ovens to the storage trays and under the door leading to the front shop. There were lots of empty pastry cases waiting to be filled and baked on Sunday for Monday's sales. We helped ourselves to a couple of brown paper bags and filled them with a selection of meat pies, scones and bread rolls. We were very careful not to make a mess and tried to leave everything as we had found it. It was our intention to use the window again in the future.

As we tiptoed out of the front shop my pal got his eyes on the cash till.

"There might be some money left in there," he whispered as he crept stealthily towards it. I had my doubts about Mr. Benny leaving any cash in the empty shop but I just humoured him.

"Go on then have a look, but mind we're not taking the lot if there is any."

John rounded the counter, keeping an eye on the shop window. We were now visible from the front street, so extra caution was necessary. He stopped in front of the till. It was just like a miniature chest of drawers with only one drawer. The outer case was made of mahogany, French polished to a deep red and lightly dusted with flour. He put his fingers into the brass-domed handle at the front of the drawer and pulled it gently towards him. It wasn't locked. We both held our breath as it slid silently open.

"Ting!"

The warning bell rang out as the drawer opened fully. It sounded like 'Big Ben' in the empty shop. You would think my pal had been shot out of a cannon. There was a flash of ginger hair as he passed me on his way to the window. I didn't hear anyone say 'Shazam' but I'm sure he changed into 'Captain Marvel'. No human being could have moved at that speed. I have to say that I was only a nanosecond behind him but it was the first time he had ever beaten me in a race. I was surprised to see how much flour dust had clung to us. We were both quite white. Well it appeared to be flour, but it could have been fear!

In spite of our rapid exit we both maintained our grip on the two bags of pastries, so all was not lost.

The window was successfully closed and locked. Everything 'looked' back to normal.

The intrusion appeared to have gone unnoticed by the baker,

but less than a week later the little window had two large screws inserted in the lower sash. Fastening the two wooden frames together in the closed position forever! It may have been just a coincidence, or even a slight suspicion, but no one ever said anything, to our mutual relief.

Eddie's elder brother Henry lived with his wife and family in the flat opposite to his parents on the same floor. He was probably old enough to be Eddie's dad rather than his brother. Henry was a bit of an amateur magician, performing several illusions with glasses of water, turning them upside down with only a sheet of paper seeming to hold the contents in the glass. His card tricks were also very good but his piece-de-resistance was mind-boggling. It didn't appear to be an illusion and trickery seemed to be out of the question. He didn't bother to warn us not to try it ourselves and several idiots, myself included, did try it with disastrous consequences.

The props were very few and very simple: a steel poker, a hanky or duster and an open fire. The 'trick' was he would lick a red-hot poker! I had seen him do it on several occasions. I watched from as close as I could get to him. I had heard the hiss of the hot metal touching his flesh. I have no idea how he did it, but I definitely saw it with my own eyes.

Several us of decided one night that we would try to solve the mystery of 'licking a red-hot poker'. This could be our ticket of admission into the 'Magic Circle'. Instead it almost ended up with us being admitted to hospital. We used Eddie's front room, the same poker that Henry used, and the same fire! The only difference was, we didn't know what we were doing.

Henna Andrews wanted to try it first. He was convinced he could do it and we all waited with anticipation as he withdrew the poker from the fire. It was white hot at the point and little sparks of burning metal twinkled like miniature stars as he turned it towards his mouth.

There was a momentary hiss as the metal touched the saliva on his tongue; this was followed by an almighty scream that outdid his very good 'Tarzan' call by about fifty decibels. He ran from the room into the scullery and almost devoured the cold-water tap. His tongue was shrivelled up at the end and a hard scab of burnt flesh had formed almost instantly. His language was the choicest I had ever heard. He spoke very quickly for several seconds and I can't remember hearing even one word of English it all seemed to be Anglo-Saxon!

The consensus of opinion was that he had done it all wrong.

"He must have licked it too hard."

"He was too quick, Henry does it much slower, that must be the trick."

These two comments certainly seemed to make sense but I was of the opinion that they were all doing it wrong. I could see what was happening. They were trying to actually lick the poker when all you had to do was to gather enough saliva on the end of your tongue and pretend to lick it without touching it. The hiss would come from the saliva, completing the illusion. I had it all worked out and I was confident I could do it.

Four of my friends had badly burned tongues. The other two decided they didn't want to try it. So now it was my turn. I drew the poker out of the fire trying to be as casual as Henry. I looked at it, tapped the dust off it on the fireplace and gingerly eased it towards my tongue. The heat was very intense. There was no audible hiss as I made contact with the hot metal but the shock of intense pain from my tongue almost rendered me unconscious. It was as if something inside my head was trying to burst out through my skull! Pain was a regular daily occurrence and was accepted with disdain, but this was no ordinary pain, this was excruciating agony. I dropped the poker onto the 'clippie' mat in front of the fire, which instantly burst into flames. No sound came from my mouth, just a long sustained mmmm… through my nose as I clamped my lips together, afraid to open them in case I should discover that my tongue had gone completely. It didn't feel as though I had burned myself it was more like having my tongue cut off. Tears were streaming down my cheeks but I wasn't crying. I had screwed my face up so tightly that I had forced every drop of liquid out of every orifice. I could smell burning. I cringed at the thought of opening my mouth. Surely it wasn't my flesh I could smell. Surely I couldn't have done that much damage in such a short time. But the smell of burning was only the mat, extinguished by several pairs of feet and a saucepan full of water.

"What a bunch of stupid shites you lot are."

Henry's voice quietly filtered through to my numbed brain.

"Do you bloody idiots not realise it took me over twenty years to learn how to do that?

No!

You buggers think you can do anything. Well am pleased you all found out how to do it! You can go and tell all your pals that you can lick a red-hot poker, and how much it bloody well hurts!"

He refused to give us a demonstration and ordered us all to visit the land of 'off'.

As we trooped out of the front room and down the stairs, Eddie who just happened to be last in line was helped on his way with an almighty kick up the backside. I always thought they were brothers but I must have been mistaken. It was obvious that Henry had no parents or at least no father judging by what Eddie called him! And he was a 'king' one as well!

My burns turned into mouth ulcers in a couple of days, then they seemed to heal up very quickly. I must have developed a phobia for hot things after the poker incident and I still avoid very hot drinks.

My mother decided it was time we took our long promised trip to Carlisle to see her two younger sisters Dot and Liz. They seemed to be happy enough but Ma was determined to see personally that they were all right. The only problem was how to get there. The farm was situated out in the wilds of what used to be Cumberland with no Bus Service; no Railway Station and we had no means of transport. A round trip of 120 miles with no way of getting there presented quite a challenge, but not to my mother. She was working in the Co-op Dairy at the time, earning just about enough money to feed and clothe us so she hit on the idea of making toffee cakes and toffee apples to raise some extra cash to pay for the trip. When she worked out the cost of paying for some means of transport, possible accommodation and a little spending money she had reached the staggering sum of twelve pounds, or over six weeks wages!

Realising that most people were sick and tired of shortages, rationing and sweet coupons etc., she thought there would be no shortage of customers for her products and she would soon have the money she needed. Apples were fairly easy to come by but sugar to make the toffee was a different story, it was rationed and there never seemed to be enough to go 'round so finding the quantity and source for the amounts we required presented a bit of a challenge.

Dad used to send us the odd pound of sugar wrapped in his laundry but it was only occasionally, not a regular supply. Something had to be done, so Ma sat down and wrote to my father explaining about the proposed trip to Carlisle and how she hoped to finance it. She told him how much sugar she needed and was there any chance of 'buying' extra supplies in the south. The response was amazing. Dirty laundry started to arrive at number 54 Cannon Street two and sometimes three times a week. Each parcel contained at least two twopound bags of sugar amongst the dirty shirts and socks. Any of my Dads friends who came home on leave would visit us, usually with two National Food Tins full of sugar, and all it cost us was a cup of tea and a sandwich or maybe a home-made meal; the supply seemed endless.

The toffee was really just sugar heated in a pan with a small amount of vinegar and water until it turned into syrup. Then we added the bicarbonate of soda. This transformed the mixture into a golden brown frothy consistency which was poured into individual cake tins, normally used to make fairy cakes, or into a large shallow oven tray to cool before being broken up to be sold by weight.

Making the toffee apples required a slightly different technique, the bicarb, was left out of the hot syrup and the apples were impaled on individual sticks and dipped into the hot liquid. A quick dip into a dish of cold water slowed the toffee as it ran down the fruit, coating it in a thick sweet layer and finally setting in a cake at the bottom. This process allowed us to stand them on end on a sheet of greaseproof paper until they cooled and were ready to eat. Everything we made was sold in minutes. Some customers even queued at the front door and waited until the next batch was ready to ensure they got what they wanted.

After a few quite successful weeks my mother decided to branch out into something else. So on the back of her toffee enterprise she introduced homemade Ginger Beer. This was made to her own recipe, which was far superior to the traditional 'ginger beer plant' method. The ingredients were purchased from a chemist's shop beside our local Fire Station. Powdered ginger, dried yeast, artificial sweeteners and a little of our precious sugar to help the fermentation, was all that was required. I was given the task of mixing the ingredients in a small dish then transferring the 'mulch' into two five gallon vats. The previous tenants had left the vats in our pantry almost six years earlier. They appeared to be brand new and didn't seem to have ever been used. One of them was pure white with a large coat-of-arms on the front; the other was dark brown. They were made of very thick earthenware but although quite heavy, they were easily moved around by tilting them onto the edge of the base and rolling them using the rim to steer. We had to put them into the pantry before we filled them, as it was almost impossible to move them once all of the water had been added to the mixture. The smell from the powdered ginger was fantastic; the fumes penetrated your scent and taste buds as the steam from the boiling water enveloped you. It only required a kettle full of hot water to be added to each vat and after stirring this in, until everything was liquefied, cold water was used to top it up to the five-gallon mark inside of each vat. A damp towel or tablecloth was draped over the top of each container and the lid was pressed firmly in place. That was it, ten gallons of ginger beer fermenting away. The fermentation was very mild and served only to aerate the liquid making it slightly sparkling. If it were left too long the fermentation would eventually change the contents into alcohol, which we would consider had 'turned bad'. There was little or no chance of this happening as the ginger beer was every bit as popular as the toffee. Several people who worked at Armstrong's factory became regular customers. They were earning very good money working sixty hours a week for the war effort and there was very little that they could spend their money on due to rationing and shortages in general. Orders were placed on the way to and from work and collected on the return journey.

As soon as the liquid was cool enough we bottled it and stood the bottles in a cool dark cupboard for a day, with the corks slightly loose to allow the gasses to escape. Next morning it was ready to sell. The corks were secured with a clever string device engineered by my mother. A noose was tied around the neck of the bottle then the string was looped over the top of the cork and fastened to the other side of the noose, ingenious, and it worked. The gas pushed the corks up gently until the string became taught, and then everything was leak proof.

We used every kind of bottle available. Sauce bottles, pop bottles, beer bottles, but always trying at all times to avoid using 'returnable' bottles, as these would never come back. Our customers could take just two returnable bottles back to the General Dealers, receive their deposit and that would pay for a bottle of our ginger beer! Ma purchased most of our bottles from the local kids, which turned out to be a nice way for them, and me, to earn a bit of pocket money. We soon had quite a little business going but the profit was very small and our savings didn't seem to be growing very quickly. Although everything was selling, the profit rapidly turned into capital, which was needed to finance the purchase of ingredients, bottles, gas and other expenses. The more we sold, the more we needed to buy! The impending trip to Carlisle seemed further away than ever and we had to make a lot more money to finance it.

Tommy Chipside was the only person we knew who had any transport. His parents owned one of our local 'corner shops', and his two sisters, Eva and Charlotte worked for them. Tommy had a small vehicle and motorcycle repair business and hired out the two cars he owned, including drivers. This was ideal for us as no one in the family at that time had either a car or a driving license. It would cost six pounds to hire a car and driver and a further two pounds for petrol. That sounds quite a bargain today but sixty years ago eight pounds represented four weeks wages. Today's equivalent would be in the region of twelve hundred pounds.

From the profit generated in our first few weeks of trading, we had managed to save thirty shillings towards our trip. At this rate it would be Christmas before we had enough money just to hire the transport.

If my mother had of been born male instead of female, I'm

sure she would have been nicknamed 'Del Boy', there was always something going on in her mind. They say that 'necessity is the mother of invention', that was certainly true in my mothers case. There's an old American Indian proverb, which goes…

'As you go the way of life you will see a great chasm, jump, it is not as wide as you think'.

She always 'jumped' and landed safely on the other side on most occasions. This latest 'jump' landed us in the carpet making business. I use the term 'carpet making' very loosely, because what we were going to make was a very large 'clippy' mat, to sell or raffle in an attempt to make up the shortfall in our savings. It was a great idea as usual but I couldn't help thinking about the long hours of sitting at the 'mat frames' poking bits of cloth through the canvas sugar bag, enjoying it for a while, then dreading it as the hours turned into days and the days into weeks. Producing a mat as large as this would take about six weeks if we could get a good supply of 'clippings'.

These were made by hand from old coats, dresses, trousers, in fact anything that was made of cloth. If we acquired several odd colours my mother dyed them black, as this was the main colour in our design. The fabric was cut into two inch by about one-inch pieces (the length was more important than the width). This part of the job took hours to complete but we had several helpers who would congregate in our house and cut and gossip and drink tea for days on end, producing thousands of clippings. Some shops sold bundles of washed rags of tailor's cuttings specifically for mat making, but these were quite expensive and we only used them as a last resort.

Second hand shops were a favourite source of material and we had several of these on Scotswood Road, one of which was less than a hundred yards from our house. It was owned by a little round lady known as "Bella Lookup", a most unusual name and it was over forty years later before I discovered it was only a nickname; bestowed on her because of the way she rolled her eyes upwards when trying to decide what to charge for a particular article. She would clasp her hands together in front of her pinny pocket and look up, possibly for divine guidance, then utter her favourite sales line.

"Eeh, ah cannit let that go for less than two shillin's."

Which usually meant you would get it for half of that if you were patient enough.

Bella was a lovely old character who ran her second hand shop for many years. She had a special corner for really old stuff, not fit to wear, which she kept for mat making. This was where most of our material came from.

There's nothing new about re-cycling; it started many years ago, borne out of necessity.

Two large sugar bags formed the main base of the mat. These were sewn together to give us the length we required and then fastened to each end of the mat frames to enable the necessary tension to be maintained. The frames were made of four oak bars, two with holes drilled out to take the pegs that were used to hold the sliding bars in position. As we completed one part of the mat the pegs were taken out, then the finished section was rolled on and re-secured with the pegs. This meant that the finished mat ended up in a neat roll.

My mother drew the design directly onto the canvas with black crayon. Making nice distinct lines that were easy to follow. The whole mat was edged with a three inch black border; a large shamrock took up most of the centre and was surrounded by smaller shamrocks in the open spaces. We began with the black clippings first. This gave us our lines to work to, and then we filled in the spaces with all different colours, making a rich contrast with the black borders. Any visitors, friend or family, usually sat down at the mat frames for half an hour or so, putting a few clippings in. It wasn't compulsory but it was expected.

The tool we used for inserting the material was called a 'progger', and good proggers were very important. You could buy them at the local hardware shop. Granda Mills made ours from old screwdrivers that he cut down to about four inches long and filed to a rounded point. They were far better than anything we could buy and they lasted for years.

As we reached the last few inches of canvas, Ma said she had a buyer for the mat. She had agreed to sell it for six pounds to my great aunt's neighbour. So it was sold before we finished it (well almost).

My mother's Aunt Flo Exley lived in Caroline Street, off Elswick Road with husband Ephraim, daughter Jean and son Ephraim jnr. It was her upstairs neighbour who had seen one of our mats, which we had made previously for Aunt Flo and had expressed interest in buying one similar. She had agreed a price of six pounds before the work started, so that was more or less a contract as far as she was concerned. Not so! Ma thought that six pounds just wasn't enough for all the work we had put in and decided that seven pounds was a much more realistic price. I agreed. We had worked long and hard at the mat frames and anyway Aunt Flo's neighbour could well afford it. She was quite well off, and even had a bathroom in her house.

When this was all explained to me I was quite happy to struggle up the banks carrying the rolled up mat, in the knowledge that we were getting a much better price for our effort.

Then the bombshell came! Ma hadn't discussed the new deal with the customer or Aunt Flo; she had in effect just been saying what she expected me to tell the lady when I delivered the mat. At first I flatly refused to do it. I knew it would be impossible for me to get the extra money just like that. Everyone had agreed the price. Ma used her usual powers of persuasion. She threatened to knock me into the middle of next week if I didn't do as she said.

Mrs Ridley was delighted with her mat, she laid it down in front of the fireplace and walked over it several times, smiling and praising us, saying what a good job we had made of it. Aunt Flo smiled and nodded in agreement, appreciating it was a feather in her cap to have such a clever niece. She asked how much I had helped, so I laid it on about my contribution hoping to soften her up before I asked for the extra money.

"Right!" said Mrs Ridley.

"That's lovely, now how much do I owe you?"

I thought Christmas had come a little early this year, I couldn't believe she was asking how much since she'd known from the start, or maybe she had forgotten, I hoped!

"Seven pounds" I replied.

Aunt Flo's mouth fell open; Mrs Ridley's hand remained in her pinny pocket (probably clutching the six pounds) as she looked at Aunt Flo in dismay.

"Oh no son, we agreed on six pounds over five weeks ago, I can't afford all that."

"Well me ma said I had to ask for seven pounds because it took much longer to do than we thought and if I couldn't get seven pounds I was to take it back home."

The poor old dear was quite taken aback and looked appealingly to Aunt Flo for support. She was furious and told me to roll the mat up and take it back to my mother. Then she entered into a quiet conversation with her neighbour with lots of 'yes' and 'no' nodding.

I took the mat back home and had to endure the ranting and raving that ensued.

"The bloody miserable old sod, she's got more bloody money than she knows what to do with, well she's not getting that bloody mat for six pounds. I'd rather burn the bloody thing!"

I had escaped any recrimination for my part in the affair, but that was about to change.

"You shouldn't have told her I said bring it back if you couldn't get seven pounds, that must have put ah back up straight away."

I moved to the other side of the table anticipating an attack, but it didn't materialise. I think she was just giving vent to her feelings.

I said…

"Look, I'll take it back tomorrow and try again. She might be in a better mood this time."

This show of initiative seemed to go down quite well and Ma even told me I could drop the price a little.

"But get as much as you can."

We unrolled the mat once again and laid it in front of the fire, it looked really lovely. When we had finished it originally, it had to be laid out for trimming; that is to say we cut all of the clippings to the same height, rather similar to mowing the lawn. Thus tidying the whole thing up. With working from the back of the mat you only found out how good or bad it was when you turned it over for trimming. Ma got the scissors out once again and clipped away hoping to improve the finish, up to the seven-pound standard!

I ended up with six pounds seven and sixpence. I think it was a reluctant surrender, but Mrs Ridley finally gave way. Her daughter gave me sixpence and Aunt Flo gave me a slice of bread and jam.

My mother was pleased with the extra seven and six and told me she had already booked the hire car and driver on the strength of it. I forgot to mention the sixpence from Mrs Ridley's daughter as she handed me another sixpence which would have been swiftly withdrawn had she found out. I looked at the two solid silver coins. George V 1926 and Edward VII 1907; I was fascinated by coins. My Granda Mills sparked off the interest when he gave me an old fourpenny piece that used to hang on his watch chain. It had a hole punched in the top and was hardly identifiable due to a long spell in circulation but I loved it and was very happy to accept it as a gift, even though he was drunk at the time. That fourpenny piece of William IIII started a love affair with coins that has lasted a lifetime. I still have it in my collection, along with coins from hundreds of other countries. They are not particularly valuable but the memories of how I acquired them, where they came from and who could have owned them, makes them priceless to me.

I have one tiny bronze coin from the reign of Herod Agripa which is over 2000 years old; when I touch it the hairs on the back of my neck stand up just thinking of who else could have handled it all those years ago, maybe even Jesus Himself.

I wanted to keep the two sixpences' just to look at them occasionally, never wanting to spend them. This feeling lasted until I passed Katie's pork shop and Bowman's fish and chip shop on Scotswood Road. The spell was broken by the aroma of Katie's hot pork sandwiches dipped in onion gravy mingled with the overpowering aroma of crispy batter sizzling in great baths of hot animal fat.

Two penn'orth of chips with salt and vinegar was too much of a temptation. George V went first and the four pennies I received in change helped to overcome the disappointment of parting company with the sixpence. I managed to 'hang on' to Edward VII until Saturday morning when he was exchanged for a fourpenny seat at the Crown Picture House. I had to see what happened to 'Jack Martin'. The week before he had ended up in a coffin, which was submerged in water and the heading for this Saturday's program was 'The Adventures of Jack Martin', Episode six 'A Watery Grave'. It was great value for money, a full-length 'Lone Ranger' film with his beautiful horse 'Silver' and his life long companion Tonto, who was said to be an Indian Chief. There were at least two cartoons, a short documentary; then the news followed by the long awaited serial; all of this for only fourpence.

The day of the Carlisle 'expedition' finally dawned. Our transport and chauffeur arrived promptly at nine a.m. and we were on our way.

I couldn't believe we were in a car. I had been in one of the lodgers' trucks when I was living in Stony Stratford, but a car was something else.

The seats were red and made from real leather, I had never seen red leather before, the door panels were the same colour red, and the window ledges were made of highly polished walnut. The driver was in a compartment of his own, separated from his passengers by a sliding glass panel that he left open so that we could talk to him during the journey.

We seemed to be travelling at a hundred miles an hour as the trees flashed by along the Military Road, stretching out for miles in front of us without another car in sight. We passed Heddon-on-the-Wall, Corbridge, Hexham and on to less familiar places like Twice Brewed and a place locals called 'The Wilds of Wannee', bleak moorlands near Brampton, about eight miles from Carlisle.

We turned northwest a couple of miles outside of the city, the driver seemed to know where he was going and I was happy just to be in the car. About fifteen minutes later the car stopped.

"This is as far as I can go", said the driver.

"You'll have to walk up to the house, this gate's locked."

We had stopped at the end of a narrow lane with a formidable looking gate blocking the way forward. A large chain and padlock that looked as though they had been made to anchor the 'Queen Mary' secured the gate. The sign read 'Private' with the usual bit about trespassers being shot on sight, or something like that. So we had made it.

We passed through the pedestrian gate one at a time and made our way towards the farmhouse in the distance. After walking for only a few minutes the high-pitched sound of "Mary, Billy" came echoing through the trees. Two wild looking figures were hurtling towards us, their hair blowing in the breeze and shouting at the top of their voices. I thought two lunatics had escaped from the local asylum, but these particular lunatics were my two aunts, Lizzie and Dot, my mothers' two youngest sisters. Although it was only a few months since I last saw them, it seemed like years. They looked wonderful, Liz's hair was a golden brown colour (this was before she bleached it) and her face had a real healthy glow, country life seemed to agree with her. Dot was the same, Rosie red cheeks, but with dark brown hair, totally the opposite to her sister. She looked more like my Nanna than any of the girls, even when she was so young and as she grew older that fact became more and more obvious.

Normally we were not a very tactile family and kissing and cuddling was not something we usually indulged in, but on this occasion I was hugged and squeezed and kissed and whirled around until I was dizzy. They were ecstatic and I have to admit I was too. I suddenly realised how much I had missed them; they were so much a part of my life and would always remain so.

The farm was run by Mr and Mrs Carruthers, two lovely people and typical farmers, she small and plump with a skin that looked as though it had been French polished and he tall and bronzed with slightly rounded shoulders. He wore an old cream coloured shirt, which may have been white at some time, and a brown waistcoat with a pipe sticking out of one of the pockets, he looked very tired. The darker brown patch above the pocket indicated that he often put his pipe away while the tobacco was still burning. When the BBC later introduced 'The Archers', Mr and Mrs Carruthers became Jack and Peggy Archer and the farm at Ambridge was the same farm as Badingstock in Carlisle. The program re-kindled memories of that trip and kept them fresh in my mind for many years.

We all sat round a large wooden table, which was littered with home baked food. Bread; still warm, scones, teacakes and a large oil lamp in the centre. It seemed so strange that Mrs Carruthers prepared all of this food when she didn't even have a gas cooker. In my ignorance I thought that this was a disadvantage to her, not realising that the huge solid fuel AGA standing in the corner of the kitchen was a wonderfully efficient cooker. After tea, with nightfall approaching, we were shown to our bedroom. Now several oil lamps were lit and the rooms took on an eerie glow, with shadows leaping out of every dark corner. I was glad to be sharing a double bed with my mother, with its soft ticking enveloping me as I snuggled under the bedclothes. It was the first time I had ever experienced feather pillows, (made by Mrs Carruthers) and the difference between those and the flock pillows we had at home can only be compared to resting your head on a large marshmallow rather than a sack of potatoes.

I thought, 'If ever I get rich I will have pillows like these, a bed like this and a house like this, but with gas lights!'

I can't remember how long we stayed at the farm, but all too soon it was time to go. I'd had such an exciting time with my two aunts, exploring all of the sheds and outbuildings, collecting the eggs from the chicken run, being careful to avoid the cockerel when disturbing his hens. My experience with Granda Mills' cockerel, Ralphy, held me in good stead.

The Carruthers were very kind to us and refused to accept any payment towards the cost of our stay with them. On the contrary, we came away with eggs, home made jam and several other items that were in short supply. The two girls were very quiet as we walked towards the wooden gate and as the car came into view the tears started to flow. They wanted to come home and I wanted them to come home too. There was plenty of space in the car so I couldn't see why they had to stay if they didn't want to. My mother gently scolded them.

"Fancy wanting to leave this lovely place to come back to scruffy old Elswick" she said, yet she was crying as much as they were and homesickness is an illness that no doctor will ever cure.

We had a different car for the return journey and the driver was 'Tommy Chippy' himself, so we had a new car and the owner to drive it. I didn't know anything about cars but this one looked like a funeral car. Tommy said it was a Rolls Royce and was only fifteen years old, he seemed very proud of it.

It was quite dark on the way back home and I drifted in and out of sleep, savouring my memories of a fantastic holiday. Ma and Tommy talked a lot through the sliding glass panel (similar to the other car), but their voices only helped to lull me to sleep.

Not long after our visit the government decided the threat of a German invasion was much less likely. The Air Force was doing really well against the Luftwaffer and although air raids still continued, the German air force weren't having things all their own way. Some children, who were evacuated during the panic of the early stages of the war, were allowed to return to their homes.

It made a huge difference to me having my family back together again. Lizzie, Dot and Robert were still at school: Jenny at Vickers Armstrong's and Grace still defending the skies against the German bombers.

My mother and me often visited Grace when she worked at the Lowther Hotel before she joined the ATS. I remember her serving behind the bar in the snooker room. Now she was serving up anti aircraft shells for the Luftwaffer.

Many of the 'stars' that were appearing at the Empire Theatre stayed in the Lowther. It was very handy, being directly opposite to the theatre, and large enough to accommodate most, if not the entire cast.

There were several theatres producing live shows in the 40's and although many of the well known performers were entertaining the troops at home and abroad there were still plenty around to do regular shows, and the war never interfered with the annual pantomime. As a child I could never fathom out why girls played the principal boys and men played the Mother Goose or Ugly Sisters, in fact it still remains a mystery to me.

My Aunt Bella (Nanna's sister) ran a small business selling comics and magazines. Her husband Jimmy Roach and the lodger Charlie Hartley used to hawk them around Newcastle town centre, making quite a nice living. Some of the local theatres and cinemas allowed her to sell them in the foyer or just outside the entrance. For some reason not known to me, the managers of the theatres in question would send Aunt Bella two or more complementary tickets, which she usually passed on to us. I can remember seeing the film 'King Kong' when I was about six or seven. I also remember how scared I was. I had bad dreams for weeks after and I still find it quite frightening. Most of the free tickets were only valid for afternoon shows but it was quite a relief to come out of the 'picture house' to find it was still daylight, especially after seeing Boris Karlof in 'The Mummy's Hand' or Bela Lugosi in 'Dracula'. I saw my first 'musical' at the Haymarket Cinema in Percy Street sometime in the 1940's. It was called 'This Is The Army' with Ronald Reagan and George Murphy and it was in glorious 'Technicolor'. The music was by Irving Berlin and he made a personal appearance in the film singing one of his own songs 'Oh how I hate to get up in the morning.' The last verse went something like this…

> Some day I'm going to murder the bugler
> Some day they're going to find him dead
> And then I'll get the other pup
> The one that wakes the bugler up
> And then I'll spend the rest of my life in bed!

The sequel to this film was 'A Chip Off The Old Block' which I saw several weeks later. I often wonder what happened to these 'movies'. I can only speculate that they must have been destroyed or lost sometime in the past. I have made several attempts to trace copies in video format but they seem to have completely disappeared. I would love to see them again just to find out if my memories of them are accurate after such a long time.

⚘

In 1941 the German air force bombed Newcastle extensively. Their main targets were the arms and munitions factories along Scotswood Road but several other buildings were also hit. One of these buildings was the Goods Station at the end of Newbridge Street. Everything was destroyed, trains, freight wagons, buildings – everything. Some of the freight wagons were loaded up with tons of sugar and this burned for days.

My mother was visiting my two half-cousins who were in

78

Walkergate Hospital at the time and she told me about the spectacular fire she saw from the bus window.

"You could feel the heat through the glass as we went past Manors Station", she recalled.

My two half-cousins were the sons of my Granny Robson from her second marriage, to my Granda Robson. Nicholas, the eldest, was born in 1932 and Ronald a month after me in May 1936. Nichol was ginger like his father but Ronnie was blonde like me. In fact we looked very much alike and were often taken for brothers. I liked my cousin a lot and we played together as often as possible. He was always clean and tidy when we started out, but not so clean when we came home. One of my favourite playgrounds was the old Elswick Colliery and it was very difficult to stay clean in that environment.

We had the usual measles and chicken pox together but he was kept in the house a lot longer than me. My Granny didn't seem too keen to let him out with me too soon. Ma used to say,

"She keeps that poor bairn wrapped up in cotton wool".

Which I thought was a little extreme for a dose of chicken pox. I had visions of him lying on the settee in the front room with wads of cotton wool sticking out of his pyjamas.

We played together in the front room while he was still poorly. Gran had lit the coal fire and we played commandos, crawling under the beds with the gaslight turned down low, capturing Germans and Japanese and generally winning the war for Britain. We had sausage sandwiches for our combat rations and Ronnie had a large bottle of Dandelion and Burdock, which I hadn't tasted for months. The sandwiches were consumed under the double bed, lying on the highly polished lino, but we had to stand up to have a drink from the bottle of 'pop'. The flickering of the coal fire on the glossy floor gave the impression of water, so we commandos had to swim everywhere to escape from the enemy. This was achieved by turning the bedside mats upside down and propelling ourselves forward with hands and feet while lying belly down on the mat.

Once we had finished off the whole German army we decided to swim back to England to prepare for the final battle against the Japanese. I knew it was a long way from France to Dover and the Channel would be very rough but I was confident that we could do it. Another Englishman, Captain Mathew Webb was the first man to swim the Channel, so if he could do it so could we!

It was turning dark outside by the time I was ushered out of the front room and sent on my way home.

"Ronnie's tired now and wants to go to bed", said my Granny.

Followed by loud protests from my cousin, who had no desire to go to bed.

"We're nearly home from the war, just leave us a little bit longer. Can Billy not stay the night? My spots have nearly gone!"

All to no avail and with the promise of,

"You might be able to go out tomorrow if you're a good lad".

He was whisked off to bed.

I didn't see Ronnie the next day as my mother had told me he was still poorly and my Granny thought it would be better if he stayed in bed. I asked if I could go and see him but was told not to. This all seemed very strange to me so I decided I would investigate for myself. I climbed up to the bedroom window of number 22 and peered through the net curtain, the room was empty; there was a fire lit but no sign of my cousin. I thought my Granny must have taken him out somewhere and the 'poorly' bit was just to put me off. I didn't mention it to my mother, not wishing to receive the usual 'clip' around the ear for climbing.

My Granda Robson's truck stayed in the back lane all that day so I was quite pleased I didn't go to my Grans' house, thus avoiding his... "Wad di ye want?"

This huge vehicle loaded up with barrels of beer was a steam powered Sentinel with solid tyres. The boiler had to be lit every morning to build up a head of steam before it could be moved. The inside of the cab was more like the footplate of a train engine than a truck. There was a large coalbunker in between the driver and his mate and the steel floor was covered in coal dust. The fuel was a mixture of coal and coke. There was no gearbox, and when a full head of steam was achieved the driver simply engaged the drive and silently moved away. There was no roar from the huge engine, just the hiss of steam and a puff of black smoke from the metal chimney sticking up through the roof of the cab. Apart from the chimney smoke it was probably one of the most environmentally friendly modes of transport ever invented. Trucks that didn't spew out diesel fumes, tramcars and trolley buses running on electricity, big, silent, clean, where did they go? Why did they go? In the name of progress?

Maybe the ozone layer would still be intact if they had stayed. It seems that progress took a very large backward step in disbanding these clean transport systems, maybe it will turn full circle, maybe someone will realise that the high price of progress doesn't always mean better!

My mother didn't come home from work that day, which wasn't really unusual, but she always told me to go to my Nanna's house for my dinner if it was going to happen. I assumed she was out socialising with her friends. She loved to go out and after all she did work hard and needed some relaxation. When she finally came home she was still dressed in her work clothes and since she was always smartly dressed when she went out with her friends, this was really strange.

"I've just come back from the hospital," she said.

"Nichol and Ronnie were taken in early this morning."

So it was true, Ronnie was still poorly and so was his brother Nichol, (I didn't like him very much). I waited for more information but none came. She seemed quite upset and I think she had been crying.

"You'll have to go to the doctors tomorrow, to be examined."

"What for? My spots went ages ago. Why have I got to go to the doctors? There's nothing wrong with me."

"You're going anyway" she replied.

"I'll stay off work and take you myself."

Now that sounded rather serious to me, mother staying off work just to take me to the doctors, 'She must really think I'm ill' I thought, 'but I don't feel ill!'

Appointments were unheard of in those days; you just turned up at the surgery and waited in a long queue until the doctor was available. Doctor Dove was a small bespectacled man with shiny black hair plastered down with Brylcreem. He always wore the same dark blue pinstriped suit, and seemed on edge, just as though he was anxious to get away, which was probably true. He sounded my chest with his freezing cold stethoscope and poked a long flat stick so far into my mouth I almost threw up. Then he took my temperature and had another look down my throat.

"No Mrs Finnegan I don't think there's anything to worry about."

No one ever got our name right first time. We had Flannery, Hannigan, Fleming and many others. Of course there was always the classic one that no one had ever heard before, 'Flannigan and Allen.' Whenever this happened my mother and I would look at each other and sing a chorus of 'Underneath the Arches,' with our eyes turned upwards in the 'Bella Lookup' style.

"Keep an eye on him for a couple of days and if he suddenly develops flu-like symptoms just send for me."

I knew I wasn't ill, so what was this all about? Why did she have to keep an eye on me?

Next day I stayed with my Nanna for the whole day. Ma was visiting my cousins again but by bedtime she still wasn't back so I was put to bed with our Robert in Nanna's front room. It was very late when Ma finally came home. She came into the bedroom and woke me up; looking very sad and red eyed. I was carried along the street to our house in my pyjamas and put onto the settee. Ma seemed reluctant to go to bed and proceeded to light the fire. I was still half-asleep and just dozed on and off till the fire was burning brightly. We had a cup of tea and a rare gingersnap. She told me that the Goods Station was still burning and the buses had to be diverted down to City Road to get to the hospital. She hesitated a little when she got to 'hospital', then she must have decided that the time was right. She said reluctantly...

"You know when you and Ronnie had chicken pox, and you got better really quickly but he didn't. Well he got another illness straight after. It gave him a very sore throat, so bad that it stopped him from breathing properly and he died tonight while I was at the hospital. That's why you had to go to the doctors, to see if you had caught the same disease and that's why Doctor Dove kept looking down your throat. Its called diphtheria and it's very dangerous."

I think I was a little too young to grieve properly but I did cry. I couldn't believe that I would never see Ronnie again but I have never forgotten him.

Nichol survived the diphtheria, probably because he was a little older and stronger than his brother, or maybe it was down to the old adage 'only the good die young'. In this instance it certainly was the case. There was something about him that I didn't like and although we had some good times it was never a close relationship.

My father didn't get on very well with Nichol either. He accepted the fact that he was his half brother but there the relationship ended. They would talk to each other without any sign of animosity but there was always that air of expectancy, waiting for one or the other to say the wrong thing. Nichol was a bully, that's the only word I can think of to describe his character, he was an out and out bully, but he disguised the fact rather cleverly. I never saw him actually take part in any bullying but I did see him incite the act on several occasions. He would stir up a fictitious feud between two youngsters until they finally came to blows, then he would stand back and shout and laugh while the two adversaries knocked the stuffing out of each other. He tried it with me on several occasions but the only time he managed to get me into an actual fight, I won, much to his disappointment. I think bully by proxy could safely identify him. On one occasion I saw him handing out short lengths of hosepipe to some of his cronies. He had hammered pieces of lead pipe into the end of the hose to be used as a cosh. He then watched as they attacked someone he didn't like, in fact the person was a little retarded, quite big and strong, but not strong enough to save him from being beaten up by four idiots armed with coshes!

Most of Nichol's friends were also my friends, but when they were in his company they were different people. They seemed to hero worship him and would do anything he asked.

I was just under four years younger than they were but I was able to keep up with them when running or swimming, or in any of the rough and tumble games they took part in. When we played 'street football' they all wanted to be in his team, which annoyed me. I was the opposite; I never wanted to be in his team. He was outwardly a very nice person, always clean, well dressed and very polite (but so was Dr. Jeykell). You had to spend a lot of time in his company to really get to know the other side of his character. What I would describe as the dark side!

One Sunday we organised a 'coal picking' trip to the Denton Burn slagheap. Six or seven of us would be going for the whole day, taking two old prams to carry the coal. As we weren't allowed to take the prams on the bus, two of us volunteered to walk to the tip, some three miles away. I didn't mind this at all as a lot of the journey was down hill, so we could ride on the empty prams. Setting off at about nine o'clock in the morning we arranged to meet the others at Denton Burn. They would start collecting the coal as soon as they got off the bus and would hopefully have a good pile before we turned up.

The tip was made up mostly of spoil from the Montague Pit, (nicknamed the Monty Pit) which had closed down several years earlier, leaving a legacy of what appeared to be several million tons of slag and coal dust. On the 30th of March 1925 the 'Monty' pit suffered one of the worst disasters in the Northeast's mining history. Thirty-eight men and boys were either drowned or suffocated when water from an old coalface flooded the workings.

The other side of Denton Dene was used for tipping household rubbish, the two heaps drawing closer and closer until they eventually met. The hot ash from the household ashbins ignited the coal dust in the spoil heap and this burned slowly, but out of control for several years. The eventual outcome was the creation of what is now a very attractive park and children's playground, a fitting memorial to the miners who lost their lives.

By three o'clock in the afternoon we had collected four bags of good quality coal between us and loaded them into our two prams. We had no money for anyone to travel back home by bus so we took it in turn to either push or ride. This worked quite well and we were back home in less than two hours.

Nichol and the others took the coal with them to sell to their customers and agreed to meet up later to share the money. After tea I called for one of the other lads who was also entitled to a share and we set off to find the others. The two prams had been left outside of our front door and as they were empty it was obvious that the transaction had taken place. My friend and I searched all night until we finally met up with Nichol and his cohorts. They were all standing outside of Arkless's fish and chip shop on Beaumont Street. Three of them were still eating fish and chips and all of them were laughing rather loudly at some private joke. When I asked how much we had coming to us they laughed even louder. They said they got a lot less than they had expected for the coal and after deducting bus fares and the cost of a loaf and two bottles of lemonade, there was hardly any money left to share out, so they just spent the rest on fish and chips. There was nothing left for us.

So after walking six miles and scratching amongst the slag and coal dust half the day we were to get nothing! My cousin never said a word; he just sat there on the window ledge of the shop and carried on eating. The other two started to turn nasty at my protestations, they said they had picked most of the coal anyway and we did nothing for the first couple of hours so the money was rightfully theirs and what was I going to do about it? This was a challenge if ever I heard one.

If I decided I was going to try to do something about it I would end up getting severely beaten, as they were all older than me and quite a bit bigger, so I had to back down. As my friend and I walked away the others laughed with exaggerated gusto, we were obviously the private joke they were laughing so hysterically about when we first saw them. They had never had any intention of sharing the money with us right from the start. I had a pretty good idea who had orchestrated the whole affair, but when I told my parents about the incident I discovered that Nichol had already told them some story that cleared him of any involvement. In fact I almost got into serious trouble for trying to get money I wasn't entitled to.

I don't know what he said but it was convincing enough and once again he came out of it smelling of roses!

The other two were normally decent types and I personally had a good relationship with them when they were on their own but they seemed to change into different people when they were in Nichol's company, constantly trying to please him with some act of bravado or, in most cases, acts of stupidity.

Jim was his favourite sidekick, the eldest of a large family; he seemed to thrive on the attention he got from associating with my father's stepbrother.

There were seven of them who were together most of the time and of course the two or three younger boys who were allowed to tag along with them, myself included. We were the 'whipping boys' for the older members of the gang and had to bear the brunt of their jokes and larking about. It was mostly good fun and being allowed to follow the 'big lads' was a privilege afforded to only a few. I liked them all as individuals but collectively their personalities changed in an instant.

On one occasion we were playing in the wheelhouse of the Elswick Colliery, a favourite meeting place of ours. Most of the winding gear that controlled the ascent and descent of the cage was still intact and was used occasionally to inspect the water level at the bottom of the shaft. We climbed up the fire escape to the roof of the building and jumped off into a pile of sand left by workmen who had recently bricked up one of the windows. It was about twenty feet to the ground and it was necessary to do a forward roll on landing to slow down our momentum. There was lots of banter and giggling amongst the older lads and they started to throw sand at us as we rolled forward. This lasted for only a short while and most of them tired of the prank except one. Jim. He persisted, and even when we stopped jumping he pushed sand down our necks, in our hair and even down our trousers.

Everyone was having a great time at our expense. I hated sand; I didn't like it at the seaside and I always kept my shoes on to prevent it getting in between my toes. It was pretty obvious to everyone that I was reacting to the tormenting more than anyone else so I was singled out for more treatment. I was pushed face down into the sand as the perpetrator was encouraged to cover me completely. By this time my temper was completely out of control. I was sobbing quietly and desperately looking 'round for something to use as a weapon. Then I spotted it, just a couple of yards away from the sand, a pile of left over building bricks, some still whole and several smaller pieces. The rest of the gang were scoffing me for crying and being soft, but I didn't care. The crying was part of the plan and as the bully turned his back on me for just a second that was all I needed. I grabbed for half a house brick and when he turned back to face me I let him have it with every ounce of strength I could muster. He was very quick and spun around shrugging his shoulder up to protect his head, but he wasn't quick enough. The missile caught him squarely on the nape of the neck. Some of the force had been taken out of the blow by his evasive action otherwise it might have killed him.

Jim pitched forward onto his face, obviously stunned but not unconscious. I didn't wait to see what happened next, I just ran to the colliery wall, which was only three foot high, on the pit side but twelve feet to the ground on the other side.

I straddled the sandstone coping stones and as I turned to lower myself to the ground I saw the injured party lurching towards me, he managed to grab my hand just as I let go but he couldn't hold me. I sprinted down Glue House Lane, followed by a hail of bricks and pebbles, but he missed and I rounded Cannon Street corner heading for my Granda Mills' house.

I didn't go out again that day. I knew I was in for some form of retribution, so I decided to lay low for a few days, until things had cooled down.

I hesitate to labour the point, but every time I got into trouble with the older boys Nichol always seemed to be at the bottom of it. I think the fact that he and my father didn't get on had something to do with it. He seemed to be getting at him through me. It was his usual cowardly way. He knew that confronting Dad on any pretext would have ended up very painfully for himself!

But it wasn't all doom and gloom and we did have a lot of good times. Also I gained a great deal of pleasure when the older boys praised me for doing something they themselves would hesitate to do, like my initiation 'task'. If I wanted to be accepted as one of the 'gang', I had to prove that I was prepared to do anything they did. Being so young and impressionable, I was anxious to be 'one of the boys'. I also thought it would help to stop the bullying by the older boys.

Nichol brought home a tray of a dozen rotten duck eggs from the butchers' where he worked. They were very large and you could smell them even before the shells were broken. My task, or dare was to throw at least two of the eggs at our local constable, some time during his tour of duty. This new 'bobby' had just arrived in our area from somewhere in the South, judging from his accent, and according to him, he was going to rid Elswick of it's 'petty criminals', once and for all!

It was no idle threat either. He hadn't joined the Police force to make friends, which was just as well; the Police had very few friends in Elswick. He made no secret of the fact that he didn't like the Northeast or the people and he seemed to hate us kids. So, for me, throwing two rotten eggs at him would be a pleasure rather than a challenge. I would have been happy to pay for the privilege. This one-man crime buster walked, no strutted around his beat as though he owned the place. If you happened to look at him as he was passing he would grab you by the scruff of the neck and demand to know what you were up to.

"Why are you looking at me? What are you up to? What are you looking so guilty about?"

Followed by a clip around the ear or a kick up the backside.

We always knew when P.C. Thompson was on duty; the cats and dogs were off the streets. Even the pigeons seemed to be anxious to get back to their respective lofts. We observed his movements along Scotswood Road from our vantage point. This was in Cannon Street behind the façade of a row of derelict houses, the inside of which had been cleared leaving a clear view right through to Scotswood Road. The whole gang had assembled to see the spectacle. The plan was to throw the eggs at the constable then run through the houses behind us on the other side of Cannon Street, into the back lane and away before he realised what was happening. Simple, he would never catch us. He would have to either run through the unfamiliar derelict buildings or right 'round the block of houses before he even reached street level. The escape route we would use would be the same one used by the gamblers on a Sunday afternoon.

They would play tossing the pennies up and betting on the number of 'heads' or 'tails' that turned up when they fell to the ground. There were often quite large sums of money involved in this illegal gambling school and it was a favourite target for P.C. Thompson and his colleagues. The game was played in the middle of the street, with touts, or lookouts, posted at either end. Their job was to alert the participants, usually by tic-tac, if the Police made an appearance. Then everyone would just stand around talking or quietly walk away looking as innocent as possible. If on the other hand the law surprised the gamblers and sealed off both ends of the street, the men would run into the houses on the even numbered side of the street, (the doors were always left open), and lock the front door behind them.

Then they would knock gently on the passage door and politely ask permission to be allowed to go through the house and out into the back lane. It was always given and sometimes the residents even invited them to sit down and have a cup of tea until the police dispersed. This would be the way we would escape, as we all had several houses we could use, belonging to relatives or good neighbours.

The flat cap of the policeman as he came into view almost fooled us. We were expecting to see the usual tall helmet; this was the first peaked cap I had ever seen. It was him, the notorious cockney copper. He looked straight at us and instinct must have told him something was up. He started running towards us shouting.

"Stay where you are you lot!"

He must have been demented.

'Stay where you are you lot' was more effective than a starting pistol. I threw my two eggs in quick succession, turned, and ran towards my Nanna's front door. P.C. Thompson was screaming out all manner of oaths and curses as he tried to pick his way through the old derelict buildings. Then suddenly he stopped, he uttered a few sickly 'errs' and 'oh no's', then nothing.

Nobody was running anymore, my accomplices were laughing and jeering at the luckless policeman.

After I had released my two 'stink bombs', one of which was a direct hit, the rest of the dozen eggs rained down on him from all angles, thrown by the rest of the gang. One of them hit the peak of his new cap and covered his face in dark green slime. I thought I was the only one who had eggs, I didn't realise I was going to be backed up by the others. It was very amusing to observe through the glassless window frames, this tall figure in a dark blue uniform gingerly making his way back towards Scotswood Road. His arms extended like a scarecrow, covered in wet foul smelling albumen. The Police didn't have two-way radios at this time so they had to resort to phoning for help or 'backup' from their blue 'Tardis' like police boxes. This was fortunate for us!

The enforcing of so-called Law and Order had reached quite ridiculous proportions. Petty little incidents were treated like major crimes; you could be arrested for riding two on a bike, or if you're red light wasn't bright enough. Chalking bays on the pavement for hopscotch was almost a capital offence! Football, the national game, was completely outlawed on the streets even though playing fields were non-existent. If you kicked a ball in the street and the police caught you, you were in real trouble.

I was standing watching some friends playing 'kick about' with a tennis ball one day. One of them kicked the ball past the 'goal' and it rolled towards me, I kicked it back to the player, who, I was surprised to see, was running in the opposite direction. I was grabbed rather roughly by the shoulder and a voice growled in my ear.

"You ran the wrong way this time didn't you!"

It was P.C. Thompson. I insisted that I wasn't running anywhere and I wasn't involved in the game of football, but it made no difference. He took my name and address, and shook me a couple of times when I refused to tell him the names of the players who had got away.

The end result was a warning letter for breach of the peace and a hefty ten-shilling fine, accompanied by some well-aimed blows from my mother. I was not allowed out of the house for over a week. So the duck egg episode was a very sweet moment for me.

We had several encounters with this particular 'Officer of the Law'. He took one of my friends, who was only thirteen, to the police station for selling firewood without a licence. He followed another friend, Jimmy James and me into Elswick Colliery and tried to arrest us for trespassing, but he couldn't find us, he even came into the main cable room where we were hiding but he still couldn't see us. There were too many places to hide that he didn't know about. It was hilarious watching him creeping stealthily about looking for us, when we could see him all the time. I felt like shouting BOO! But my friend kept saying.

"Don't be so stupid me Gran'll kill me if I get caught in here".

'Cocky' Parks was the local bookmaker who operated from someone's back yard near my Nanna's house. Betting anywhere other than on the racecourse was illegal then, so P.C. Thompson was very keen to put an end to 'Cocky's' career. He tried everything. Surprise raids, stakeouts, even posing as a punter in civilian clothes, but he failed miserably. 'Cocky' had too many friends and P.C. Thompson had none!

We had a resident 'Lady of the Night' in our street called Peggy and her favourite name for our friendly policeman was 'piss quick'. She called him that everytime their paths crossed, and seemed to have a total disregard for him or his uniform. After one particular outburst of derisory remarks he threatened to arrest her for 'abusive behaviour' and she almost died laughing at him. She spent more time at Elswick Police Station than he did.

Several people would have good cause to report him today, for assault, wrongful arrest, harassment etc., etc., but this was long before human rights or citizens advice bureaux' or anything of that nature even existed. The Police thought nothing of giving you a 'clout' round the ear or a very large boot up the backside. They were the Law and nobody reported them, it was much safer not to.

Then one day it was all over (no, not the war) P.C. Thompson vanished without trace. Rumour had it that he had asked for a transfer but no one knew for sure, he just never appeared again.

A young man named Storer, who lived on Glue House Lane, became our new 'Bobby'. He was well liked by everyone, even though he was still 'the law' but he was fair and gained a lot of respect within the community.

Chapter Four

My fathers' two brothers were exempt from military service for health reasons. They were both epileptics. Benny the elder of the two seemed to cope with his affliction much better than his brother Christopher, but they both managed to work for their living. Uncle Benny was a cook in a works canteen and Uncle Chris a porter for the London North Eastern Railways. Coincidentally, most of the cutlery used in all of our houses was stamped L.N.E.R.

There has always been a social stigma attached to epilepsy and its sufferers. Being possessed by demons was a popular diagnosis in medieval times and faith healers often enhanced their reputations by driving the devil out of some epileptic, when in fact the subject was probably coming out of the seizure looking non-the worse for the experience.

Epilepsy is not a disease. You can't catch epilepsy, but it can manifest itself in anyone at any time. It can be triggered off by an illness such as meningitis or any other ailment that may bring on a neurological disorder. There are no visible signs that sufferers have epilepsy, so they don't receive the same sort of sympathy afforded to other forms of disability. Drugs seem to be the main form of treatment, but in recent years huge advances have been made in surgery as a possible cure, with varying degrees of success.

I had my first experience of epilepsy in my Granny Robson's house when I witnessed my Uncle Chris having a seizure. It was a very frightening experience to see someone who is normally very quiet and shy, suddenly change into what I thought at the time, was some kind of madman. He was foaming at the mouth and threshing about uncontrollably. A lot of seizures are quite mild and often take the form of a momentary loss of awareness. Some sufferers can even tell when a fit is coming on and are able to steel themselves to fight off the attack, or find somewhere safe and quiet to take refuge until it passes.

Once when he was working for a pipe manufacturer Uncle Chris felt a little unwell, so thinking that the inevitable attack was imminent, he crawled into a large concrete sewer pipe to lie still for a few minutes, in the hope that it would pass. On this occasion he lapsed into unconsciousness rather quickly, which was not uncommon, but when he woke up sometime later he found himself on a building site in Darlington. The pipe along with several others had been loaded onto a wagon in Gateshead and delivered to the client in Darlington. My Uncle was totally unaware as to what had transpired and when he realised where he was he treat the whole incident as a huge joke. He took great pleasure in re-telling the story over and over again.

It became a family joke and Chris laughed about it as much as anybody. The punch line was:

"It's a good job they weren't sending them bloody pipes to Germany!"

There were several other light-hearted stories about things that went wrong for him because of his condition. He filled a petrol driven car up with diesel when he was a petrol pump attendant during a mild fit. But a lot of the time more serious attacks caused personal injuries and an awful lot of stress.

Uncle Benny was a much stronger person. He seemed to be able to summon up tremendous will power when trying to combat a pending seizure. Shaking with determination he kept on repeating:

"You're not going to have a fit, keep hold of yourself, you're not going to beat me."

Unfortunately it often did and he would fall back writhing and bucking, still trying to beat it. The Doctors described his form of epilepsy as Grand Mal with Furore. His fits only lasted for a few minutes or often only a few seconds, but he came out of them with his eyes popping out like organ stops and his face twisted with rage. It was mainly verbal anger with a lot of arm waving and nose-to-nose confrontation, but on the rare occasion he did become physically violent.

Once during an argument with my father, Uncle Benny suddenly fell forward on his face. Dad put a folded handkerchief into his mouth to stop him from biting his tongue and rolled him over onto his side into the recovery position. Several minutes later he sat up, looked around and while still slightly dazed, started to get to his feet using the fender to steady himself. With his legs fully upright and his hands still clutching the steel fender he unfolded his body 'til he was at his full height, but with the fender hoisted above his head. He lurched towards my father. The wild look in his eyes was the only warning Dad needed. He picked up a piece of wood, intended for the fire, and aimed a blow at Benny's arm. It missed, but travelled a little further and hit him full in the face, knocking him to the floor. When his brother finally recovered Dad convinced him that he had injured his face during the seizure as a result of falling against the fender.

After a long series of bad attacks and constant refusal to take his medication Uncle Benny was committed to a Mental Institution. The whole family was devastated. They all knew he wasn't mentally ill but no matter how they tried, they could not convince the Authorities and he was locked away.

It was many years later that my father discovered his mother had signed the necessary papers to have her son sectioned. The incident was often mentioned to her in the heat of subsequent family squabbles, but she would never admit it. Dad could never forgive her. It seemed to drive a wedge between them and he talked about it until the day he died, with obvious pain and anguish!

Uncle Benny's stay in the asylum was very short indeed. He absconded shortly after his committal and stayed with his sister Edie until the authorities stopped looking for him. When anyone came to the house enquiring about him Aunt Edie would roll back the carpet, remove two loose floorboards, and hide him under the floor until they left. This went on for over a month. Many people who were wrongfully locked away managed to escape, and if they could avoid being re-captured and stayed out of trouble for twenty-eight days or more they were considered to be free. It was generally accepted that anyone who was able to do this was sane and responsible, and able to take his or her place in society, posing no danger to the public.

In spite of the epilepsy my two uncles managed to work most of their lives. Both married and raised several children between them. They were never a burden to the state or their families in spite of everything.

$$\text{☀}$$

During 1944 our family seemed to go through rather a bad patch. Dad had been in the Army for nearly five years and my mother was working in the Co-op dairy. She was hardly ever around. She started work at five in the morning and on most days she went out with her friends straight from work. I took care of the house and made my own breakfast each day. Ma arranged a credit account for me at the local corner shop, so I was able to get anything I needed on 'tick'. My aunts took care of the main meals and I thought things were going along quite nicely, but I wasn't aware of what was going on behind the scenes.

My mother loved to go out socially and was always ready to have a good time. We had several parties at our house for all of the family, but occasionally one or two strangers would be invited, including American servicemen. I was always there and Ma even took me with her when she went for a ride in the local Coal Merchants truck. I can't say one way or the other if any improprieties took place during these meetings, but my mother was still quite young and attractive, and my father had been in the army for almost five years.

Her lifestyle didn't seem to bother her side of the family and she even went out with her sisters occasionally. It was not the same on my Dads' side. Ma was very quickly gaining a reputation for being a good time girl and my Granny Robson made sure my father was made aware of it. She wrote and told him what sort of life his wife was leading and embellished it with 'facts' that she must have concocted. Whatever she wrote certainly had the desired effect.

It was a Saturday evening and I was in my friend's house. It must have been after 10.30p.m, when someone knocked at the door.

Mrs Thorburn answered the knock and said it was someone for me. I wasn't expecting anyone to be looking for me, Ma was out as usual and I would be in bed long before she came home. It was my fathers' half-brother Nichol.

"Yih better get yersell home quick, yah da's home and yah mother's gannah kill yih."

Now what was she going to kill me for this time? It was only half past ten and that wasn't really late for a Saturday night!

I walked quickly along the street towards our house, my bare feet making no sound. I tried to find a reason for my impending 'murder' but there didn't seem to be one. I thought if anyone has got two pins on them; please don't give them to my mother!

The front door was open as usual and so was the kitchen door. The light from the kitchen illuminated most of the passage and I saw what remained of my mother's new costume. The coat was torn to shreds and the black velvet lapels were ripped from the front of the sky blue jacket. The loud shouting and screaming from inside was like some Saturday afternoon football match. My Granny was calling my mother all of the foul names women used in those days but always avoiding the four letter words used by men. I walked into this cauldron of fury just in time to see my Granny pick up a cup from the table and make to throw it at my mother. Dad jumped up from the arm of the easy chair and shouted.

"Now that's-a-bloody-nuff, you've all had your say, now just bugger off and leave me to sort this out meself."

Granny was quite taken aback and hastily put the cup down. She and Dad's younger brother Chris and his wife Anne all left, muttering to themselves as they made their way out of our house.

I was very pleased to see my Dad, but he didn't seem at all pleased to see me.

"Look at the state of him," he said, mainly to himself.

"Where's your bloody shoes?" Followed by

"Have you been washed the day?"

I was about to answer each question in turn when my mother decided to throw in her two penn'orth.

"Wait 'til I get my hands on you, you little sod, I'll throttle you!"

I thought 'now this is where I find out what I'm going to be

96

killed for'.

"I told you to get a loaf the day, there's not a thing to eat in this bloody house, and a'm getting the blame for it".

She made to rise from the armchair but Dad held her back, not too firmly but just enough to let her know that he didn't want any more violence.

Ma's eyes were red and still wet with tears; Dad sat on the arm of the chair with his arm around her shoulder. He had been granted compassionate leave to try to sort out his domestic problems, one of many thousands in the same boat, torn apart by the war and the long periods of separation. No one had known he was coming home. He just wanted to 'surprise' everyone. He was waiting in the house when Ma came home, much earlier than usual for a Saturday, smelling of alcohol and dressed in her new clothes. I hadn't made the beds that day, so that was another fault. The house was clean, but a little untidy. Dad didn't wait to give her a chance to say where she had been or with whom, he just proceeded to give her a sound beating. He ripped her new clothes to pieces and threw them out into the street, shoes and all.

Granny, Chris and Anne were soon on the scene, shouting encouragement and urging my father to throw Ma out once and for all. But that wasn't the reason for his coming home, he wanted to save the marriage, not end it.

When it all calmed down, I was sent to bed in the only bedroom in the house, and Mam and Dad stayed up all night trying to sort out their problems. It must have worked for them because they stayed together for over fifty years after that.

Oh, and nine months after the big row a little baby sister arrived.

Chapter Five

The war in Europe and the Middle East had ended, but the Japanese were still a problem in the Far East. We had enormous bonfires to celebrate the end of hostilities but there was no magic wand to wave everything back to normal. Rationing would continue to be a problem for a long time to come. Food parcels still arrived from Canada and Australia and everything was still in short supply.

We burned effigies of Hitler and Mussolini and our bonfire was still burning a week later. We roasted potatoes on the hot embers and we kids stayed up till after midnight. The adults were singing and dancing, kissing and cuddling in the streets and 'everybody got to know everybody pretty well'.

The dropping of two Atomic bombs on Nagasaki and Hiroshima signalled the end of the war in Asia. This new method of mass destruction pioneered by Germany caused untold death and destruction. I remember as a small boy, the feeling of relief, that this weapon was ours and thinking that no one would dare to start another war with us, as long as we had it.

After the celebrations died down the full horror of what had been going on in Europe was revealed. Pathe and Movietone news showed reel after reel of the suffering of the people in the concentration camps. I will never forget seeing the piles of bodies being bulldozed into mass graves. Hundreds of men, women and children; they hadn't even been dead long enough for rigormortis to set in; they were still warm and loose, and still looked human!

We decorated the streets with 'Welcome Home' banners, flags and bunting in anticipation of the return of our local hero's. It made no difference how long they had been away or where they had served, they were all   heroes. Several had not been heard of for a number of years and there were numerous emotional scenes as loved ones stepped off the trams on Scotswood Road.

My Granda Mills' cousin had been posted as missing and for several months was thought to have been killed. When he returned we found out that he had been a prisoner of the Japanese. Although he was still only in his late thirties, his hair had turned completely white. A few days later his eldest son also came home, from a prisoner of war camp in Germany.

Uncle Billy Martin was married to my Dad's sister Edie. He was called up shortly after the war started and posted to France to face the might of the German Army. During the evacuation of Dunkirk he was one of the unfortunates who was left on the beach to be captured by the enemy. Nobody knew where he was, not even the Army. After extensive enquiries he was classified as missing presumed dead. Although none of the family believed it, there was no word of his whereabouts for over four years. In the meantime Aunt Edie took in a lodger to help supplement her income. A very nice little man called Hugh Lofthouse.

Hughie settled in very well and was well liked by Uncle Billy's children, Willy, Matthew and Edie. He became more of a father figure to them than a lodger did and when he and Aunt Edie began co-habiting it was with everyone's blessing. During the years that followed they produced four more children and Hughie proved to be an exceptional father and husband. It seemed like the perfect 'and they all lived happily ever after' ending to a film or love story, but fate was to deal them a very cruel blow.

It was well into 1946 before all ex-prisoners of war were repatriated and some even later, depending mainly on their state of health, both physically and mentally.

Then, like a bolt out of the blue, my Aunt Edie received a letter from the War Office, stating that her husband, Private W. Martin had been released from a German P.O.W. camp and was in hospital having an operation on his right knee. The knee had been badly smashed by a German guard with a rifle butt. This was the first time Uncle Billy had been heard of for over four and a half years. Although my Aunt Edie and Hughie had never married and consequently had not committed bigamy, their situation was pretty desperate. They were very happy and wanted to stay together, so the most obvious thing to do was to file for divorce and make their relationship into a legal marriage. Uncle Billy's attitude towards this suggestion was very surprising. He visited the couple shortly after his release from hospital and after a long emotional discussion, agreed to their proposals. Aunt Edie would apply for the divorce on the grounds of committing adultery with Hughie and Uncle Billy would not contest it. It was a very traumatic time for the whole family but happily it all ended amicably. There were many similar stories after the war and it is only possible to appreciate how it affected the lives of the people involved when you had experienced it first hand.

My father and Billy Martin were very good friends for many years before the war, and when my Dad realised he would probably never see him again he was very sad.

"The poor bugger spent nearly five years as a prisoner of war and when he finally gets back home he finds he's got no home, no family, no wife and no bloody where to live, it's not bloody fair!"

When everything was sorted out Uncle Billy visited us to say his goodbyes. He was resigned to the fact that he would eventually loose touch with everyone, but he wanted to let us know that there were no hard feelings. He was quite optimistic about making a new life for himself.

I hope he did.

꙳

My new baby sister was crying quite a lot through the night, and as her cot was in the same room as us, mother and I got less and less sleep. Finally Ma decided that she wasn't feeding her enough with natural milk, so she thought she would try her with a bottle feed to see if she would sleep any better. It worked like a charm. Once she got used to the unfamiliar bottle, she slept for much longer periods, so it must have been hunger that was making her so unhappy. Once she was on the artificial milk the breast milk didn't seem to be to her liking and she refused to take it. This turned out to be quite a serious situation for my mother. She was producing natural milk and the baby wouldn't have it, so something had to be done.

The answer to the problem was pretty obvious; the excess milk had to be disposed of in some way, so Ma borrowed a device that I can only describe as a glass Claxton horn! It was a very strange looking object, made of glass and shaped like the end of a trumpet. A large red rubber bulb was attached to the other end of the trumpet and when I squeezed it I expected it to make a noise like the old car horns, (the type they used to have on the model 'T' Fords). I had no idea what it was, but I was soon to find out.

My Mother explained that the device was used to 'express' milk. When breast-feeding babies refused to suckle, the milk had to be drawn off with this 'trumpet' to prevent the mother contracting milk fever. The bell or front of the glass trumpet had to be placed firmly over the front of the breast and the rubber bulb squeezed almost flat. Then holding the glass end with one hand the pressure was released from the bulb with the other hand. This operation drew the air from the glass into the bulb causing a vacuum, which in turn aspirated the breast. That was the theory of it, but in practice it was a little different. My mother wasn't able to manage the whole process on her own, so I was recruited to help.

I was confronted with these two enormous mammaries, red and swollen, the skin tight and shining like two huge abscesses. It was difficult to say who was the more embarrassed.

I was just past my ninth birthday and I'd never seen anything like this before, not even by accident. After fumbling about in several futile attempts I finally achieved success! Ma winced as I released the pressure on the rubber bulb but the relief from the pain when the milk started to flow showed immediately. We both forgot our embarrassment and I was delighted that we had managed to overcome the problem. I was very surprised at how watery and translucent the milk was and thought it was little wonder my sister didn't like it. The 'milking' had to be performed quite regularly until the supply dried up naturally, helped on by some tablets from the doctor.

This was by no means the end of my post-natal duties. I had to apply a very large binder around Ma's waist every couple of days. This was supposed to help her to get her figure back to normal, so she said, but I think it had more of a medical function than that. Whatever it was supposed to do, it was my job to put it into place. I learned more about the female anatomy in those few short weeks than some people learn in a lifetime. To say I was old beyond my years would be no exaggeration, I knew far too much for a nine-year-old! My mother had a huge scar on her abdomen. It was about twenty inches long and travelled in a curve down the right side of her stomach and ending up just below the navel. She told me it was where she was operated on to have her appendix removed. In these days the scar left after a similar operation would be no more than two inches long.

The arrival of my sister heralded a new era in my life, the era of baby-sitting. The baby was wrapped-and-strapped into her pram and I was told to push her till she went to sleep. I didn't mind the new duty at all; it opened up several new avenues for me both in work and play. On the 'work' side, I was able to take the pram to the Butcher's on Saturday mornings and load the meat into the pram beside my sister. Then I could go straight to the greengrocers for the vegetables and on to the Co-op for the groceries. I was now allowed to do all three jobs in one go and the pram was ideal for carrying everything. Several of my friends had siblings to take care of, so we used to meet up with our prams and have races 'round the block, pretending to be Roman chariots or 'Wells Fargo' stagecoaches being chased by Indians. The odd crash went unrecorded and thankfully none of the babies were hurt. Sometimes just for fun we would swap the babies around, putting them into different prams and taking them home. The expression on my mother's face was priceless when she picked Veronica George out of the pram instead of my sister. I tried to look as shocked as she was but I couldn't hold my laughter in. She was not amused, Ma didn't like that kind of shock humour and I received the compulsory 'clout' for my pains! But it wasn't really too hard and I believe I detected a slight smile on her face.

I had one of my friends in my sisters' pram one day; we had

taken the padded panels out and he was sitting in the bottom. The hood was up and he had the blankets pulled up around his neck. We were just larking about and he was making stupid baby noises, when an elderly neighbour came out of her front door.

"Is this the new addition to the family Billy?" She asked.

"Let me have a look at her," she said as she took a sixpence out of her purse.

"Oh, I think she's asleep," I lied, hoping she would pass the money over to me. But she insisted on having a look. She bent down to look under the hood and my mate said.

"Hello Mrs Reeves!"

The poor old dear nearly had a heart attack. She jumped back with a loud:

"Oh!" as she pressed her hand up to her chest.

I couldn't do anything for laughing and poor old Mrs Reeves just waddled off looking rather perplexed as she put the sixpence back into her purse. My friend's mother had been watching all of this from her bedroom window and she shouted.

"You two sods will get something for that, that poor old bugger nearly died."

She was trying to admonish us while desperately trying to hide the amusement on her face.

My friend in the pram was Henry (Henna), the eldest of four brothers and one sister. We were blood brothers. We had both cut our hands and clasped them together until the blood from the wounds mingled. This was the North American Indian way of cementing a close friendship. We had seen it happen at the Crown Picture House in several Cowboy and Indian films. Of course our 'cuts' were more like deep scratches, but at least it made us feel good.

'Henna' was a master of making 'bone-shakers'. These were made from old bike frames stripped of everything but the handlebars. The name 'bone-shaker' is in fact the name given to the forerunner of the modern bicycle. It consisted of a frame with handlebars, two wheels and a saddle, which resembled a horse saddle. There were no pedals to propel the machine and the 'riders' had to push with their feet in order to move forward. The ones Henna made were very similar.

Two old pram wheels took the place of the original wheels and the brake (not brakes, as there was only one) was a piece of wood jammed into the back forks and pressed down against the rubber tyre on the pram wheel which slowed the bone-shaker down quite efficiently. As there was no means of propulsion, other than using your feet or taking turns to push each other, we turned to the hills for our power.

Elswick and Low Benwell were built on the side of a hill. Everywhere you went was up! Up to the butchers, up to the doctors, up to school. The Fire Brigade and the Police Station both had the same station name, Arthur's Hill, right at the top of the West Road. Scotswood Road was at the bottom of the hill, Elswick Road was halfway up and the West Road was the summit, the highest point in the city.

Henna and I decided we would try a run from St. John's Road, down Edgeware Road turning into Cannon Street before reaching the bottom. This was about half a mile of steep hill, but the road had recently been tarmac'd over the sandstone cobbles, making for a very smooth run We only had one bike so we 'tossed' a coin to see who would go first and he won. I thought that was only fair considering he had built the machine. If it needed any modifications after the run, he would find out what they were. There were three streets running off Edgeware Road to the left on the way down. If he felt he was going too fast or a mechanical problem arose he could turn off into Beaumont Street or Glue Terrace therefore shortening the journey before he picked up too much speed. I think that was a very credible safety plan for two kids. We were often accused of being reckless or even mad, but we always tried to avoid accidents for obvious reasons.

So off he went pushing the bike up Edgeware Road, past the dairy and on to St. John's Road. I stayed at the bottom end of Cannon Street, as I wanted to see how well he would negotiate the turn into the street. I also thought if he was going to come off, this would be the place for it to happen!

Henna's loud Tarzan cry pierced the air as he came hurtling down the bank at a fantastic speed. He was way past the first and second safety zones and it was obvious from his excited cries that he had no intention of stopping until he reached the bottom. As the 'bone-shaker' and rider came into view his jet-black curly hair was flowing behind him like an Indian headdress and his shirt looked more like a parachute as it ballooned out, full of air. He would have to put his foot out to steady himself, like a speedway rider, if he was going to turn into the street at that speed. But how could he? He never wore shoes, only to go to school. He was in his bare feet! The bike wobbled a bit as he pressed his bare foot on the wooden brake. It started to slow down but he had waited too long. He leaned over at a very acute angle and sparks came off the crankcase at the bottom of the frame, as it touched the ground. After that everything seemed to happen in slow motion. The machine slewed sideways towards the pavement. The two pram wheels struck the grey granite kerbstone simultaneously and my friend was catapulted through the air turning a left over right cartwheel type somersault. He seemed to be in the air for several minutes before finally landing in a jumbled heap of arms and legs and bike (which had rapidly followed him in his flight). Henry was anything but a softy, but on this occasion his Tarzan call degenerated into a high-pitched scream.

"Me leg, me leg, me f-----g leg," he shrieked.

"A'v broke me f-----g leg!"

He had an'all. His left leg was lying at a very strange angle and his foot looked as though it was back to front. Several neighbours came out to see if they could help but Henna's Uncle Cecil who lived just opposite to where the accident occurred was the first to reach his nephew. He picked him up (ignoring his screams) and carried him back into his flat. As my friend was being attended to by his family I retrieved the 'flying machine' and went home. I was told later that he had his left leg in plaster up to his thigh. 'Uncle Cecil' had taken him up to the General Hospital in an old pram where, they confirmed that his leg was fractured in two places. Sympathy was in very short supply and Henna got very little from his family. His mother said….

"Ah knew that this would happen, you and that Billy Flannigan are bloody barmy the way you ride them stupid bikes. He nearly smashed his neck last week when he crashed his bike."

She was referring to an incident, which had occurred a few days earlier. I came down Edgeware Road on a borrowed bike, sitting on the pannier instead of the saddle, this allowed me to lean right over with my foot on the ground and do a very fast 'speedway' turn in the width of the road. Only I misjudged it slightly and although I had full size wheels and proper brakes, I still managed to hit the lamppost beside Granny Robson's front window. I didn't hurt myself too much, only my pride!

Cecil had been looking out of his front room window when the crash took place.

"A've never seen owt like it in my life. Wore Henna looked like a bloody rag doll as he went flying through the air, it's a good job he landed on his heed or he might a hort hesell." He said with mock concern.

The broken leg was rewarded with six weeks off school, in which time my friend had three new plaster casts. The first re-newal came only three days after the original. He picked away at the plaster until it was down to the gauze.

"Ah couldn't stand it any langer, a flea must have got doon inside the plaster and it nearly drove is barmy," was Henna's excuse.

The second one was just below the knee, so he was able to shove a knitting needle down when the itching started. This was much better as he was now able to bend his leg, allowing him to sit in an old pram so we could push him around. The third one was the best of all. It had a large lump of plaster at the heel with a piece of metal running through it to be used for walking. So Henry could now get about on his own, instead of having to be pushed around in a pram. But he still didn't go to school!

We played several games that had originated in our locality, most of which required no equipment, save the odd tennis ball. 'Lampoil', (the name had nothing to do with the rules) was a form of Rugby League, without the ball and we used the name 'Lampoil' only to identify the game when deciding what to play.

The game started off with only one member on one side and as many as possible on the opposing side. The pitch was the distance between two lampposts, about fifty yards. The idea was each team member had to run from one post to the next and touch it to be home. The opposing team member had to prevent the first player from reaching the sanctuary of the lamppost. If he failed then that was the signal for the rest of the team to make their way past him en-masse. If however he was able to prevent the player from making contact with the post, he claimed him as a member of his own team. The more he stopped getting through, the bigger his side became. This went on until only one man was left on the side doing the running. It was up to him to make one final run through the opposing team, if he achieved this his whole team was freed from the other side, and he had won his first run. It was extremely rough. Bloody noses were commonplace, and having your shirt ripped off your back was almost obligatory, but it was always good humoured. I cannot recall even one incident of anyone loosing their tempers. There were plenty of injuries, but no individual was ever to blame, the game itself was always the cause.

The duration of each run was governed by the number of players and the number of 'runs' depended on how much stamina they all had. It often went on for hours. People living in the street had a grandstand view from their front room windows; they shouted encouragement and generally enjoyed the spectacle.

The Police often tried to intervene, but when the players failed to run away and with the absence of any ball, they retreated to the jeers of the spectators.

There were many other games with strange names, for example; 'Cannon' 'Stairs' 'Bays' 'Spanny' 'Doors' 'Pitchy' and a very firm favourite with everybody, 'Monnakitty' or sometimes pronounced 'Mountakitty'. The name being a derivation of 'Mount a cuddy', which is Geordie for mount a horse.

The cuddy, or horse was usually played by one of the stronger boys who had to bend double with his head pressed against another boy's stomach. This acted as a bolster. The other players ran and jumped as far up onto the 'horses' back as they could to leave as much space as possible for the next 'rider'. Everyone kept on mounting the horse until someone fell off. The fallen then became the second part of the horse. Sometimes the horse would grow to three individuals. Making it more and more difficult to reach the front section and causing numerous collapses. When all the riders had mounted the 'cuddy' they shouted in unison.

"Monnakitty, monnakitty, one, two, three, butchers' shop and away."

If they managed to complete the chant before anyone fell off, they were entitled to another go. I doubt if anyone knew where the chant originated but it was always the same. It never made any sense to me, but on the other hand neither did the game.

On Sunday when the pubs closed, if there was no 'gambling school' operating, the drunken men used to play 'Monnakitty'. This was a spectacle to behold. Ten or twelve men, all under the influence of several pints of beer, playing our game. It was tremendous fun to watch but suicidal to take part. They played for hours. Several cases of concussion ensued and someone always ended up in the General Hospital. They argued like school kids about things like, 'not finishing the chant before someone fell off' or

"Ah saw your foot touch the groond before you got to 'butchers shop', never mind away".

It was unbelievable; they even had referees to ensure no one cheated. I watched them in 1967 and I was convinced that someone would be killed before the game ended. Their wives and girlfriends were all there as spectators and the noise was deafening. I ended up taking someone to hospital in the back of my mini traveller. He had a bad cut on the back of his head, but when we got to St. Johns' Road he said.

"Just drop me off here cock, I'll just get the wife to put a sticky plaster on when I get home."

He seemed to be slightly confused as he swayed along the pavement, but no more so than usual for a Sunday afternoon.

Holidays meant only one thing to my friends and me and that was six weeks off school. There were very few people who could afford to go away on holiday and those who did, usually combined it with fruit or vegetable picking or some kind of paid employment. Our excursions were confined to a trip to Whitley Bay or Tynemouth, and occasionally a weekend at my Uncle Tommy's, in Wallsend.

The public was allowed onto the beaches once more as they had recently been cleared of barbed wire and tank traps etc. The sand was fresh and clean, having been out of bounds for several years. In 1939–40 the 'impending' German invasion had prompted the government to order the fortification of our beaches. I don't suppose it occurred to anyone that the enemy was quite capable of doing the same 'trick' as they did when they 'penetrated' the 'impenetrable' 'Mageno Line' when they invaded France. They simply went round it! Surely they would do something similar if they invaded Britain. Maybe just fly over it?

Well that was all behind us now and the seaside was available to us once again. Everything was still in short supply and about the only thing you could buy was hot water. Most people took a small amount of their precious tea ration with them, so with a hot drink and a couple of sandwiches, impregnated with a few wind-borne grains of sand, seaside picnics were high on the entertainment agenda. I liked the rock pools, and picked winkles and looked for crabs, but I just couldn't put up with the sand. I preferred the dene at Wallsend and always felt relieved when my mother said we were going to Uncle Tommy's for the weekend.

Uncle Tommy Jackson was really my Great Uncle, being my Nanna's brother, but I always looked on him as my uncle for the fifty years that I knew him. He worked at Swan Hunters shipyard as a riveter and was exempted from military service during the war because he was doing essential war work. I always looked forward to seeing my two cousins Tom Junior and Denny his younger brother. We got on very well and always had a great time together. It was such a change from Elswick. Playing in the Wallsend dene amongst the trees and bushes, there was even a small stream, which lent itself to several exciting games and adventures. Their house was in Mullen Road, number 28, just off Station Road and quite close to the Rising Sun Colliery. The back garden was huge and backed onto a very large field, which was used for grazing horses and cattle. Uncle Tommy said the landlord who owned all of the houses in their street had offered to sell him the house they were renting but my uncle declined the offer, he thought £380.00 was a bit much!

The green house, in the back garden was about twenty-five feet long and it was full of tomato plants, and various other things. The two boys used to climb over the hedge into the field and collect dry 'cow pats' and horse manure to make compost for the plants.

Not being used to farm animals, I declined their offer to join them on their manure collecting, I was rather wary of the 'things' with the large horns. How could they tell they weren't bulls?

Uncle Tommy had a secret recipe for feeding his tomato plants. He soaked the dry cow dung in a bucket of water. Then he put his hands into it and squeezed the solid matter until it had 'released all the goodness' as he said. The mixture was then poured into another bucket through several layers of muslin to remove all of the seeds and undigested particles. Now it was ready to 'serve'. The plants must have loved it. They responded with huge trusses of large bright red tomatoes that people came from far and near to buy.

I watched from a safe distance as my two cousins shovelled the dry cowpats into their bucket, but I was also watching the antics of one of the horses. It seemed to be looking directly at us. I was glad I was on the other side of the fence. The two boys had also noticed the interest the animal was showing and decided to join me back in their garden. The horse ambled up to the hedge. There was no sign of aggression – it just looked curious. He was a huge beast, probably over sixteen or even eighteen hands high and had no difficulty in poking his head right over the fence. What happened next was quite bizarre. He may have picked up the scent of the vegetable patch or something. He craned his neck forward, pushing his head nearer and nearer towards the plants, all of the time leaning his chest against the fence. The Hawthorn bushes which had overgrown the original wooden fence were very tough and mature, but the sound of wood cracking warned that it was beginning to succumb to the pressure of half a ton of horse. Uncle Tommy poked at him with a clothes prop but that just snapped like a matchstick. We all shouted and waved our arms about in an effort to scare him off, but nothing worked.

Then Aunt Vicky took charge of the situation. She was a very organised person and calmly walked into the greenhouse, reappearing with a hosepipe seconds later. This was hastily attached to the outside tap and turned on full. The jet of cold water hit dobbin right between the eyes. He threw his head up and backed away from the hedge, he hesitated for a second, but another well-aimed burst did the trick. He'd had enough, and retreated to the other side of the field. Aunt Vicky said nothing. She rewound the hosepipe and returned it to the greenhouse, then as she walked back into the house she said, rather smugly.

"Tea's ready."

Her contempt for our feeble efforts to deal with the horse was painfully obvious.

We stayed at Wallsend for the whole weekend and although Aunt Vicky was a scrupulously clean housekeeper she never seemed to mind how grubby my two cousins and I got. When we came in very dirty, she filled the bath and dumped the three of us in together. It was very strange having a bath more than once a week and especially in a proper bathroom and a proper bath. My bath night at home was in front of the fire in a zinc bath tub about three feet long. This had to be filled with a relay of pans and kettles of water heated on the gas cooker. On rare occasions I was allowed to take a bath in our local 'Bath House' above Elswick swimming pool, but that cost fourpence, which was quite expensive when you consider it cost the same for a loaf of bread, a Mars bar, or a Saturday Matinee at the local cinema.

All good things come to an end and all too soon we were on our way back home to Elswick. The bus from Wallsend dropped us off near the Central Station and we got straight onto a tram for the last part of the journey. Our 'stop' was at the bottom of Edgeware Road, just opposite the Forge Hammer public house. A lot of pubs were named after the armourment business, or machinery used to produce the tanks and guns at Vickers Armstrong. There was The Gun, The Rifle, The Hydraulic Crane, The Crooked Billet and of course The Forge Hammer.

Built in the reign of Queen Victoria the Hammer was named after the massive forge hammer used in the Armstrong factory on heavy engineering work at Elswick. The hammer worked day and night, stopping only momentarily to change shifts or make slight adjustments. It was audible as far as two miles away. The loud crash as it landed on the white-hot ingots of steel, accompanied everything we did. It could be heard in the cinema, in church and we even went to sleep to a lullaby of one thud every few seconds. The noise was so loud it had to be cast out of your consciousness or it would have driven you mad. It had to become part of the 'background music' of life. So that is exactly what happened. No one noticed it, even though it was always there! Then one day in the 1950's, it stopped forever. The reaction from the local people was amazing. There was an eerie silence, even more audible than the hammer. No one could sleep without the heartbeat of Elswick works ringing out. Everyone missed 'the hammer'. It had always symbolised the prosperity of the area, but now, even more so it was to herald its decline. Heavy industry on Tyneside was on its way out. The workforce would be reduced to less than five percent of the twenty thousand then employed. Elswick was to be transformed from almost full employment to one of the country's un-employment blackspots. The three and a half miles of Scotswood Road would soon resemble a ghost town. Shops, pubs and factories from Marlborough Crescent to Scotswood Bridge were soon to become a thing of the past. This was unthinkable in 1946. Even though the signs were there, everyone expected life to go on in the same old way. Born and bred in Elswick, lived and worked in Elswick, died and buried in Elswick.

I was happy to be part of that culture, as was everyone else at that time; the 'Road' seemed busy and prosperous. Several new businesses had sprung up and a lot of old shops were re-opened. Pennocks the cobblers opened a china and kitchenware shop. Todd Brothers had a good display of clothes in their windows again and the old pub The Miners Arms had been taken over by a joinery firm to be used as a workshop. The smell of freshly cut timber and French Polish filled your senses when passing the open door; which also revealed their main source of business, rows of newly made coffins leaning against the walls, waiting for their white satin interiors and brass handles to be fitted. The old pub was never again referred to as The Miners Arms; it was now 'The Coffin Shop'.

The thought of this all coming to an end was as far from our minds as flying to the moon. The Public Houses were all being re-painted. The old wooden cobbles were taken up and the roads re-covered with lovely smooth Tarmac, making cycling much more comfortable. The old granite cobbles were still part of the roadway up to the Elswick subway, but after that the mile and a half to Scotswood was a cyclists paradise. It was a joy to take a bike ride without being shaken half to death.

The White City Dog Track at the other side of Scotswood Bridge was re-opened and the stadium painted gleaming white. This was a regular haunt for my friends and me as it was only thirty minutes walk from Elswick. Situated at the south side of the bridge nearer to Blaydon than Scotswood, the stadium looked spectacular. It was very large and the white paintwork gave it a majestic air. Saturday afternoons were very popular and the ground quickly filled with spectators and gamblers. The minimum age for patrons was eighteen, so that left all of us out in the cold. Not that we had any intention of paying to get in anyway.

An old down-and-out was at every meeting. He would buy a programme for six pence, copy the names of all the favourites onto small pieces of paper and sell them to the gamblers as 'tips'. We often helped to write the names out for him, so we were able to see the whole programme free of charge. Once the spectators were settled into their particular vantage points, the old boy lost interest in the proceedings and disappeared over Scotswood Bridge and into the 'Ord Arms'. Obviously he had sold enough 'tips' to afford himself a little liquid refreshment.

Large advertising hoardings surrounded the West Side of the stadium and the owners had very kindly interspaced these with aluminium trellis. This looked very smart and also made climbing to the top very easy, in fact only a lift would have made it any easier. We had the best view in the house. Sitting on top of the wooden framework was as comfortable as the most expensive seats, and we could see much more than any of the paying guests. We chose our favourite dogs and bet hundreds of fictitious pounds on them. It didn't take long for us to realise how easy it was to loose a fortune by gambling, or how difficult it was to win one! Only the Bookmakers ever win, the 'punter' has enormous odds stacked against him. The occasional win was not uncommon, but the number of betting slips that littered the ground at the end of each meeting bore testimony to who the winners and losers were.

My favourite dog was called Bedan. He was all black and usually ran out of the number six trap. He was a lovely looking animal and I always backed him with a lot of fictitious money. I did bet on him with real money once and won a princely two shillings and sixpence.

After our Saturday outing to the dogs we always played a game we had made up called, 'dog billiards'. Alex Morgan had a small snooker table with a full set of snooker balls. He would set the table up in the dining room with a slight downhill tilt, from the balk end to the bottom cushion. The coloured balls were lined up in the balk end of the table to represent the six dogs in a normal race, black-white-red-yellow-blue and green, in a straight line held back by a snooker cue. We placed our bets on the colour of our choice, and then the cue was lifted up allowing the balls to roll quickly down to the bottom cushion, which was the finishing line. Betting was quite heavy and I had put six of my best marbles on the black at 'even money', but on this occasion 'Bedan' let me down and I lost. Alex was usually the 'Bookie' covering all bets himself. Some of the older lads bet with real money but we youngsters were only allowed to bet with marbles, cigarette cards or milk bottle tops. This was a bit of a shame really, we were allowed to buy our lost possessions back if we wanted to, and so what was the difference, money still changed hands.

Bella Morgan was the youngest sister in Alex's family. She was always very pale and never seemed to have much energy. During one of her brothers 'dog meetings' she came out of the bedroom looking really poorly and asked us if we could make less noise. We didn't even know that she was in the house let alone ill in bed, Alex had omitted to mention the fact. It was only a couple of weeks later that the curtains were drawn at number twelve. Bella had succumbed to whatever illness had engulfed her. She had been very young and very pretty. I asked her eldest sister Janie if I could see her. She was in my Nanna's house at the time, everyone seemed quite surprised at my request, but Janie agreed quite readily. I followed her up the lino-covered stairs. The whole place was in darkness except for the flickering candles dotted around the house.

Bella was lying on a long table dressed all in white, with a transparent veil over her face. As her sister drew the veil away memories of my Nanna came flooding back to me. She looked just like her. Her hands clasped in front of her with a little posy of blue and white flowers placed between them. I didn't say anything, I just wondered why? Why had this happened to such a young person? Surely God could have done something, she was a good Catholic and the whole family were good Catholics. He had taken my Nanna, my cousin Ronnie and all of those poor people who died in the war, why? It would take many years of soul searching before I was able to even contemplate what the answer might be.

I often found myself thinking 'how can anyone expect God to do anything, look how He let His own Son die in such a horrible way. I suppose it's what we call 'child logic', naïve, mis-guided, maybe, but honest!

The Morgan's House was out of bounds for a few weeks after the funeral, so we had to be content with our Saturday trip to the dogs. The 'Venture' Bus Company had a service that ran right past the White City Stadium, so we decided that we would travel in style. The information panel above the drivers' cab said 'Consett via Clara Vale' and the first stop on this route was just over Scotswood Bridge, which was confirmed by the conductor. The bus fare was nearly three times what we paid on the tram, but someone must have come into some money because my fare was paid for me and I can't remember who paid it. The buses were almost brand new and very comfortable, nothing like the hard wooden bench seats on the trams. They were upholstered with a soft crushed velvet fabric with marble effect patterns, and trimmed in maroon leather. It seemed a shame to get off after such a short journey. It was even more of a shame when we reached the Stadium. It was closed. A large sign on the door said 'Due to a fault in the starting traps, next Saturdays meeting is transferred to Gosforth Dog Track'.

'Next Saturday' was in fact 'this Saturday', so the temporary closure must have been announced at Wednesday's evening meeting. Typical, a luxury bus ride to nowhere. No one wanted to go home so several suggestions were made and after a short discussion we agreed unanimously to go to Lemington Glass Works near Newburn Haugh.

The Glass Works had a huge spoil heap for broken glass and we were going to search amongst it for 'pea shooters'. These were made of lengths of small-bore glass tubing obtained from the heap. There was usually plenty to find and as 'pea shooters' were not available in the shops at the time, the kids clamoured to buy them from us.

There were certain risks attached to gaining access to the glass spoil site, such as getting caught or falling into the river at Bells' Close, a stretch of water, which we had to cross in order to reach 'Chinky's Island'. The Island was really a small peninsular, but the Glass Works had taken up most of the land for it's factory, marooning the last couple of acres, which could only be reached either through the factory or over the water at Bells' Close.

'Chinkys' Island', I suspect gained its nickname from a company close by which manufactured toilets. They also had a spoil site made up mainly of broken pots, affectionately called china. So the mountain of broken china possibly lent its name to the Island, 'China Island'. This would naturally have become 'Chinkys' Island' in the local dialect.

There was a narrow bridge constructed from old railway 'sleepers', it was only a foot or so wide and attached to four large wooden posts which had been pile driven into the riverbed. The 'sleepers' were roped to the posts and floated on the surface of the river when the tide came in. It was too risky to try to walk over when they were floating so we waited until the ebb tide, when they settled down on the thick silt. The 'bridge' resembled a suspension bridge in miniature. The ropes were fastened to the top of the wooden posts then slotted through holes cut in the 'sleepers' keeping them in position. Walking over them was still a little hazardous, but holding on to the ropes as you rounded each post helped you to maintain your balance. I negotiated the first two uprights without much trouble but the third one was still quite wet from being submerged at high tide. I decided not to 'bear hug' the post to get round it but to use the rope and sway out and step past without actually touching it. I had followed the same procedure on numerous occasions without any difficulty and confidently swayed backwards holding the rope, which was quite taught. I made to take the single step onto the next 'sleeper' but the rope kept on stretching. The water had tightened it much more than I realised and my weight was making it act like a piece of elastic. I was gently deposited, seat first, into the thick brown stinking mud. When the surface was broken it revealed a black oily substance, which smelled even worse. I instinctively put my left hand out to push myself back up, but it just sank into the mire up to my elbow. Fortunately my feet were still on the bridge and I had a tight hold on the wet rope with my right hand. With a little help from my friends I was able to scramble back to safety. The seat of my trousers was covered in soaking wet black mud and smelled rather high, so I decided to take them off to let them dry. I wiped the mud from my left hand and arm with dry grass and washed myself with water from the river. My friends had lit a fire and my trousers were hanging from a gorse bush near the heat. The incident didn't spoil our day, or even interfere with it. We played our usual games of Cowboys and Indians, Hide-and-seek etc., plus a successful trip to the glass dump. I didn't even think about my trousers until it started to get dark.

We made our way back to our campfire, which was still burning brightly, but not quite, warm enough to dry wet mud. One of the younger lads was holding the trousers closer to the fire; I asked him how the drying was going, to which he replied.

"They're nearly dry, there's just one little patch here, that's still wet."

He poked his finger at the 'wet' patch and it went straight through the material. The 'wet' patch turned out to be a scorched patch, not wet, but burned as black as coal, which just disintegrated as soon as it was touched. The whole of the seat became two large holes! My friends were very sympathetic and some of them even shed tears at my misfortune…tears of laughter! This frivolity erupted into hysterics when I put my trousers back on and with laughter being so infectious it wasn't long before I joined in. On the way home I wrapped my jacket around my waist and tied the two sleeves together like an apron in reverse, preventing the public display of my rear end and not-too-clean underpants.

I received the usual verbal roasting from my mother when she saw the state of my clothes. Fortunately for me we had company, so no physical violence took place. The incident was mentioned on several occasions, but not too seriously.

"When I saw the state of them good trousers, I could've flattened you. You'll never know how lucky you were."

Oh but I did!

ॐ

The Bedford family lived at number 56 in our street, they seemed quite well off compared to us. Mr Bedford was a pit deputy at one of the local collieries and their three daughters and Mrs Bedford's brother who lived with them, all had good jobs. We often swapped some of our freshly laid eggs for a couple of buckets of coal to supplement our meagre fuel ration. The Bedfords got a free coal allowance, we got free eggs from our hens, and so no money ever changed hands in the transaction.

One day I had just finished emptying the two buckets of coal into the coalhouse when my mother shouted my name.

"Billie."

My heart sank. I had a feeling she was about to send me on my second most hated errand. First on my most hated list was the pawnshop, second was asking some friend or neighbour to lend her some money.

"Go and ask Mrs Bedford if I can borrow two and six 'till next week."

"Oh, can you not ask her? You've just been talking to her and she seemed to be in a good mood. I hate asking her, she always tuts and moans...

'What does your mother think I am, the Bank of England?'

My mother gave me that 'death-by-a-thousand-cuts' look, so I didn't argue anymore. I just went and did her bidding. I shouted up the stairs of number 56.

"Mrs Bedford, me ma says can you lend her half a crown 'till next week?"

I thought to myself, wait for it, wait for it, and sure enough it came!

"Ah don't know, what does ya mother think I am, the Bank of England? It's hard to tell who this bliddy half crown belongs to, me or her."

I had heard this refrain so many times before; you would think she would learn some new lyrics. She appeared at the top of the stairs.

"Here, and I want it back next week mind you, tell your mother we are as hard up as anybody."

'Oh God, spare me the lecture', I thought. Just give me the money and get it over with.

The half crown landed at the bottom of the stairs. I picked it up saying.

"Ta, I'll tell her Mrs Bedford."

The coin was another George V, dated 1922, made from solid silver and worth much more than the two shillings and sixpence it represented. All 'silver' coins from Roman times onwards contained some of the precious metal. Many lower denominations were made from an alloy containing a percentage of silver. It did not take long for the unscrupulous to realise that by melting down early silver coins you could increase their value by as much as one hundred percent. The Royal Mint also realised that the price of silver was rapidly increasing, so in 1926 they reduced the silver content to about fifty percent and silver coins became silver alloy. This lasted until 1946 when silver ceased to be used at all for coinage. All coins are made from an alloy made up of copper and nickel, known as 'cupro nickel'. Precious metals like Gold and Silver are reserved for special commemorative coins and medals but not for general circulation.

I took the money to my mother and relayed Mrs Bedford's comments.

"Aye, she didn't say that last week did she when I sold her that two pound ticket for thirty bob? She makes me sick sometimes, hard up! She doesn't no what hard up means."

This was my mother's way of showing how grateful she was at having been granted the loan of the two and sixpence.

The two-pound ticket had come from a 'Tally' lady called Miss Engleton, she ran a small credit business with her sister and issued 'tickets' for various amounts of money, which had to be redeemed in shops or stores participating in the scheme. They were known as 'ticket shops'. My mother had sent me up to Miss Engleton's house in the very posh Wingrove Road, to ask her if she could let us have a two-pound ticket for Todd Brothers. The Victorian terraced house was huge. It was three stories high. The door opened into a short passage with a thick coconut mat at the entrance. The hall door had leaded windows in the top half with beautiful stained glass designs, more suitable for a church than a house. All the woodwork was dark mahogany, richly polished and smelling of furniture wax. The light from the kitchen gave the parquet floor a look of water reflecting

Miss Engleton's image as she walked towards me. She was a very regal looking lady, wearing a pale green cardigan over a white blouse and a string of pearls almost down to her waist. I gave her the note from my mother. She clipped a pair of spectacles onto the end of her nose and sighed a couple of times as she read it.

"You know your mother hasn't paid off the last ticket yet and we never give anyone more credit until their account is clear." She said, shaking her head as she spoke.

I knew there was a reason behind my being sent on this errand. Ma was trying it on again, and I was the one who had to do the dirty work.

"Yeah I know that but me Ma says if you give her the two pound ticket she'll pay for it separately."

I didn't know what I was talking about but it sounded good. I was still standing in the hallway when another lady came in. She was wearing a maroon coloured coat with a whole fox 'round the collar, the head as well. I had only seen her once before, in our house but I recognised her straightaway, it was Miss Engleton's sister, they were just like twins. They immediately went into a little huddle, obviously discussing the note, which they read over, several times. Miss Engleton disappeared into the reception room on the right of the passage. She called me into the room. She was sitting at a large desk with an electric light above it; everything on the desk was in order, neat and tidy, not a thing out of place.

"My sister and I have decided to let your mother have the ticket, but this will be for one time only and she's not to ask us to do it again, she must pay for it separately and it must be finished before she asks for any more, understand?"

"Yes, yes I'll tell her when I get home." I answered.

'Not that it will do any good' I said to myself.

Mrs Bedford duly paid my mother one pound and ten shillings for the two-pound ticket and Ma had ready cash to buy whatever she wanted.

The half crown was handed back to me along with a list of things she wanted from the Co-op Stores. It was most unusual to have to do a mid-week errand to the Co-op but I didn't mind, it would probably mean less to carry on Saturday. I left by the back door flipping the silver coin up in the air and catching it just before it reached the ground. I dropped it a couple of times but there were no 'fever grates' in the back lane, so there was no danger of losing it. I met one of my friends as I was walking up Glue House Lane and he decided to come with me to the Co-op.

There was a long queue at the grocery counter so I entertained myself, flipping the half crown up in the air with one hand and catching it in the other. Then spinning it on the wooden counter like a 'top', to the annoyance of the elderly gentleman in charge of the 'fats'! I was trying to throw the coin up in the air and make it go up my sleeve as I pretended to catch it. I managed to do the trick a couple of times impressing my school friend with my 'magic'. Old Grumpy on the other side of the counter said, rather loudly.

"Next" just as I threw the half crown into the air once again. I took my eyes off it for a fraction of a second and heard it as it hit the wooden floor between the footprints in the sawdust. It was my turn.

"Just a minute, I've dropped me money."

"It serves you right, you've never stopped playing with it since you came in. Next!"

I had lost my turn and I was now on my hands and knees looking for the missing half crown.

"It must be here, it just dropped in front of me."

I said to myself, as I swept away the sawdust. My friend was doing the same, but it wasn't there. We asked people to move away until we looked under their feet but it had just disappeared.

By now I was beginning to panic so I asked one of the assistants if she could help me. She seemed very concerned and suggested that I should wait until five o'clock when they closed; then she would get someone to sweep the sawdust into one pile, put it through a sieve and the coin would probably turn up. I thought this was a brilliant idea, the money must be here and this would be the best way to find it. I still had quite some time to wait until the shop closed so I asked my friend to let my mother know I was going to be late, but not to mention the reason why.

Promptly at five o'clock two men in brown warehouse coats came into the shop and started to sweep the sawdust up from one end of the floor near where I was standing. The shop was huge, more like a Cathedral, with a glass-domed roof that must have been thirty feet above the floor. The three counters were at least thirty feet long on each side with over three feet of counter between the customers and the assistants. I followed the two sweepers every inch of the way scouring the floor expecting to see old George the fifth at any minute. But he didn't appear. It had never entered my head that the coin may have gone forever; I was full of optimism. It must be here.

As the last remnants of the greying sawdust was carefully sifted, doubt began to creep into my mind. It wasn't here. Someone had found it, and kept it. Although I would probably have done the same thing I thought 'what a dirty trick; this was stealing'.

The two entrance doors suddenly rattled. I looked around to see my mother's anxious face peering through the plate glass window halfway up the door. She must have thought that someone had spotted her ration book 'fiddle' and that I had been detained because of it.

"What's wrong?" She said as she was let in.

"What's happened? Why have you been here so long?"

The change in her was quite frightening when I explained about the lost money. Her anxiety quickly turned to anger.

"How many times have I told you?"

That was all I heard as the blows rained down on my head and face.

"You can't go a message without…"

Again I only caught part of the sentence as she dragged me out of the shop. An old lady chided my mother as she marched me down Glue House Lane.

"Arr pet there's no need for that, he's only a bairn."

"Mind your own bloody business, he's my child and I'll do as I see fit."

She must have realised she was making a spectacle of herself, so she stopped hitting me, but she wouldn't let go of my shirt collar. She knew I'd be off like a shot.

Finally we reached home. I was literally thrown down the four stairs into the sitting room, landing face down on the coconut mat. The weight of my mother sitting on my back knocked the wind out of me. She straddled me horse fashion as she rained blows to the back of my head. She was completely out of control. The sound of each punch or slap echoed in my head as waves of unconsciousness washed over me. It wasn't hurting anymore. I just lay there with my face pressed into the rough weave of the mat.

I think my sister saved my life that day. Her crying distracted my mother for a second, which must have brought her back to her senses. She picked the baby up out of the pram and gently rocked her back and forth in her arms.

When I gained enough courage to look up I discovered that not only was my sister crying but Ma was crying too. My head felt as though it was about to burst, but I wasn't as badly hurt as I had thought. I often got bad headaches due to sinus trouble but this was the worst one I'd had for a long time. I'd had several 'good hidings' in my short life but the latest one topped them all. I knew it was my own fault. I knew I shouldn't have messed about with the money. I knew how hard up we were. But I still didn't think that justified the severity of the beating. I decided there and then that if I ever had children of my own, I would never send them on messages, never beat them or humiliate them. I had something knocked out of me that day and it took me a long time to find out what it was. My mother lost my respect, it's sad to say. I became very resentful, insolent and very aggressive. I looked for trouble and would fight anyone. There didn't have to be a reason. I just had to feel threatened; that was enough. I felt as though I had to show everyone that I was not one to be messed with. On one occasion I fought with one of my best friends for over twenty minutes. He was giving me a rare 'going over' but I wouldn't stop. All of his family were there giving him support, even his parents. I was on my own. His father was telling him what to do and it was working, I was on the retreat. My opponent was Billy Ball and we had been friends since we were two years old. He was a month younger than me but quite a bit taller. Billy was a little slow at times, normally very placid and we had always got on very well.

One day when he was eating a toffee apple I jokingly said to him.

"You should have been called 'Toffee Apple' instead of Billy, you eat that many."

The name stuck and he hated it. If you wanted to annoy him

you just had to say it. Well on this day I had said it and I was beginning to regret it. I had never seen him so mad. I'd had lots of hard fights and could handle myself pretty well but I was right on my back foot in this one. My arms were numb from blocking his punches but he was showing signs of tiring. He kept dropping his guard and shaking his arms before launching another attack. He did it again, down went his hands, but I didn't wait for the flurry of punches that was about to follow. Instead I stepped forward and launched a viscous straight right to the throat followed by a left hook to the side of the head. The right was all that was necessary; the left was just a little bonus. Billy clutched at his throat and fell to his knees coughing and retching. I thought 'will I hit him again while he's on his knees?' I felt like it and it certainly would have ended the proceedings, but I'm glad to say I didn't. He'd had enough and so had I. After all the tears had been dried and we had dusted ourselves down we just stood and looked at each other, as if to say 'what was that all about'? We both knew it would never happen again. Billy has remained a dear friend, one of nature's gentlemen, loved and respected by everyone. I think I must be one of the very few people ever to have fallen out with him, but that was the one and only time. It never has, and never will happen again.

I was challenged to fight on several occasions and readily accepted every time. I now had a reputation and was expected to live up to it. I fought the Newton brothers together. It actually started out with the elder brother, but his younger brother joined in when he saw I was gaining the upper hand. It didn't do either of them any good. I thrashed them both.

My family were not aware of what was going on and I didn't tell them. In fact I have never told them. Every time a fight was arranged I was sure I was going to win, never even contemplating the thought of defeat.

Eventually I decided to try the 'noble art' on a more formal basis, fighting in the ring with boxing gloves, three-minute rounds and rules. It all seemed a bit soft to me at first, but the more I studied it the more I began to realise that boxing was a very scientific sport. Being able to fight someone for three, three-minute rounds, without loosing your temper and being awarded prizes for doing so, was strange but very enjoyable.

My street fighting helped me a lot in the sport and a few years later I fought for and won the Northumberland County Welterweight Championship, at the age of seventeen. I beat a twenty-one year old miner in the final, which was held in New St. James' Hall, (Now Gallowgate Metro Station).

Many good boxers were born on Tyneside, and right from the earliest 'bare knuckle' days to the present, we have produced our share of champions. The one man who stands out, way above the others in my estimation is 'Seaman' Tommy Watson, who in 1932 became British Featherweight Champion. It was a very strange coincidence that he spent his early childhood at No.55 Cannon Street, and I lived at No.54, just across the street.

Watson joined the Navy at sixteen years of age but bought himself out three years later to become a full time boxer. He had a very successful career and became the first North Eastern pugilist to win a Lonsdale Belt. He lost only nine fights out of ninety-two and even fought the world champion, the legendary 'Kid' Chocolate, losing on points after a very close contest. When he retired from boxing he became a very successful referee. He ended his days as manager of The Gun Hotel on Scotswood Road only yards from where he was born. The sign outside proudly boasted 'Manager: 'Seaman' Tommy Watson former British Featherweight Champion'. He died in 1971, aged only sixty-three.

I had my first 'taste' of boxing gloves long before I took up the sport seriously. It happened one night in 1947. I was having an argument with one of my pals in the local boy's club where my father's younger brother Christopher was assistant club leader. The argument was becoming quite heated so my Uncle Chris decided it would be better if we settled the dispute in the boxing ring, under his supervision. I have to admit I wasn't too keen at first as my adversary was older and taller than myself, and while I was able to shout as loud as he could I had grave doubts about my chances of beating him in the ring.

We agreed to fight for only one 'round', which would last for as long as it took for one of us to say we'd had enough. The gloves were made of cotton and were stuffed with horsehair. I can remember it as though it was yesterday, the pungent smell of stale sweat and dust that had impregnated them over the years of use and abuse (they were more often used for kicking around the hall as a substitute for a football). I hesitate to describe the fight, suffice to say it was horrendous, which is from the Latin word 'horrendus' meaning 'to be shuddered at': very appropriate. No one won or lost in this encounter, we just hammered each other till we were both covered in sweat and grime caused by the dust that erupted from each glove with every blow struck. I always maintain that I won, but that was only to preserve my unbeaten record.

⁂

The changes were beginning to take place on Scotswood Road. The trams had been replaced with double-decker buses and the tramlines were taken up; a sure sign that they would never return. The yellow and brown granite cobbles were replaced with Tarmac, but were stored by the council and used years later to create fancy pavements.

A Chinese Restaurant opened opposite the Cattle Market, one of the first in Newcastle. They had old second hand tables and chairs, no tablecloths and only one condiment set.

The Cattle Market was being used less and less. The days of hundreds of beasts being bought and sold seemed to be over. My Aunt Bella had a small boarding house just opposite the main entrance to the market and I spent many hours watching from the windows as the cattle, sheep, and pigs were unloaded for auction. Sometimes the animals were taken straight from the sale to the slaughterhouse, to be converted into meat.

My aunt looked after three old gentlemen, two First World War veterans and an ex-bare knuckle boxer, named Geordie Miller. He was over sixty years of age and worked at the local Blind Society workshops, chopping firewood. It seemed to be a very strange occupation for someone with no sight at all, but he never had an accident all the time he worked there.

The Boarding House was next door to the Ord Arms public house, which was just off Scotswood Road and therefore didn't qualify as one of the twenty-seven public houses along Scotswood Road.

The other two lodgers, Jimmy Roach (who she later married) and Charley Hartley received disability pensions from the Army after being injured in the First World War. Jimmy had been badly burned and Charlie had a steel plate in his head. He also suffered from shell shock. Each lodger had his own room but they all had their meals together in Aunt Bella's dining room. Geordie's room was on the first floor at the front of the house. The large sash window was a marvellous vantagepoint to observe the Cattle Market. I often spent time listening to Geordie's stories of his many ring battles; some of which lasted for two or three hours. He didn't lose his sight through boxing but he did have his arm broken in one fight and it never healed properly. It left a large lump on his elbow and restricted the movement in that joint for the rest of his life.

Boxing started over three hundred years ago and was originally called 'Prize-Fighting'. There were some rudimentary rules at the outset, but basically anything but shooting each other seems to have been allowed. A round lasted until one of the contestants was knocked or wrestled to the ground. He was given thirty seconds to recover and if he failed to do so, the other fighter was declared the winner. Most contests were held outdoors well away from the prying eyes of the law. A line was scratched in the centre of the ring and both men had to stand toe-to-toe on the line before a round could begin. This was known as 'toeing the line', a euphemism widely used today to describe someone's willingness, or unwillingness to abide by the rules.

After a knock down it was up to the handlers, or seconds, to bring their man up to the scratch line within the required time. As we all know, not being 'up to scratch' covers a multitude of reasons, either in sport, health, ability etc., for performing below expectations, a legacy from the old bare-knuckle breed.

In 1867 the Marquis of Queensbury presented his rules to the boxing 'fancy'. Each round should consist of only three minutes duration, after which time the contestants shall have a one minute rest, being allowed to sit on the bent knee of one of his handlers. The two contestants or their representatives shall agree the number of rounds of the contest before the day of the fight. Gloves or mufflers to protect the hands are to be worn for the entire contest.

Although many fights still took place under the old Prize Ring rules it was not long before the governing bodies worldwide adopted the new rules. All of today's boxing matches are held under Marquis of Queensbury rules. The last world championship fought without gloves was held in 1889 and was between John L. Sullivan and Jake Kilrain. After a battle lasting over two hours, Sullivan was declared the winner. He vowed he would never fight bare knuckle again.

The new rules brought a bit of respectability to the sport, leading to its eventual legalisation.

My father always maintained that boxing could never be classified as a sport.

"How the hell can two men trying to beat each others brains out, be called sport?"

"He was never much of a sports fan. He didn't go to football or cricket matches and only watched me run two track races in my thirty-five years as an active runner. We sometimes went to the wrestling on a Saturday night at New St. James' Hall, but that was about the limit of his interest in sport.

When Dad was finally released from Military Service on the 22nd of April 1946 the war had been over for almost twelve months. I was ten years old and my sister was just three weeks away from her first birthday. It was great to have him back. It gave us a warm feeling knowing that there was someone there to protect us. The country was billions of pounds in debt and the road back to prosperity was going to be long and arduous. Work was very difficult find. Many ex-servicemen were looking for jobs and the Northeast in particular, seemed less able to provide employment for them.

When war veterans left the services they were given a small amount of money known as a gratuity, to help them to ease their transition back into civilian life. After being told what to do and how to do it for such a long time it was often very difficult for them to have to think and act on their own initiative. Initiative is a dirty word in the Army. No one, from the highest rank, down to the lowly private, acts on initiative; soldiers act only on orders! They are given the orders, and then they are expected to carry them out with blind obedience. One light hearted story often recounted by my father summed up the indoctrination process employed by the army to achieve this.

During a physical training session the instructor in charge brought the whole squad to attention.

"Right you 'orrible lot, when I shout 'one', you will all jump up in the air. When I shout 'two', you will come down!

One!

What are you all doing back on the floor, I didn't shout 'two', get back up where you were!"

It was only a joke, but what made it an even bigger joke was the sight of thirty squaddies trying to stay up in the air until they were told to come down!

The small amount of money Dad received as his gratuity was soon put to good use. He purchased several pieces of leather and started repairing shoes again as an extra source of income. Being a very accomplished cobbler, he found no difficulty in re-kindling the skills taught to him by his father. I used to watch him for hours, fascinated by the technique required just to 'sole and heel' a pair of shoes.

First of all the choice of leather was very important. Dad knew which piece of the hide was best for soles and which for heels. The sole needed to be flexible but hard wearing, while the heel had to be firm. Some of the shoes people brought for repair were almost falling to pieces, but he always managed to do something to save them. He used to say.

"If the uppers' are still there, I can mend them."

The 'upper' being the part of the boot or shoe that the sole and heel was attached to.

First the old sole and heel were stripped off. A thin piece of flexible leather was nailed or hand stitched to the full length of the upper and filed down to the shape of the shoe. Dad would then cut out a sole to match the shape of the foot, leaving enough space to fit a new heel later. A line was drawn on the piece of leather about a quarter of an inch in from the edge and round the whole of the sole, making it appear as though a smaller one was to be cut out. An incision with a very sharp knife was made at a slight angle, following the line but penetrating only halfway through the leather. Dad then prised the leather upwards like a trap door, revealing the deep cut. The sole was placed onto the upturned shoe and nailed into position.

A metal 'last' was used to fit inside the shoe. This flattened out the nails securing the leather in the process. When all of the nails had been inserted, the upturned leather was firmly hammered flat and as if by magic there was the new sole firmly attached to the shoe, with not one nail visible. The heel was made of four layers of thick leather with a small 'heel plate' inserted at the back to protect the layers and prolong their life.

When the repair was complete, the leather was pared with a cobbling knife to remove the excess, and then smoothed down with a heavy file called a rasp. The next stage was my job. Dad heated a small tin of 'heel ball', which was a black waxy substance. This had to be applied to the edge of the new leather with a hot iron. The iron, being only about one inch long, was attached to a long wooden handle. I would dip the hot iron into the 'heel ball' and rub it over the coarse edges. The wax penetrated a fair way into the leather dyeing it black or brown. A final rub down with fine sandpaper and a second coat of 'heel ball' made the shoes look like new. For all of that work and the skill necessary to accomplish it Dad was paid the princely sum of three shillings. But he never complained. He used to say…

"That's three bob more than I had when I got up this morning, and three bob further away from the workhouse!"

One of the best things about having my father back home, apart from the obvious ones, was the lack of violence from my mother. I can't remember ever being beaten by her when he was around. Oh, I got the odd slap or punch, but no hysterical assaults.

They both argued quite frequently, so I would slip away unnoticed, not returning until things had calmed down. The rows usually started with light-hearted banter and lots of pushing and laughing, but invariably one or the other would say or do something out of place and the 'slap and tickle' would end in a full scale 'battle'. Ma's temper was still very volatile, but now it was mainly directed at my father, not me. On one occasion she threw a tin of tomatoes at him, hitting him between the shoulder blades as he turned away. My Auntie Dot, who was present at the time, recalled…

"That was the first time in my life I had ever seen a fully grown man knocked down by a pound of tomatoes, mind you, they were still in the tin at the time!"

I had enormous respect for my Dad, but our relationship never seemed to be a close one. He never laid a hand on me in his life, and we never had a cross word between us, but there still seemed to be something missing. We never had anything in common. A conversation with him was more like filling in a tax form. I think the six years he spent in the army ruined the chances of us forming any kind of a bond, in fact I often felt as though I was in the way and intruding on his and my mothers relationship.

I bought my first gramophone record when I was eleven years old. I saved my pennies and ha'pennys until I had the four shillings and ninepence I needed. I walked into Newcastle town and made my way to 'Windows' in the Central Arcade. This was my first experience of buying a new record and I felt a little apprehensive as I approached the dark mahogany counter.

"Yes young man, what can I get for you?"

She was a lovely lady and I could smell her perfume as she leaned forward over the counter.

"Em, have you got Caruso singing 'On with the Motley', please?" I asked.

"My now, I am surprised. I thought you were going to ask for Vera Lynn singing White Cliffs of Dover," she said, smiling.

I blushed beetroot red, and then I realised she was only joking.

As she removed the record from the paper sleeve I marvelled at how pristine it was, shiny black with the HMV red collectors label printed with gold lettering. She held it by the edge not wishing to touch the precious recorded part of the shellac.

"Booth number three is available so you can have a little listen and see if you like it. The sound of these old recordings are not as good as the modern one's but I'll let you hear it and you can make your own mind up."

I followed her to number three booth and we both went inside. It was large enough to hold three or four people, and her perfume again filled the air as she placed the record onto the turntable. She smiled through the glass door as she closed it behind her and I sat in raptures as Caruso sang Vesti la Giubba from Leoncavallo's Pagliacci. It was magnificent. I didn't even notice the surface noises from the old acoustic recording. It was the voice that mattered and this voice came straight from Heaven. I had heard snatches of Caruso's recordings on two-way family favourites, but this was the first time I had been able to listen to a full recording played just for me.

I wiped the tears from my eyes as the last strains of the orchestra died away. The lump of emotion in my throat almost choked me and I just sat and stared at the record as it slowed to a halt.

"Did you enjoy that, then?"

The kind ladies' voice jolted me back to reality.

"Oh yes, I think it was marvellous."

"Good, I'm glad you liked it, but you don't have to buy it you know, it is a lot of money for such an old recording."

"Oh no, I'll have it please." I said, and followed her back to the counter.

The record didn't sound as good on our old wind-up gramophone, but the voice still sounded wonderful. I was astounded to discover that Caruso was my father's favourite tenor and he had once owned several of his recordings. This kind of information was never forth coming from either of my parents, it was always a chance remark or a direct question that was necessary to get them to open up and let me into their little world.

My Dad's best friend was Billy Hall, Uncle Billy to me, and he was somewhat of an expert on the workings of the wireless. So when Dad decided to buy a second hand 'Cossor' Uncle Billy was there like a shot to help him to install it. Radio's were very complicated pieces of apparatus in those days and had to be powered by batteries, as no one in our locality had electricity.

The 'Cossor' stood about three feet tall and it took two adults to lift it. The cabinet was made of thick plywood veneered with walnut. The inside of the cabinet housed the battery, grid bias, accumulator and all of the valves and wires required to receive sound. This was then transmitted to a very large loudspeaker in front of the workings to output the signal.

Dad and his friend worked on it for several days but all they got was loud whistles and foreign sounding voices that seemed to come from outer space. Uncle Billy flicked the inch of ash off the end of his cigarette and stood back from the radio, then looked at my Dad.

"Well yi bugger Bill" he said pushing his cap to the back of his head.

"What a pair of bloody idiots we are. Yih kna' wharrit is, we've been trying for three bloody days to get something on this wireless wih nee bloody aerial in."

I couldn't quite catch what was said after that, but they both laughed. It sounded a bit like...

"After all that mucking about!"

The missing aerial was plugged into the back of the radio then passed through a hole in the window sill to be attached to a long clothes prop fastened to the side of the house. The result was instantaneous loud music as clear as anything I had ever heard. I felt a tingle of excitement at the prospect of hearing Caruso with such clarity. I had listened to radio shows on my Granda Mills' wireless, or in some friend's house, but this was ours, our first radio.

I soon became a fan of all of the popular programmes such as 'The Charlie Chester Show', Itma, 'Much Binding in the Marsh', and 'Twenty Questions'. This was hosted by Stewart McPherson and later by Gilbert Harding. It was a whole new world of entertainment. One night of the week I was allowed to stay up late and listen to 'The Man in Black' with Valentine Dyall. He frightened me half-to-death with his deep basso-profundo voice, creating terrifying pictures as he narrated the short plays. It was often what he didn't say that was more frightening.

Then there were the Carrol Levis' Discoveries, Friday Night is Music Night, and a new comedy show from Wales called 'Welsh Rarebit' with Ozzie Morris and a little fat comedian who sang a duet with himself, singing both the tenor and soprano parts. This little fat comedian was later to become Sir Harry Secombe, one of the most loved entertainers of all time.

The characters in each show took on their own identity. Dick Barton Special Agent, became a Douglas Fairbanks Jnr. type hero, and not even his photograph could change that image. I remember one of the characters from Tommy Handleys' 'Itma'. He was supposed to be some kind of spy who turned up in the most unusual places. His catchphrase was 'this is Funf speaking' and I always imagined him dressed in a long black overcoat, a black Homburg hat and a grey scarf wrapped around his face. I never discovered what he really looked like, but it wouldn't have changed my picture of him anyway.

In many ways radio was better than television. It wasn't necessary to see a tap dancer to know how well he was dancing and lots of characters were more convincing in the imagination, than they were in reality.

We had our share of singers too, Heddle Nash, John Hanson, the wonderful Jewish tenor Jan Pearce, and of course Beniamino Gigli, who was still the leading tenor in the world of tragic opera.

Comedy was always high on the entertainment agenda and most of the comic actors and comedians had been busy entertaining the troops during the war. There was now a multitude of talent available as they left the services. Frankie Howard, Ted Ray, Arthur Askey, Vic Oliver, Frank Randal Norman Evans, George Formby, Arthur Lucan and Kitty McShane as 'Mother Riley' and daughter 'Kitty' and scores of others. They all seemed to be saying 'the war's over now, so let's have a good laugh for a change'. Even a ventriloquist's dummy had his own show, 'Educating Archie', with Peter Brough, Archie Andrews (the dummy), Max Bygraves, and the teenage soprano Julie Andrews (no relation to the dummy) who was destined to become a super star.

Our new 'Cossor' was never turned off. The accumulator was the power source needed to run the radio and it had to be recharged at regular intervals, rather like a car battery. There were several shops that provided a charging service and it cost about sixpence per recharge. We had three accumulators, one on charge, one in use and one in reserve in case the power ran out over the weekend. It was marvellous to have so much entertainment at the flick of a switch.

My Parents went out most Saturday evenings, while I stayed at home with my sister, I didn't mind at all. I could listen to all of my favourite programmes, and if my sister was a bit 'twisty' I used to get her up out of her cot and let her listen also. It was a very effective way of getting her back to sleep.

My father finally found employment with a painting contractor. The firm had won a contract with Vickers Armstrong to remove the camouflage from the factory roofs.

They had all been painted in various shades of green and brown to blend in with the landscape. This was supposed to confuse the German pilots on their bombing raids. It was partially successful, but they still managed to hit the factories on several occasions.

As this was no longer necessary, the government decided to have all traces of the war removed. Some roads had been barricaded with concrete and steel, the coast was dotted with machine gun bunkers commonly known as 'pill boxes', some of which survive to this day. The air raid shelters were demolished; this provoked a nostalgic air of regret when they disappeared.

The 'togetherness' spirit that had prevailed during the conflict was about to die, never to be resurrected. Everyone remembered the long nights during the air raids, singing our own propaganda songs.

'We're going to hang out the washing on the Siegfried Line', 'Run Rabbit Run' and the rude version of 'Colonel Bogie'. No one seemed to mind us youngsters' singing:-

Hitler has only got one ball
Himmler has two but very small
But Goballs, yes Mr Goballs
Oh, poor old Goballs, has no balls at all.

'Goballs' was really Marshal Geobbels, one of Hitler's henchmen, but the way we pronounced his name made it fit the song perfectly.

Dad came home on his first payday at about half past five. He hung his coat up on the inside of the cupboard door and sat on the fender in front of the fire. His white boiler suit was covered in khaki scuffs and splashes. My mother came in from the scullery and sat in the armchair; I was on the sofa beside my sister, who was sound asleep. The brown envelope in Dad's hand seemed to have mesmerised us all. No one spoke. He shook it a couple of times and smiled as the coins jingled inside, then he tore it open at the top. He took out four beautiful blue pound notes followed by a smaller red note with ten shillings printed in the centre of the floral design. They were all crisp and brand new.

The Bank of England had introduced blue pound notes in 1940 to protect our currency from German counterfeiters. It was also the first paper money in the world to have a metal security strip embedded into each note.

Dad tipped the packet upside down and two half crowns, a

threepenny piece and four large copper pennies tumbled into his hand. Four pounds, fifteen shillings and seven pence, a fortune!

"That's a lot more than you thought you would get." said Ma, "you said about four pounds for a forty four hour week."

"Aye, that's true," he replied.

"But they don't pay you so much an hour any more, well not this firm anyway. They give you a price for doing a certain number of roofs in a week, and if you do really well and get them finished quickly you can start on another lot straight away. The more you get done, the more you get paid. It's called piece work."

Ever practical Ma asked...

"What happens if you don't get them done in time?"

"Well then you don't make as much."

Dad explained, "It's a bit of a risk, but it seems to be working out okay for our squad."

Three of the pound notes were handed over to my mother. She was smiling broadly as she slipped them into her red leather purse. Three pounds to keep us for a week, it was a King's ransom. No more pawnshops, no more 'tick', no more borrowing from the Bedfords. All of these things flashed through my mind. Dad put the other two notes into the breast pocket of his overall and the two half crowns along with the odd coppers went into his trouser pocket, or at least they appeared to. As he stood up he put his right hand back into the trouser pocket and fished out one of the coins.

"Here," he said.

"Don't spend it all in one shop."

My heart leapt as I saw the half crown in between his fingers and thumb. Two and six for me, I couldn't believe it; I didn't know what to say. I just mumbled "Ta Da," as I turned the coin over and over in my hands.

Later I could hear my mother remonstrating with my father. Her voice came clearly through the closed scullery door.

"That's far too much money to give a ten year old, half of that would have been quite sufficient."

"Well so what, we'll see what he does with it. Anyway I owe him some 'back' pocket money, he got very little while I was in the army, and he might not get the same every week."

The contract with Vickers Armstrong lasted for several weeks and I continued to receive my half crown pocket money every Friday.

While my Dad was working on the Elswick factory I was employed to deliver a large enamelled jug of boiling hot water every day to the site.

The men filled their tea cans with the water and hung them over an open brazier to 'mast' the tea. I was paid threepence from each member of the squad, which added up to another one and six a week. I thought I was in clover, until I got back home. My mother insisted that the money was to pay for the gas used to heat up the water. She took the shilling and let me keep the sixpence. I suppose I was lucky, - she could have taken the lot! I worked it out at one penny a day, Monday to Saturday. It was only a ten-minute walk each way, but it was the lowest paid job I ever had.

I mentioned the incident to my Dad and he told me not to worry, he would sort something out.

On my next payday the men gave me an old pay packet with some money inside.

"That's for your mother, and that's for you."

Dad said as he pressed a shilling into the palm of my hand.

"Don't tell her how much you got, just give her the envelope."

It made me feel really grown up to be sharing a secret with my father; it was to be the first of many.

One morning when I arrived at the Elswick works one of my Dads squad met me at the gate to collect the water.

"Where's me Da?" I asked.

"Oh he had a little accident this morning, nowt serious, he just got some caustic on his fingers."

'Nowt serious', I thought, then why isn't he here? He wasn't the type to stay away from work if it was 'nowt serious'! I hurried back along Scotswood Road and through the old buildings to our house. I had to let my mother know what had happened. I burst into the kitchen anxious to tell my tale, but Dad was already there. Sitting in the armchair in front of the fire. He was still dressed in his white overalls but both of his hands were bandaged. Each finger individually bound in white gauze. He looked as though he was wearing white gloves. His face looked a little pale, but otherwise he seemed all right. I didn't ask him what had happened, I was just relieved to see he was okay.

Later he explained that while he was washing down part of the roof with a solution of caustic soda and carbolic acid, he had slipped and put his hands out to save himself from falling face down. He'd had the presence of mind to put only the tips of his fingers onto the wet slates as he realised he was about to touch the corrosive liquid. When he regained his balance he immediately wiped his fingers, but he was too late to prevent them from being burnt.

The hospital had given him a roll of gauze and a bottle of 'Acraflavine' and told him to change the dressings twice a day. Later that evening Ma started to unwind the bandages one finger at a time. When I saw the injuries he had received I was absolutely shocked. He had no fingerprints left on any of his fingers or thumbs. The end of each digit was completely gone. They looked as though they had been pared away with a cobbling knife. The flesh was deep red, glistening with the fluid weeping from each wound, the bone clearly visible just below the surface. Dad laughed as he saw the colour drain from my face.

"What's the marra wih you? It's only the end of me fingers."

I couldn't believe how he was able to joke about it. I thought, 'he must be as tough as nails'.

"Does it not hurt?" I asked.

"Aye, it does a bit," he replied.

"But moaning about it won't make it any better."

Next morning he was back at work. Ma washed his face for him and off he went. He didn't even have a day off, and by the end of that week he had no bandages on his hands, just a small Elastoplast on the end of each finger.

When the camouflage contract was completed the company informed the men that there was no more work for them on Tyneside, but several jobs were available in various parts of the country, working on painting contracts they had recently won. This meant working away from home for several weeks at a time. Not the kind of situation families wanted to be in after the several years of forced separation during the war. Our family was no exception. When Dad asked Ma what she thought about him working away, she almost hit the roof. It wasn't an argument; it was just a very loud and straightforward statement.

"There's no way you're leaving me and the kids again," Ma said.

I don't care if you never get another job, you're not working away!"

In the years that followed, there were many similar tearful confrontations. Dad worked away on regular occasions for over twenty years. He spent some time in the Northeast, but most of the well-paid jobs were out of the area, so he followed the money!

Ma soon got used to having the extra money that came every week and I'm sure it helped to ease the pain of not having Dad at home.

It was a bit of a wrench when my father first worked away. After being used to having him at home, then suddenly to find he wasn't there anymore, made me feel rather empty. I had enjoyed the way he treated me as one of the squad, not bothering to restrict his use of swear words when I was in earshot. He had made me feel very grown up. Now it was back to normal. Ma was very demanding, 'Billy do this, Billy do that, Billy go here, Billy go there', I was constantly at her beck and call, and was fed up with it. So I decided I would run away from home and live in a cave, like Wilson of the Wizard. One of my friends said he knew of some caves near Hamsterley Mill, so my mind was made up. I would go during the summer holidays, so as not to miss school!

Three of my closest friends had decided they had had enough of life at home and they would join me on my adventure. We had all seen Mark Twain's 'Huckleberry Finn', at the pictures recently and we were all confident we could emulate 'Huck'.

The four of us left home just before nine o'clock one Sunday morning. I had my Dads old army respirator holder full of food and vital tools, such as his cobbling knife, a knife, fork and spoon with L.N.E.R. stamped on the handles. Billy Thorburn had an old shopping bag with a large white loaf, a bottle of Puroh milk and a bag of sugar. Henna Andrews had brought a green ration book, some loose tea and a jam jar to use as a cup. I couldn't believe what John Hodson had in his bag. I explained to him that we were actually running away and not playing away, and what the hell had he brought his football boots for! As if to add insult to injury, he produced from inside one of the boots, a small piece of Fairy washing soap!

Dad had found an old French bayonet on the beach when he was doing his army training in Cornwall and he had brought it home as a souvenir. It was over thirty inches long and I had to walk like 'Long John Silver' when I secreted it down my trouser leg, in case we encountered any policemen as we made our way to Elswick railway station.

It was a lovely sunny day and the stationmaster was in a good mood.

"Hamsterley Mill, now how can we get you there?"

He looked through his timetable, but kept on shaking his head.

"Not from here lads, you'll have to go to the Central to get a train or you could go by bus."

"Could you tell us what bus to get from here? There's a bus stop just outside the station" I said, feeling really stupid. Here we were running away from home and we had no idea how to get where we wanted to go to!

He explained that we needed to be on the Consett or Shotley Bridge bus.

"But make sure you get off before Medomsley or you'll have a bloody long walk back down the bank."

As we waited for the right bus to come along we decided we would only go as far as Winlaton Mill, an area we were quite familiar with. We were sure we would be able to find a cave, or a least somewhere to set up our camp! Also there was a very kind lady living close by who, had been very generous to us in the past, with her bread and jam.

We lit a fire beside the stream and prepared our first meal. Four runaways determined never to return to our homes. Determined to live off the land. Fishing, catching rabbits, collecting wild mushrooms and blackberries etc., it was all very exciting stuff.

"Who's got the kettle?"

"Kettle, wha'di'we want a kettle for?"

"Well it's handy for boiling watter."

"Ah no, clever Dick, but so's the pan, yi don't need a kettle!"

"All right then did yi bring a pan?"

"Nee body told me t' bring a pan, ah thought ye would bring one."

"So wha'da we ganna boil the watter in t' make the tea?"

The old reliable National Food tin came to the rescue once again. Filled with water and pushed onto the hot embers it seemed to take no time at all before it was bubbling away. The dry tealeaves were put straight into the boiling water and stirred briskly until it turned brown. It smelled fantastic.

We had three tin mugs and one jam jar, so tea for four was served up with rich creamy Puroh milk and a dessertspoonful of sugar in each pot. The bread didn't cut very well with Dad's cobbling knife; so four slices took almost half the loaf. A jar of crab paste was spread over the four thick slices of bread and we devoured the lot very quickly.

We sat quietly round the fire, watching picnickers making their way home and wondering where we were going to spend the night. It was still daylight but it was getting quite late.

"Where 'we sleepin the neet then? Anybody got any ideas?"

"We could try the owld mansion in Gibside woods."

"Ah naa, that bloody gamekeepers crackers, he fired his gun at some kids a few weeks ago."

"How aboot the owld farm hoose just ower the railway line, that's not far, and its quite big inside."

"Aye but it's got nee bloody roof on. We'll get bloody soaked if it rains."

That was surely tempting providence.

The hiss of large spots of rain as they fell onto the hot stones around our fire, told us there was no <u>if</u> about it, it <u>was</u> raining.

We gathered our things together without looking at each other. No one spoke as we took our coats off and draped them over our heads and, as if by command we all trudged to the bus stop.

Four very wet individuals sat in silence as the bus crossed over Scotswood Bridge on its way back to Elswick. The revolution was over!

Every couple of weeks I would help my Granda Mills to clean out the chicken run. Most of the hens had been reared from day old chicks and he knew them all by name. Ralphy was the cockerel and he was vicious. He attacked anything or anyone who invaded his domain, including cats and dogs. I was very wary of Ralphy, and never ventured into the yard without my Granda. He would just shout at the cock and it would stand still and follow you with its eyes, feathers all fluffed up and his red comb standing erect on his head. He never attacked any of the family, probably because we were wise enough to take a shovel with us whenever we ventured out into the yard. I think he knew that shovels were formidable weapons from past experience. His only friend was 'Blackie', the black and white Dutch rabbit with whom he shared the yard. They never seemed to bother each other and Ralphy even tolerated him feeding from the same dish as the hens. The rabbit was almost as bad as the cock for attacking people. He would run straight at you and butt you on the legs, or bite your shoes. On one occasion he came charging towards me as I made my way to the outside toilet (Granda had told me to take the yard broom with me in case Ralphy or his friend gave me any trouble). I pushed the broom in front of me, as though I was sweeping the yard and Blackie ran headfirst into it. The impact was quite severe and stopped him dead in his tracks. He rolled over on his side, his back legs twitching, and then he lay quite still. I prodded him with the broom shank but there was no response. 'I've killed him' I thought.

There was no sign of life; I couldn't detect any breathing or anything. I picked the limp body up by the ears and threw it into the coalhouse. On my way back from the toilet I ventured another look at the black and white corpse. It was still lying where I had thrown it. I didn't know what to do, so in a panic I scooped out a shallow grave in the coal dust and buried it.

Granda had finished his cup of tea, so we both made for the chicken run, to finish the mucking out. One of the older hens was broody and she had made a nest out of wood shavings and straw. We had put some boody eggs under her along with a couple of real eggs from the grocers, just to keep her happy.

"Do you think we'll get any chickens from them shop eggs Granda." I asked.

" I doubt it", Granda replied.

"But let's have a look anyway."

He took the two warm eggs from the nest box and shook them beside his ear.

"There's nowt in them, they're still wet inside," he said, as he poked at one of them with a six- inch nail. It seemed very tough, so he exerted a little more pressure.

"Splatt!"

The egg burst open. The smell was incredibly vile. Granda was covered in the bright green foul smelling slime, memories of P.C. Thompson and the duck eggs flashed through my mind. I was almost sick with the stench, but Granda just roared with laughter. He chased me up the yard with the rest of the eggshell, but I was too quick for him and was out of the back door in a flash. When I peeked back into the yard he was in the scullery washing his hands at the sink, so I just carried on with cleaning the hen cree, but I kept one eye on my Granda in case he decided to let me have it with that other rotten egg.

By the time he got himself cleaned up and changed his shirt I had finished cleaning the chicken run. I had put fresh sawdust down and it had a nice clean smell.

"Well done lad, you've made a canny job of that, so I think we should call it a day."

He was still laughing about the egg and he promised me he had put the second one in the bin, but I still kept an eye on him.

"Get me that little shovel will you son? I'll take a pail of coal in to chuck on the back of the fire."

He opened the coalhouse door and stooped forward to fill the shovel. He jerked back with a start.

"Bugger my, I nearly bloody died!" he exclaimed.

"Have you ever seen such a bloody stupid animal in all your life? He's must have been in there for ages trying to dig his way out, look at the size of the hole he's dug up."

The black and white rabbit was now <u>all</u> black. I hadn't killed him; I had just knocked him unconscious. I didn't mention the incident to my Granda. I thought it was much better to let him think that Blackie had been accidentally locked in the coalhouse rather than buried alive by me!

My Uncle Robert had hung a football on the clothesline in Granda's yard. He and I used to punch or head it, as practice for playing football. I wanted to be a goalkeeper and Rob wanted to be a centre forward. The ball had wound itself round the line until it was slightly out of reach. Robert decided the best way to reach it was with a cricket bat. He swung the bat and knocked the ball over the line a couple of times until the string held it at shoulder height. Then he hit it with a wild swing, 'thud'; it flew into the air, snapping the string. He followed through with the bat, turning completely round. There was a second 'thud' as the bat struck me on the forehead.

I didn't feel a thing. There was a loud explosion in my head, then total blackness. When I came round I was sitting on a chair with a sea of faces all staring at me. The room seemed to be made of elastic and I was finding it difficult to focus.

Someone gave me a drink of water and I began to feel a little better. I stood up with a little help from my mother and looked into the mirror on the windowsill. There was a huge red lump on the right side of my forehead and I put my hand up to touch it, I swear it hurt before I actually made contact. Butter was gently applied to the swelling, which was supposed to stop it from getting any bigger. It certainly didn't stop it from hurting!

I had a wonderful headache for a couple of days but that was all. There didn't appear to be any permanent damage, although there are many who would dispute that. I remember our Robert laughing about it later, as he told his mates what had happened. I have no recollection of him ever saying he was sorry. I got my revenge a couple of weeks later when he tried to push me out of the passage and into the street. He was much stronger than I was but he had been off school for a few days with an earache, so as I wrestled with him I punched him on his bad ear. It was the one and only time my Grandad shouted at me. He tried to grab me as he consoled my uncle.

"You bad little sod, I'll tan your arse when I get hold of you."

"Well he hit me first Granda" I said tearfully.

"Go on, get away and don't bloody come back!"

That rather upset me, Robert started it and I was getting all of the blame. Everyone knew we were always fighting, and I usually came off second best.

Next day Grandad told us both off, and threatened if we didn't stop arguing he would send us both to a 'training ship', and we would have to stay there until we left school. A training ship was a kind of approved school or Borstal, with a very severe disciplinary regime. Not the kind of place I wanted to visit let alone reside in. So Robert decided he would only torment me when we were out of site of any of the family in the future.

Chapter Six

When my mother and I returned to the Northeast in 1942, we brought two kittens back with us from the litter born to the white Persian, owned by our landlady. The cats were all different colours and had obviously been sired by some stray Tomcat. 'Topsy' was black and white and 'Tibby' all black. Tibby settled in his new home right away but Topsy never seemed to settle at all. He was always crying, and it was just as though he was fretting for his family. One day he went out into our back yard and just disappeared, we never saw him again.

My mother acquired a green budgie from somewhere and it had become quite a pet. She used to let him fly around the house during the day, much to the annoyance of our cat. He watched every move the bird made, licking his lips in anticipation. Ma would look hard at him and say in a threatening tone.

"Just you dare."

The poor cat seemed to understand what she was saying and would skulk away with his tail twitching angrily.

I couldn't stand the constant squawking but Ma was besotted with 'Joey', as she had named him. One lunchtime as we were having our meal the budgie was walking around the table, helping himself to a pea from my plate then a piece of potato or something from Ma's plate, then he'd take a little flight around the sitting room, and back to the table. He flew onto my mother's shoulder and pulled a couple of hairs out of her head.

"Hi," she said.

"Stop that."

But he was in one of his mischievous moods and tried to nibble at her ear. She put her hand up to lift him down from her shoulder but he flew away and landed on the floor beside the armchair.

"Now come on Joey, you know you shouldn't be on the floor, if Tibby comes in you've had your chips!"

There was complete silence. No budgie squawks or whistles.

"Where's he gone?" asked Ma, looking under the dining table.

"He must be under the wireless table."

There was no sign of him.

"I hope he hasn't got out, but how could he? Every door in the house is shut."

"Do you think he could have gone up the chimney?"

I offered in desperation.

"Ee could of but I'm sure we would have seen him, anyway he's scared of the fire."

He seemed to have completely disappeared. Then I spotted the black tail protruding from behind the settee.

"Tibby, come here."

He slowly walked behind the full length of the settee, poking his nose out at the other end.

"If you've touched that bird, I'll murder you," said Ma angrily.

I've never heard of cats being able to change their facial expressions, but I'm sure he was smiling. We didn't know he was in the house when the budgie was flying about or we would have taken some precautions. It was too late now. There wasn't even one feather left to prove that we had ever had a pet bird. Tibby didn't even bother to stay in for his dinner; he had a little drink of milk and went out.

Over the years Tibby became more feral than domesticated. He stayed away from home sometimes for several weeks and we often thought he had been killed. He returned one day after an absence of over two weeks. It was on a Monday and my aunts were doing their weekly wash in our yard, when he appeared. Grace shouted through the window to me.

"You better come and have a look at your cat, he looks as though he's been poisoned." It was not uncommon for cats to be poisoned in our back lane, as there were over a dozen pigeon fanciers in the locality who often put poisoned bait down to get rid of stray cats. Unfortunately several pets had suffered the same fate.

Tibby was on the roof of the outside toilet. He was making baby-like cries tapering off into a throaty growl. I wasn't afraid of him, but I approached him with caution, not wishing to be bitten or scratched by a poisoned cat. Saliva was hanging down from his mouth in long strings and his fur was soaked with it. I called his name and he turned and looked straight at me. I thought he was a 'gonna'!

"I think your right Grace, look at the way he's slavering."

The poor animal got to its feet and walked up the toilet roof and along the back yard wall. I thought he was going to run off, so I called him again. He came down from the wall and stood on the dividing wall between our yard and our next-door neighbours. I stroked his head and he just stood there. He didn't look ill at all, he just seemed to be having difficulty closing his mouth. Grace held him by the scruff of the neck while I prised his mouth open to see if I could see any signs of poisoning. In between his back teeth was lodged a whole Cod vertebrae. I put my finger and thumb around the bone and worked it up and down a couple of times till it finally broke free.

You could almost see the relief on his face as I wiped him down with an old towel. He was a lot thinner than he used to be, so I suspect it had been some time since he'd eaten before he came home. He drank a full saucer of milk and looked for more. He was in no hurry to leave. I gave him a large piece of cucumber (his favourite delicacy) and half of my chips at dinnertime.

For the next couple of days he just hung around the house and ate everything we put in front of him. It was like having a new pet cat; he was much more settled than he had been for some time. He even fell asleep on my lap, which was most unusual. I think he had been in danger of starving to death, with that bone stuck in his mouth and was now content to stay where there was a regular supply of food.

As Christmas 1946 approached, everyone was looking forward to the first Christmas since the end of the war. Rationing was still firmly in place, but some things were beginning to return to the shops. 'Eldorado' were producing ice cream again, but demand was so great that they had to allocate only a small amount to each shop. When a delivery was made everyone had to stand in a long queue to purchase the two slices allowed each customer. The ice cream came in blocks about the size of a house brick, and were in fact called bricks! The shopkeeper cut the bricks into inch thick slices, wrapped them in greaseproof paper, then they had to be taken quickly home before they melted. Most of the ice cream that was available during the war was made from cornflour and flavouring, it was awful. 'Eldorado' tasted marvellous!

When Chipsides had their delivery from Eldorado I was sent to stand in the queue for our two slices. Tommy Chipside cut one slice from the block and what remained was given to me as my second slice. He wrapped them up in greaseproof paper; I paid him the shilling and sprinted back home.

I waited in eager anticipation as Dad opened the paper.

"What the hell's this?" Dad exclaimed.

"Does he think I'm paying full price for half a piece of ice cream?"

The second slice had been cut like a wedge, probably due to the slight deviation of the knife as the other slices were being cut.

"You can take that back and tell 'Chippy' I want a proper slice."

I looked at him in dismay.

'Oh not again', I thought: if there's anything wrong with anything, just send Billy to sort it out. By the time I had run back to the shop all of the ice cream had been sold. Tommy said.

"Tell your Dad he got the end of the block and was just unlucky. I bet he wouldn't have sent it back if it had been the first slice."

Back I trudged, not running anymore, but the ice cream was. It was rapidly returning to its liquid state. I told Dad what Tommy had said, but it made no difference.

"I'm not paying for half a slice of ice cream, you can tell him I'll have my money back."

Off I went again. The ice cream was no longer a slice, but more of a pat, getting thinner all the time, but much wider. I sat on the edge of the pavement in the back lane and opened the paper. I had made my mind up. I ate it, I say ate it, but I almost had to drink it. It was

149

delicious. I licked the greaseproof paper until it fell to pieces.

"Now what?"

I rummaged through the cigarette cards, tram tickets, and milk bottle tops in my pockets until I found the sixpenny piece I was looking for. I made sure there was no trace of the offending ice cream on my person as I skipped down the back yard steps and into the scullery.

"Mr. Chipside say's he's very sorry you got the end of the block and you can have your money back."

"Aye, too bloody true he's sorry, he must think a'm bloody stupid or something, that's his bloody last!"

Whatever that meant!

The other slice was gone. My parents had consumed it while I was practising for the marathon, running back and forth. I wasn't too bothered; I'd had my share. Even if I did have to pay for it myself, it was worth it.

Mam and Dad were very strange about certain things. If they bought a bag of sweets to eat while they were playing cards or dominoes you were only offered one or maybe two. If it was a bar of chocolate you were given one 'square', they ate the rest. During the Christmas festivities the house smelled of fruit and sweets but none of it came to light. It seemed to be spirited away. I was constantly searching for their hiding place but it eluded me until one day I looked in my Dad's old army kit bag. I was amazed to discover a hoard of fruit, chocolate and other confectionery. Needless to say I helped myself to as much as I thought they wouldn't miss. The next time I tried, the bag had a long reach padlock slotted through the metal eyelets at the top, making it impossible to open or even to squeeze one hand through. I think Houdini would have been hard pushed to open it.

When Dad bought a bottle of 'pop' no one was allowed to have a drink without his permission. He even marked the level of the contents after he had taken a drink, but he never seemed to notice when it was slightly diluted with water! When my sister married and left home, she wasn't allowed to take any of her personal possessions with her. All of her childhood birthday and Christmas presents had to be left behind. I could never understand why. Surely when you give someone a present it becomes his or her property. I couldn't believe someone could give a present with one hand and take it back with the other!

I had my own private shelf for my toys and books etc., in the cupboard next to the fireplace. I was a compulsive collector and hoarded anything that looked interesting or had some potential value to me. I possessed a large collection of 'Picture Post' and 'Illustrated' magazines. They were full of stunning photographs and articles on worldwide news and events. I kept all of my old tram tickets, bus tickets, cinema tickets, cigarette cards, milk bottle tops, marbles, empty cigarette packets, and a new craze of collecting the labels from cheese segments. These had been available before the war but I had never seen them. Now they were coming back into the shops and were very popular. A circular box held about eight or ten segments of cheese all wrapped in foil, each piece individually labelled. The labels were very easy to remove and were printed in bright attractive colours. One of my favourites was 'Velvita'. The cheese was very soft in texture and was coloured more of an orange than yellow. It had a strong mature flavour and reminded me of the small tins of army cheese Dad used to send to us. Each triangular segment was enough to cover one slice of bread; I used to spread mine over the whole slice then put another slice on top to make two sandwiches. Cheese was still rationed so you only got one segment per meal.

Most of the things I hoarded were of no value at all. Some came in handy as incentives if I was engaged in one of the swapping transactions I often indulged in. It worked this way. If one of my friends had something I wanted I would let him know of my interest. He would then decide whether or not he wanted to sell the article or do a swap.

Tommy Casey was much older than my friends or me, but being a little immature preferred the company of younger people. He was just like a larger version of one of us and took part in our games with as much enthusiasm as any of us. His paper aeroplanes were masterpieces of Origami and his kites were just as good. Tommy had a collection of stuffed birds, an owl, a hawk and several smaller birds. They were all housed in glass-fronted cases and I thought they were magnificent. The Owl had taken my fancy, so I asked him if he was interested in doing a swap deal. He seemed a little reticent, which I put down to his reluctance to part with any of his birds, but finally he agreed to come to our house on Saturday morning.

As Christmas was drawing near my mother had acquired her usual ticket from Miss Engleton and would be out shopping at Todd Brothers and Parishes for most of the day. Since my father had left the Army and our income had increased, the size of our tickets had also increased. Today she would have an account with these stores, but in 1946 it was done with a ticket.

I assembled my collection of books and objet d'art in a very tidy arrangement on our dining room table. I had some nice things along with the junk and hoped to acquire the owl with some of each.

Tom showed very little interest in anything I had to offer, but I was surprised to find that he had brought the whole collection of stuffed birds and not just the owl. I was a little suspicious. I didn't know why, I just had a little twinge of unease. So I asked…

"Are you sure these birds are really yours?"

I didn't want his mother coming to me to retrieve them if they were really hers.

"Well, they've been in my bedroom for years and me mother says she'll be glad to see the back of them."

That made me feel a lot better and I felt more confident of striking a deal.

By about twelve o'clock we had agreed on a swap. I was to give my army jack knife, several out-of-date comics, three 'Tommy' size handfuls of my best marbles, a pipe housed in a red velvet lined box the same shape as the pipe, which also had real silver bands around the bowl and the stem. Last of all, my black 'Zorro' hat. I thought it was a bit much but I was very keen to get the owl. His initial lack of interest in my 'swaps' had prompted me to be a little over generous, but I was still pleased with the result.

As he was about to leave, his pockets laden, and my 'Zorro' hat perched on the back of his head, I asked.

"Are you coming back for the others later?"

He had made no attempt to take the other two boxes with him. A strange smile spread over his face.

"No, you can have the lot. Me mother said if I brought them back to our house once more she would make me eat them."

I couldn't believe my good fortune. I had the whole collection.

'What a dealer', I congratulated myself.

I quickly cleared the top of the sideboard and proudly placed my trophies in position; the owl on the left; the hawk on the right and the larger case, housing the collection of small British birds, in the centre. What a display!

"Ma's in for a big surprise when she comes in and sees these."

I bought six pennorth of chips from the money my mother had left me to get my dinner. With the other threepence I played a game of marbles, called 'jinks', for money. A chalk circle was drawn in the centre of the marble pitch and each player had to put three ha'pence into the circle. The object was to roll your marble over the money and back out of the circle causing a 'jink' sound as the marble touched the coins. This entitled you either to take one ha'penny out of the circle or to take another shot at one of the other player's marbles, moving it further away from the money. The game ended when one player knocked the other two out of the pitch boundary three times. He was declared the winner, taking whatever money was left in the circle. 'Jinks' was only one of several games we played for money. Threepence could last all day, and winning any more than a few pence was rare.

I was still playing marbles when I spotted my mother coming along the street. She was carrying several brown paper carrier bags.

"Have you had your dinner?"

She enquired, nodding towards me.

"Yes."

I answered, not looking up. I didn't want her to see the smile on my face. I could hardly wait for her reaction when she saw my surprise. I hung back until she went inside then I crept along the street to listen.

Her scream was very loud and it didn't sound like a scream of delight. It sounded as though Boris Karloff had just turned up in his 'Mummy' outfit.

"Billy!"

Not the usual, 'You're late Billy'; it was more your 'Come here till I wring your neck, Billy'.

"Get these bloody things out of this house now!" She demanded angrily

"I'll give you ten seconds and if they're still here I'll throw them out into the front street and you after them!"

I thought 'this sounds serious'.

"All right, keep your hair on, how was ah supposed to know you didn't like stuffed birds?"

"Don't tell me to keep me hair on you cheeky sod, you're so bloody clever you didn't even know that they're bloody well unlucky. For two pins I'd bloody well make you eat them!"

"Unlucky, how's that? They're dead you know."

I avoided the swipe Ma took at me.

"Don't you bloody argue with me, just get them out now!"

Her face was bright red.

"Nobody in their right mind would have them in the house."

She looked apprehensive as I piled the cases on top of each other, and she moved quickly to one side as I walked past her. I was tempted to make some horrible noise when I was close to her but I think she would have fainted. Then there would be the normal very painful interlude to follow.

I went straight to Tommy Casey's house with the birds.

"You'll have to take these back Tom, me mother nearly had a fit when she saw them. I still like them but I didn't realise they're supposed to be unlucky around here."

He laughed quite openly.

"You must be joking, I've been trying to get rid of them for months! Me mother threatened to throw me and them out together if I didn't get 'shot' of them."

I didn't know what to do next. I was stuck with these three boxes of birds that no one but me seemed to want. In desperation I took them to a second hand shop on Scotswood Road, owned by a well-known local family. The owner said I would have a job getting rid of them around here because everyone believed them to be unlucky. He was right about that; they were certainly being unlucky for me. I asked him what he would give me for them.

"Well now, I think I could manage five bob, but if Mrs Durkin comes in she might change me mind, she doesn't like them either."

It wasn't much of an offer for these works of art but beggars can't be choosers, so I agreed.

"I think I'll be able to shift them in a week or two, maybe at one of the auctions out of Newcastle." He more or less said to himself as he went through into the back shop. I could here him rummaging about in some tin obviously trying to find enough 'change' to pay me. I fully expected him to come back and say, 'I'm sorry but I've only got four shillings in change', knowing I would have to accept it.

He re-appeared and dropped the money into my hand.

"Here son, and mind you don't lose it."

I ran out of the shop and halfway home before I stopped to look at the money again. Six half-crowns. He had given me six half-crowns, five shillings for each box, not five shillings for the lot. Fifteen lovely shillings!

"Unlucky? Who said stuffed birds were unlucky?" I said aloud.

When I returned home I was subjected to a long lecture on bad luck, bad omens, black Friday, walking under ladders, breaking mirrors and stuffed birds.

"If you find a sixpence you must give it away, its bad luck to keep it.

I thought, 'what a load of rubbish'. Give a sixpence away after you've just found it, she must be out of her mind; it's bad luck all right, bad luck for the poor sod who lost it. If I had another chance to acquire some unlucky stuffed birds I would collect them on Friday the thirteenth, walk under a ladder on my way to the second hand shop, break the nearest mirror and come home with another fifteen shillings (and sixpence) in my pocket. 'Roll on bad luck'!

My mother could never understand my total disregard for superstition. If I left two knives crossed on the dining room table she would shout...

"Get those knives uncrossed, that causes fights."

There must have been a pair permanently crossed somewhere in our house, judging by the number of rows I witnessed. My parents didn't need crossed knives to have a fight; they managed very well without them or anything else. They were married on Boxing Day, which I always thought was very appropriate, as they usually ended up having a full-scale row or a least a disagreement, on every anniversary.

It always started out as a joke.

"Aye it was the best thing that ever happened to you when you married me."

One to Ma!

"You must be joking, your father had chucked you out, that's why you came to me."

One each.

"No he hadn't, he only chucked me out when I told him I was going to marry you."

Two to Ma!

"Aye, that was just because he didn't want to help pay for the wedding."

Honours even! It was all light hearted and my Dad could hardly get the words out for laughing.

"You've never been so well off in your life and it only cost seven and sixpence for the privilege."

"Aye, that's true, seven and sixpence down, then everything you earn for the rest of your life."

Seven and sixpence was the price of a marriage licence.

"Everything you earn, you bloody liar I've never seen how much you earn for bloody years."

It was warming up and the odd swear word was beginning to creep in.

"Listen, if I earned a thousand pounds a week you would spend a thousand and one."

"Aye, and you'd make sure ya bloody mother got her share as well."

That was it. Ma's temper had got the better of her once again.

"You've never gone short because of what I've given me mother, so just cut that out."

"You make me sick, you cannot wait to get along to your mothers every night, why don't you go and bloody live there."

That was a small sample of what crossed knives can do. The arguments usually ended with a couple of hour's silence. Then they would gradually start talking again, and soon it was all forgotten.

The Christmas tree was in the middle of the floor and Christmas decorations were strewn about the house. Donald Duck took pride of place right in the centre of the tree sitting with his legs astride a branch. He was all that remained of a clockwork toy someone had given to me on my third birthday. It was a three-wheeled bike with a box on the front; similar to the type used to sell ice cream. The lettering on the front read, 'Stop me and Buy one'. Donald sat on the bike with his hands on the box and pedalled the whole thing around when it was wound up. Sadly only Donald survived, but I'm happy to say, he still does to this day.

The Fairy was perched on the topmost branch, which went vertically up her dress. When Dad came home he always made his usual bawdy remarks about the big smile on her face.

We had two wooden hoops placed one inside of the other to fashion a circular cross. This was called a 'mistletoe'. It was decorated with bright coloured crepe paper, Christmas toys, (baubles) holly and a sprig of mistletoe, then suspended from the ceiling. A pre-war Santa Claus and Snowman stood at each end of the sideboard, and the Christmas tree replaced Ma's tea caddy in the centre. The tea caddy was really a silver plated soup tureen, but served us well in its present role, holding our tea ration. Dad's army kit bag was looking rather bulkier than usual. The bumps and lumps around its misshapen circumference looked suspiciously like Christmas presents. I could still make out the fading white lettering which read, 'PTE. A.W.FLANNIGAN. C.M.P. SER No.13075089.'

After his induction medical in 1940 Dad was officially graded C3 which almost made him exempt from military service, but the Doctors decided that because of his above average intelligence and one green and one blue eye, he was a perfect candidate for the Pioneer Corps. This branch of the services was named 'the unskilled army'. Their roll being the clearing up after the troops, or digging latrines and trenches, clearing bomb sites and generally labouring, in order to relieve the fighting men to do their job.

After several encounters with headless corpses and badly mutilated children during cleaning up operations my father asked for a transfer. He had heard that the Military Police were looking for volunteers, so he applied. He easily passed the entrance examination and spent the next five years in that branch of the services. His main function was to direct traffic or guard special areas of high security. I

157

discovered many years later that he was a dog handler guarding the now famous Bletchley Park were the Enigma code-breaking device was invented.

He always said the best job he ever had in the army was Officers Mess Cook. This position became the source of our extra rations, which he sent home at regular intervals.

When the Christmas tree was in place, I suggested to Ma that the owl would have looked great on top instead of the fairy, but she didn't agree, in fact she was downright hostile. I won't repeat what she said, but she was certainly using a lot more four-letter words than usual.

Although my mother was quite superstitious and afraid to 'tempt providence', she had no fear at all of vermin or 'creepy crawlies'. She had no hesitation in picking up spiders or cockroaches and even dead mice. The house we lived in was very old and we had our share of household pests.

Originally my parents had lived in Coatsworth Road in Gateshead but moved to No 3 Cannon Street shortly before I was born. From there we rented a house in Tulloch Street near my Great Grandma Mills, but again this was only temporary, and we moved to No 54 Cannon Street in 1938. I can remember my Uncle Billy Hall, the wireless expert, pushing a handcart along the street with a double bed spring, brass bed ends, a mattress and me on top. I was just about two and a half years old but the picture is quite vivid, either in fact or in my imagination. The doors in the new house were painted light blue with four cream panels, and the scullery walls were painted with red ochre. We had our own toilet in the back yard, which meant we didn't have to share it with our neighbours as we did in No 3.

I remember Dad pulling the floorboards up a few months after we moved in. The floor was four feet below the level of the back yard and over the years moisture had seeped through the outside wall and slowly settled in a pool below the flooring just under the window. Dad and his friend re-pointed the outside wall, removed all of the water and wet soil from under the floor and we never had that problem again. The landlord wasn't interested in any problems you had with the property, he was only interested in the rent, if you didn't like it you could leave. Several families did leave but mainly for economic reasons, and they usually left late at night, before the Rent

Man called next day. It was commonly known as 'doing a moonlight flit'. My parents were fortunate enough not to have to indulge in this activity but they knew and helped several people who did.

The cat we owned at this time was a ginger Tom and naturally enough he was called Ginger. One night after Ma had finished baking he caught and devoured eight mice in and around the gas cooker. That was his record for one day, but he caught several more over the ensuing months. The cooker was an obvious place for attracting vermin. The smell of food cooking and the residue from scones and buns was more than enough to tempt the pests.

My friend Kenny who lived across the road from me in No 57 had a Tabby cat, which was also very adept at catching mice. His favourite hunting ground was inside the coal-fired oven over the fireplace. He would sit inside with the door open and wait patiently until a mouse dared to venture out for a meal and then he would pounce! Unfortunately for him, he was accidentally locked in on one occasion and almost roasted alive. His cries of distress became louder and louder as the temperature built up towards cooking point. When someone finally heard him and opened the oven door his fur was sticking up like a hedgehog. It was crisp and spiky for weeks after, and he was very reluctant to go anywhere near the oven for some considerable time.

Kenny was a great friend of mine but he never took part in the rough-and-tumble games that we played. He preferred playing cards or marbles and he even liked reading!

His father, Geordie Flynn was one of a large family of brothers and they all had pet names for each other. The youngest was Tommy and he was the strangest of characters. He was loud and 'cocky' but lacked intelligence when making sweeping statements about his ability in some field, only to fall flat on his face. 'Dissy' was the eldest brother, 'Bisto' was next then 'Hocky'. Where these nicknames came from remains as much a mystery today as it was then. The only one of them who ever had a regular job was 'Bisto'. He delivered coal for many years, but none of his brothers worked.

Geordie was the second eldest brother and the only one with a family. He was registered as a partially sighted person and used to wear two pairs of spectacles at the same time while reading the racing results. He was also one of the top club darts players in Elswick. He used to say…

"It's just instinct, ah cannit see the board, but ah nah where it's supposed to be."

The whole family used to visit No 57 every Sunday afternoon to play cards if it was raining, or 'scraper' if it was fine.

'Scraper' is a game which I believe originated in our community, or at least in the Northeast. The 'scraper' pitch was made up of a metal water drain that ran from the wall of a house to the edge of the pavement. The water that drained from the roof, down the cast iron drainpipe, was channelled away into the road, this ended up running into the 'fever grate'. The water drain was usually full of black sooty sludge and had to be scraped clean often, which possibly accounts for the name 'scraper'.

The rules of the game were quite simple. Each person put two pennies into the 'pool'. Then all they had to do was throw, or pitch as many pennies as possible into the slot of the drain, from an agreed distance. The slot was less than one inch wide and very difficult to hit from eight or ten feet away; but the Flynns were experts. I once saw Geordie put six pennies into a single Woodbine packet and pitch it straight into the slot to beat the previous best shot of five. If two players scored the same amount of hits, they were considered to be 'in the same boat', or level. The term they used for this situation was 'paddlers'. If someone was paddling with another player and both had the highest score, they could either share the prize money or have a head to head to determine the outright winner. Games often lasted well into the evening on light summer nights. It was always good humoured and the money was the last thing that mattered, it was the game that was important. The wisecracks and banter between the five brothers was akin to having a pantomime in the street.

"If ah was as blind as ye wore Geordie, ah could tell the colour of Hitler's eyes from a black an white pitcha!"

The next generation of the Flynn's family was well established by Geordie and his wife Mina. I believe her full name was either Jemima or Willemina. Their offspring consisted of Kenny, the same age as myself, Joe, Alan, Audrey and Pat. They were a lovely family, extremely poor but really nice people. I often stayed over at No 57 and Kenny's dad would wake us at five o'clock in the morning to take us mushroom picking. We all wore flat caps and a pair of socks on our hands for gloves. Geordie always cracked the same joke as we entered the fields with the usual collection of cowpats.

"If you drop ya cap be careful when you pick it up; last time ah dropped mine ah tried six on before ah foond the reet one."

I always found it extremely funny, possibly due to my vivid imagination. I could easily picture him trying on the dried up cowpats.

Sleeping at the Flynn's was real fun. It was only a one-bedroom house and we all slept in the same room. It was a big room with about four beds. Kenny, Joe and I slept in an old double bed that had no mattress, we lay on old coats spread over the bedsprings and I often woke up with an arm or leg sticking through the wire. No one seemed to mind being poor, I suppose what you are always used to, you just accept as being normal. Poverty can sometimes be a great character builder, and as the years passed this family proved that to be true.

The prospect of having two weeks away from school for the Christmas holiday was even better than getting presents. I found schoolwork to be fairly easy but I couldn't raise any enthusiasm for it. I was useless at woodwork. Everything I tried to make was a minor disaster. Bad dovetail joints, bad fitting half-lap joints and my mortise and tenons were just a joke. Strangely enough I still got pretty reasonable marks, mainly for the 'finish' I achieved with my French Polishing.

My Granda Mills had taught me how to make a polishing 'pad'; how to fill it with polish and wrap it tightly in lint free cloth, then squeeze it gently until the polish seeped through. I could French polish really well before I could write properly.

I enjoyed most of the school lessons, but history was my favourite, until our Head teacher decided to introduce politics into the history lesson. I found this kind of history totally boring.

We were under Roman domination for over four hundred years. Ruled by the most powerful nation on earth. We used their coinage, we still do. L.S.D. our pounds, shillings and pence, is based on their 'libra', solidus and denarius. They gave us roads, public baths, the Roman wall, and here we were rambling on about the Woolsack and Black Rod.

I was almost falling asleep in one lesson when the Head, Mr Stephenson walked between the rows of desks and bent down to look me squarely in the eyes.

"Are you bored boy?" He asked.

"No Sir." I replied, hoping he would fail to realise how untrue that was.

I longed for tales of Captain Cook, Horatio Nelson, The Duke of Wellington, Robert the Bruce, William Wallace and Rob Roy, but I had to wait many years to quench this thirst for knowledge.

Science was quite an interesting lesson, mainly due to the teacher, Mr Carter. He constantly played tricks and pranks on us under the guise of education. His favourite source of entertainment came from a small hand operated generator. This had two metal handles attached to two lengths of wire. One handle was placed in a bowl of water, the other was held by a boy. Four other boys joined hands with the first boy holding the electrode. Mr Carter then placed a shilling into the bowl of water. He said to the last boy in the line.

"If you can get the shilling out of the bowl you can keep it."

There was no shortage of volunteers; a shilling was a lot of money.

As the boy's hand entered the water the teacher turned a little handle on the generator. The result was hilarious. The current from the little machine shot through the five guinea pigs, the water magnifying the power ten fold. It was really funny to see five pupils dancing up and down, unable to release their hold on the electrodes and their hair almost standing on end!

English was a mixture of essay writing, poetry and reading. I found it quite difficult to understand where and when to use verbs, nouns, pronouns, similes etc. I knew I was using them, but identifying them was my problem. I did enjoy poetry, but where I lived it was unwise to admit that to anyone. You could be branded a 'softie' or even a 'queer' for showing such interests. We had a poetry competition just before the Christmas break, so I tried my luck and entered. It was just a bit of fun, not an official contest, but nevertheless it had to be treated as a serious lesson.

The teacher in charge of the entries was Mr Scottie and strangely enough he was a Scot. A few days after I had entered my poem he asked me to come to his classroom after school to talk about my entry. I was quite surprised, but also pleased, to think it had been singled out.

"Now then Flannigan, this poem of yours."

The soft lilt of his Scottish accent sounded so reassuring, but the raised eyebrows suggested that there was some doubt in his mind about something.

"I'm very impressed with your effort, but I feel I must ask, is it all your own work? Or maybe you've remembered it subconsciously from some book or story you have heard in the past?"

"No sir, I wrote it all on my own." I replied.

I felt a little aggrieved at his questions. I did write it myself and I knew I hadn't copied it from any book, surely he didn't think I would be as stupid as that. It was no masterpiece anyway, so why all the fuss.

"Well now, that's fine." Said Mr Scottie.

"I'll be putting it into the competition tomorrow, but I thought I'd better clear that up first."

I could still detect a slight element of doubt in his voice, but my conscience was clear. The next morning the Headmaster announced during assembly, that the winner of the poetry competition would be reading his poem out to the whole school the next morning. It had not been decided who the victor was, but the decision would be made that afternoon.

After lunch the school secretary summoned me to the Head's office. She was a very cold, starchy sort of a woman and didn't speak at all on the long walk back to her office.

I knocked on Mr Stephenson's door.

"Yes, come in." He sounded chirpy.

I entered slowly, looking around the door before I put a foot inside.

"Come in, come in, don't worry you're not in any trouble, come in."

I had never seen him with his jacket off before. He looked

much smaller in his cream shirt and brown waistcoat. His silver watch chain was gleaming.

"Well now, this poem of yours. I'm very impressed and not least of all pleasantly surprised."

He was doodling with a pencil and seemed a little nervous or apprehensive.

"I know Mr Scottie has spoken to you about the authenticity of your entry and I would just like to stress that we are all agreed that it would be a shame if it was found to be similar to another work. It is very easy to think you have an original idea, but we can often be miss-led by our own memory, or something someone has said, like your parents or friends."

"Yes sir, but I did write it myself. My parents don't even know I've done it."

"Excellent, excellent, excellent, that's all I needed to know. Now I'm very pleased to tell you that you have won the competition. It will be my pleasure to announce the result to the whole school during assembly tomorrow morning. You will then read your poem out after the Lords Prayer. My congratulations to you."

I didn't fancy that at all. Everyone would think I'd gone soft, writing poetry. How was I going to get out of this predicament? I would have to get my thinking cap on before tomorrow.

My friend Henna once told me how sore his throat was after doing his Tarzan yodel for any length of time. I thought,' It might work'. If I try hard enough, I might even lose my voice. It was worth a try. It was desperation!

I shouted and screamed all night long. The old Elswick colliery echoed to my cries as I tried desperately to lose my voice. It just didn't work. My vocal chords must have been made of piano wire. I normally had tonsillitis two or three times a year, but not this year – all of my viruses had deserted me.

Next morning my mother woke me up for school as usual. She asked me if I wanted any breakfast, and what would I like? I said nothing, no not nothing for my breakfast; I said nothing at all because I couldn't speak. I had lost my voice. I croaked out.

"Just a bit of toast."

But it was hardly audible. I was delighted. My little scheme had worked. Surely no one at school could ask me to read out my poem with a throat like this.

"Good grief, your throat sounds terrible. The sooner you get your tonsils out the better." Ma said.

I was already on the waiting list for the operation, but the N.H.S. had yet to be introduced, and the waiting list meant exactly that. Waiting! We think we are badly done by today waiting a few weeks for surgery. I recall waiting over two years for a hernia repair and that wasn't exceptional.

"I think you should go to the Doctors this morning. There's only another couple of days till the school holidays, so you won't be missing much."

Everything was just falling into place; I could not have planned it better.

Doctor Dove said it looked like laryngitis, not my usual tonsillitis.

"Just stop talking for a day or two and gargle with salt water. That should do it."

He didn't prescribe any other medicine, so I left the surgery and made my way back home.

My mother was out by the time I returned, but she had left a note propped up against the tea caddy, saying that I was to stay at home and not to bother with school for today. I decided that that was not the best thing to do, so I ignored the note and went to school. I had no intention of staying there, I just wanted the Headmaster to see for himself that I had a problem and that was the reason why I had missed assembly that morning.

Mr Stephenson was very understanding and remarked on how refreshing it was to have someone actually turn up to show it was a genuine case.

"Very unfortunate, very unfortunate, yes, very unfortunate."

His triple tonguing was better than ever; he would have made a great trumpeter.

"Nevertheless we will have your poem read out tomorrow morning, last day of term, and I'm sure Mr Scottie will be very happy to do the honours."

I was allowed to go home with the blessing of the Head.

"If you feel well enough tomorrow you may attend assembly to hear the reading."

This consideration coming from such a strict disciplinarian was very surprising. I put it down to the Christmas Spirit; or was it. Did I detect a slight chink in the tough 'armour' usually worn by this man? Maybe!

The dulcet tones of Mr Scottie's warm velvet voice drifted over the assembled throng.
"The Blind Man by William Flannigan"

I am so poor not a penny have I
I only wish that I could die
To free me from this blackened life
Of everlasting toil and strife
I've stuck it now for Fifty years
Sometimes with laughter
Sometimes with tears
I had a house not long ago
And lived there with my dog, Black Joe
An old oak tree outside my door
Was struck by lightnin'
It fell onto my house
The roof and walls caved in
Black Joe was cold and dead
The tree had crushed his head
Now I'm alone forever
Wishing to be dead.

If they were my words I hardly recognised them. Mr Scottie made them so different, so sincere and so moving.

I know it wasn't much of a poem when you think of the great works of Keats, Wordsworth, Browning, Rupert Brooke etc., but on that Friday in 1946 I felt every bit as proud of what I had written as any of the afore mentioned would have been.

When the applause died down Mr Stephenson said.

"Well now, what did you think of that?"

I was surprised at the reaction of my friends. I expected the usual jeers and sniggers about poets, but it didn't happen. They all thought it was great, but every one of them asked me where I had copied it from!

When I sat the Eleven plus Exams I had been absent from school more than I had attended. I had continuous trouble with my nose and throat. Tonsillitis was the main problem but I was also suffering severe attacks of sinusitis, a problem, which has persisted to this day.

I failed the exams miserably, but I was neither surprised nor worried at the outcome. I didn't really want to go to some Grammar or Technical School, where you had to wear a school uniform and do homework. I was quite happy at Cruddas Park. I played goalkeeper for the junior football team, wicket keeper for the cricket team and represented the school in the long jump.

I was quite good at Art and Science; my position in the class was always around the top six. I got on very well with most of the teaching staff, and the prospect of ending my school days at Cruddas Park was very appealing to me.

Unfortunately things don't always turn out the way we would like them to; therefore it was quite a shock for me to discover that although I had failed the exams, I had been recommended to be considered for a place in either a Commercial or Technical School for Further Education. The idea of going to a 'posh' school didn't appeal to me. We were poor; I spoke with a Geordie accent. I thought, 'I'll never fit in, I couldn't pass the Eleven Plus, so how am I going to manage a higher standard?' My family was delighted. You would think I had been chosen to go to University. I was very surprised at their reaction and wallowed a little in the glory.

We would never be able to afford a school uniform, there was no doubt about that but, as usual my enterprising mother scoured every bit of literature on school grants and assistance for people in our circumstances, and came up with a free uniform. The only drawback was that I would have to attend my new school for six months before I qualified for the grant.

'Pendower Secondary Commercial School' what a mouthful. It was too long to fit into the panel on the front of the bus. 'Pendower' was all they could manage. It sounded quite intimidating; I didn't fancy it at all. They did Algebra, Logarithms, Trigonometry, Geometry and even Short Hand and Typing, and if you were very good and ate all your vegetables, you could even qualify for an A class, where they did French. French! What use was French to someone who was struggling with English? The only people who needed to speak French were the French, and they already knew it. The only thing I would ever be likely to say to a Frenchman would be.

"Can you tell me the way back to England?"

First year students were called 'Fags'. They were expected to run errands or do small jobs for the older boys; a bit like 'Tom Browns School Days'. Anyone who refused to comply was taken to the nearest toilet block to have his head pushed down the pan and 'flushed'. I knew I was in for some trouble and I wondered to myself how the perpetrators would react to having the same thing done to them.

I learned very quickly that the first day of term was 'fun' day for the senior boys. Several of them were hanging about the school entrance ordering shy little lads to 'carry our bags upstairs' or 'nip along to Benwell Post Office and get me a penny long stand'. Several were escorted to the toilets to be 'ducked' and everyone was having a whale of a time, except the youngsters.

It was inevitable that my turn had to come, dressed as I was in my light brown herringbone suit.

"Here you, get this bag up to form 4A and put it on the second desk up in the first row."

I just ignored him.

"Hey, are you deaf or something? Didn't you hear what I said?"

"Is this your first day?"

"Yes it is."

"Well then you must know that first year students have to learn to do as they're told."

I didn't answer.

"Now here is my holdall, take it upstairs and put it into Mr Coagin's class, 4A."

"I don't know where it is."

"That's not my problem, find it and don't be so stupid."

I took the bag and walked up four flights of stairs. As I reached the fifth landing I took the holdall and dropped it down the well of the staircase. It landed with an almighty thud that echoed up the open stairwell. I sprinted up the other four flights of stairs to the roof playground only to find the exit guarded by two other boys about my age.

"Come on you, we saw what you did," they said, as they took me by each arm and frog-marched me towards the toilet block.

My two captors were laughing and giggling at the prospect of giving me a soaking, and talked excitedly to each other as though I wasn't there.

"Should we give him one flush or two?"

"Oh I think two would be more appropriate, he does look a little scruffy."

My mind flashed back to 'Tom Browns School Days' once again.

I thought, 'these two bloody idiots think I'm just going to stand here and let them push my head down the pan without trying to stop them. What a mistake they've made!'

As we approached the cubicles I pulled my right arm free from the taller of the two, whom I had already nicknamed Elsie, and grabbed the other one in a very sensitive area as I shouted.

"Not so bloody fast 'Doris'!"

Elsie and Doris 'Waters' were two very popular female 'comediennes in the 1940s.

I pushed Elsie into the toilet and sat him down between the pot and the wooden partition. Then I shoved Doris's head down the 'loo' and flushed it before he could do anything to stop me. I pulled him out and threw him on top of his mate. They were both coughing and spluttering even though only one of them had been in for a dip.

"Listen you two I'm not a fag! This is my first term but I'm not in the first year and if you or any of your queer friends try anything like that again, you'll get more trouble than you can cope with. You won't just get a little wetting, you'll get a bloody good hiding."

By this time quite a large crowd of boys had gathered in the toilets, and judging by their reaction I had made several new friends.

Elsie and Doris just happened to be in the same form as me; 3B, and I continued to call them by those names for the duration of my stay at Pendower.

I tolerated most of the pupils in my class but made friends with very few. Most of them were from much better backgrounds and tended to look down their noses at people like me.

The lack of a school uniform was the bane of my life. Ninety-nine percent of pupils wore grey trousers and a navy blue blazer with the school badge sewn onto the breast pocket. The school motto was 'Per Ardua Ad Astra', which translated roughly into 'Through difficulties to the Stars'. I was wearing a light brown herringbone suit and a yellow T-shirt. My new uniform wouldn't be available for six months, so until then I was a target. I stood out like a sore thumb, and became the object of some of the teachers' scorn.

The Head singled me out for special attention, and although I was on my best behaviour I was frequently accused of doing things I was not responsible for. He seemed to take an instant dislike to anyone who wasn't sporting a uniform and that just happened to include most of my new friends.

One morning whilst marching out from assembly he dragged three of us out of the line and took us to his office. He insisted that we tell him what we were talking about on the way out of the hall. I believe he thought we were discussing the way he had allowed his nose to run during prayers, not bothering to wipe it until it was nearly down to his chin. This was not true at the time, even though everyone in the school was talking about it later, including the staff. In actual fact the three of us were singing the 'Oxydol' jingle, but he didn't believe us. So my two friends, Dick Chamberling Arthur Fathergill and myself had to write out one hundred times. 'I must not talk during assembly'. What a way to be educated. I thought, 'this school is more like an infants school, it's so bloody childish!'

The lessons were not as difficult as I had anticipated and I even found Algebra to be quite easy. This was probably due to the fact that the teacher was superb. We had a different teacher for each subject and 'Doc' Dawson the Maths teacher, was the best. He explained everything to us new boys in such a clear and simple manner that we were able to take part in the lessons immediately.

My Woodwork and Metalwork improved very quickly, and generally I felt as though I had begun to settle at this school. I was reserve goalkeeper for the school football team and played goalkeeper and wicket keeper for the form team. It was just the Headmaster. He didn't seem to like anyone and his face was like thunder all of the time. He seemed to be at odds with life and gave the teachers as hard a time as the pupils.

I applied for permission to use my bike to travel to school on the grounds of hardship. It was costing sixpence a day for bus fares and we simply could not afford it. The fare was threepence each way, I walked home and back at lunchtime, this was a distance of seven miles in all.

The application went to the Head for consideration and it was turned down. The reason given for the refusal was that pupils living further away from the school had submitted other applications and they must have preference. Spaces in the school cycle sheds were very scarce and this was another reason why I was turned down. I think my herringbone suit was the main reason.

I decided at this point that I'd had enough of this school. I had no intentions of spending the rest of my school days at Pendower. I stopped doing my homework; I stopped playing football for the school team, and worst of all I stopped behaving myself. After trying so hard to fit in, I realised it would never happen. I longed to return to my old school.

Although my previous Headmaster was a strict disciplinarian he didn't persecute people. He was firm, but fair.

I began to get a reputation for being a bit of a 'tough guy' and was challenged to prove it on several occasions. The venue was always the same, half past four behind the Green Tree public house, in Benwell Village. My friend Brian Bateman accompanied me on each occasion to make sure no one tried any funny business. He was almost fourteen years old, but was over six feet tall and weighed nearly twelve stone. I was eager to get to the Green Tree to show everyone what a real fistfight was like. I had seen a couple of fights in the school playground and I couldn't recall one clean blow being struck. They pulled each others hair, scratched and clawed like a couple of girls, and when one boy fell to the ground his assailant grabbed hold of his private parts and squeezed till the victim screamed in agony. Then he let go and ran away. I made it my business to have a word with him later. His name was Eric Smart and our paths crossed several times in later life. I told him:

"If you ever did that to me, I would follow you to the ends of the earth till I made you pay for it. You're just a bloody coward. Fancy doing that to somebody who was already on the ground and then running away. You wouldn't be able to run far enough from me!"

He was one of my first 'Green Tree' candidates. We agreed to meet next night and this was one encounter I was really looking forward to. I believed I could flatten most of them without too much trouble and I even fancied my chances with some of the older boys, especially if Brian was with me!

Out of my three visits to the Green Tree, I had three total disappointments. No one turned up. I couldn't believe it. I was anxious to show them what a Cruddas Park scruff could do, but I wasn't even allowed to do that. I had never experienced this level of cowardice before. Where I came from, your name would be mud for the rest of your life if you didn't turn up for a fight.

If I had any trouble with anyone after that I just thumped them on the spot, no more Green Tree. If they wanted to do something about it, there was no time like the present; it worked much better that way.

My school uniform finally materialised. It was very smart but I didn't have much enthusiasm for wearing it. I think I had a bit of a 'chip' on my shoulder about where I had come from. The blue jacket and grey flannel trousers took on the spectre of conformity and I wasn't about to conform. Oh I wore it all right, but it didn't match my yellow T-shirt, and once again I ended up in the Head's office. A long drawn out lecture ensued. I was sick and tired of the droning voice.

"In future we will have to consider very carefully any applications from Cruddas Park to admit pupils for further education."

He had just received a request from another former Cruddas Park pupil to be allowed to return to his old school.

"There seems to be an undesirable element amongst pupils from that area we could well do without. If you persist in wearing a yellow T-shirt as part of the school uniform I will have no hesitation in sending you home to replace it with a shirt and tie."

The fact that I didn't have a shirt and tie didn't seem to penetrate his brain.

My next lesson was physical training, or PT. The gymnasium was very well equipped and the teacher was a former gymnast. I could not take him seriously. I had about as much co-ordination as a two-legged tortoise, and the things he was trying to get me to do, were just out of the question. So I just clowned my way out of it. Every time he explained something I piped up.

"Aye, but what happens next?"

The whole of the class was in hysterics. The teacher tried desperately to ignore me.

"You reach as far up the rope as you can with your left hand."

"Aye, but what happens next?"

He glanced sideways at me but said nothing.

"Then you pull yourself up, draping the rope over your right instep."

"Aye, but what happens next?"

"You place the heel of your left foot on top of the rope, which will prevent it from slipping as you push yourself further up towards the top."

"Aye, but what happens next?"

"Ahhrrrrr you ... Get out! Get out! Get out of the gym altogether."

His face was scarlet and the blow he aimed at me would have knocked Muhammad Ali out of the ring.

He missed of course as I ducked and turned away, but his plimsolled toe caught me squarely up the backside.

"I'll show you what happens next," he raved.

"You go out of the door."

I was unceremoniously bundled out of the double glass doors and ordered to: –

"Stand there and don't move!"

I didn't know he had it in him. He was usually so placid. I had obviously sent him over the top and he had completely lost control.

I couldn't do anything for laughing. Everyone else was the same. I think they were laughing more at the way the teacher had reacted than at my antics.

The lesson was over in real terms. The class was almost out of control and the laughter continued to break out intermittently. One boy climbed half way up one of the ropes, started to giggle and ended up dropping on top of his two mates. He also received a nice bright red rope burn on his way down.

It was quite cool in the gloomy passage and I jogged up and down to keep warm. I was so preoccupied that I failed to notice the arrival of the 'two thirty' from Transylvania. The black cloak billowed out like two large wings and the rubber-soled shoes made no sound at all. I didn't even hear the coffin lid close.

"And what are you doing out here Flannigan?" Demanded the Head with his usual cheery disposition.

'I knew I should have put my garlic necklace on this morning, but its too late now', I thought. 'I'll probably end up with two holes in my neck'.

The PT teacher appeared as if by magic.

"I sent him out Sir, to get some fresh air, he was feeling a little queezy."

Well, there's a turn up for the book, a teacher lying to save me from the wrath of the Head.

"Are you alright now Flannigan?"

"Yes Sir." I answered.

"Then get yourself back inside."

I gestured to the rest of the class as I re-entered the Gym, and mouthed silently, 'The Head's outside'.

They all settled down and waited quietly for the teacher to re-appear.

It seemed to be quite some time before he came back, looking a little tense, but he acted as though nothing had happened. We put the apparatus away, rolled up the coconut mats and pulled the beams up to the ceiling. I was just tying the safety rope to the wall bars, when a voice behind me murmured...

"I hope that will be a lesson to you Flannigan!"

When I turned he was walking towards the two glass doors and I didn't have time to reply, or I might have said...

"Yes sir, and thank you for being such a sport."

The urge to return to my old school was getting stronger every day. Walking to and from school was beginning to get a little too much.

I was doing a three and a half mile journey four times a day now, as I was saving my sixpence bus fare to buy an air pistol. But fourteen miles a day was taking its toll. I was wearing a pair of size seven brogues that had been stretched to fit my size eight feet. I could have worn my sandshoes, but that would have landed me in more bother at school. 'Not school uniform', as I had been told on so many occasions.

My mother was against my leaving Pendower, so I wrote to my father who was working in Liverpool at the time. I told him why I was unhappy and why I thought it would be better for me to return to my old school. He backed me up fully. He did not want me to stay at a school that made me unhappy, and told me to leave as soon as I wanted. He also said that if I had any trouble with Mr Green, I just had to let him know and he would get in touch with him.

The Head was in a very grumpy mood, even more than usual. I waited outside of his office with grave doubts about what to say. I wanted to leave his school as soon as possible, but I had a feeling he may not agree to let me go, just for spite. My request had to sound genuine, with no reference to his attitude towards me, and nothing had to emerge about the snobbery or superiority complex of some of his staff and pupils.

The office door opened and two boys, snivelling quietly and almost hugging each other stumbled out. The secretary gave me a long cold stare and asked brusquely:

"And what is your name?"

"Flannigan."

"Flannigan what?" She retorted.

"Flannigan William." I replied.

She sighed deeply.

"Don't you know how to address people?

When you speak to a teacher don't you say 'Sir' or 'Miss'?"

"Of course I do, but you're not a teacher, so why should I say sir or miss to you?"

She almost exploded.

"You ins…I hope … you st… She spluttered on but failed to complete the sentence as she knocked on the Heads door.

The sombre voice rumbled from within.

"Come"

The secretary opened the door and slipped inside through a gap that seemed to be about four inches wide. I could hear her doing a demolition job on my character; I could have saved her the trouble, he had already made his mind up about my character and anything she had to add would make little or no difference at all. She came from behind the door with a satisfied leer on her face and gestured for me to go in.

He was sitting on his black leather swivel chair with both elbows on his desk. His hands were clasped fingertips to fingertips with his two index fingers touching his nose.

"Well, what is it?"

'Charming as ever', I thought.

I quickly launched into full flow. I liked the school and the lessons. I got on well with the staff, but travelling and trying to maintain the standard of dress required was a major problem. My shoes were wearing out too quickly and my family could not afford to replace them. My old school was only ten minutes walk from home and you didn't have to wear a uniform!

He held up his hand as though he was directing traffic.

"Stop, stop right there. This is all because you were refused permission to bring your bicycle to school, that's it isn't it?"

I couldn't believe he could be so stupid. He didn't like me, and I didn't like him, yet he refused to accept the real reason for my wanting to leave. He was the reason. How naïve can anyone get?

"You can go today if you wish, I will be glad to see the back of you. I will write to the Headmaster of Cruddas Park and give him a full account of your conduct and attitude towards this school. I'm sure he will know what to do. Now go! Just get out of my sight."

I grinned broadly at the secretary as I passed her office. She looked at me as though she was about to be sick, but she said nothing. It's just as well; I was ready to give her a right mouthful. The lads had nicknamed her Miss Fortune, but if she'd said anything else to me I think it would have been changed to Miss Take!

I returned to my class, which was in the middle of a science lesson. Mr Coagin had a large thick glass jar on what looked like an old gramophone turntable. He was drawing the air out of the jar through a hole in the turntable to create a vacuum. The lesson was to show how the force of gravity would make it impossible to move the jar once all of the air had been removed.

He gestured for me to sit down.

"Please sir, I've just come to tell you I'm leaving the school today."

"Are you now? Well you may as well sit down and watch the fun before you go."

I sat next to my friend Brian Bateman who whispered.

"Well done," as I scraped the stool closer to him.

Mr Coagin's voice was loud but more authoritative than aggressive.

"Quiet you two."

He pointed to my friend and me.

"Let's get this experiment out of the way, then you can talk as much as you like."

Several boys tried to remove the jar from the turntable, which was bolted to the laboratory bench, without success.

"Bateman, come out here and give us the benefit of your size. See if you can lift it!"

Brian put his two huge hands around the jar and strained upwards. The turntable had been greased with Vaseline to make it airtight and there was a loud 'plop!' as the seal broke. The jar shot up and hit my friend in the mouth, bursting his top lip.

"Good God, I underestimated your strength boy." Said the teacher as he examined the cut lip.

But he was fine; the injury was only superficial, although the profanities that followed cast doubts on the purpose of the experiment.

True to his word Mr Coagin allowed us to talk amongst ourselves while he cleared up for the next lesson. My friends were all proud of what I had done, but it was all tinged with sadness. I suddenly realised that I may never see any of them again. I had come quite close to two or three of them and I knew I would miss them. Even Elsie and Doris said I should re-consider, after all the school had a great reputation for producing high standards of achievement.

Trust those two!

I would have to face Mr Stephenson at Cruddas Park, which

was a little daunting, but my mind was made up. I would also have to face Mrs Flannigan at No 54 Cannon Street; this was even more daunting. After that it would be up to me to prove that I had made the right decision.

My form teacher at Pendower was Mr Garrick, the music teacher. He was a very kindly sort of person and I never had any trouble with him at all. He was very fair and treated everyone the same, no matter what their backgrounds were. I said my goodbyes to him and my friends and left the school forever.

It was to be almost fifty years before I saw Mr Garrick again.

I was in 'Windows' Music shop in Newcastle, when I spotted him as he flicked through the classical CD's.

"Excuse me sir, but is it Mr Garrick?"

I asked feeling like a schoolboy again.

"Yes it is, do we know each other?"

After two or three minutes of conversation his eyes suddenly widened and seemed to twinkle. A broad smile lit up the old wrinkled face and little tears of nostalgia hovered on his lower lids.

He remembered everyone. Every name I could recall brought another little nod of delight.

I would say…

"The two Hoods."

He would say.

"Parting."

"Bateman."

"Jennings."

We went on to name almost the entire class.

The handshake was firm and sincere as we parted. I watched him as he walked slowly away, leaning heavily on the walking stick in his left hand. I wondered if the limp was due to the injury he had sustained during a teachers-verses-pupils football match many years previously.

He hesitated a couple of times, shook his head and left the shop. I can still see him sitting at the school piano during a music lesson. Dressed in light beige trousers, tan sports jacket, leather patches on the elbows, gazing up to the ceiling as he played Beethoven's 'Moonlight Sonata'.

I once asked him if he knew, 'I'm always chasing Rainbows'. Of course he had no idea what I was talking about. Now if I had asked him if he knew Chopin's 'Fantasy Impromptu', the answer would have been very different. At that early stage of my musical knowledge neither he nor I knew they were the same piece of music.

I have spent many an hour in 'Windows', hoping he would turn up once more, but he never has.

My Parents decision to Marry on 'Boxing Day', turned out to be very Prophetic! (*If used as a verb*).

Mam and Dad - *married two weeks and still friends.*

Grace, Mam, the Twins Jean and Ronnie and Sister Marie.

Mam with Uncle Tommy Nannas brother.

Mam and Dad - *at Battle Stations once again.*

Granda Mills with two legs.

Granda Mills with one leg.

Great Grandma Mills with
daughters Florence and Elsie.

Granda Mills' sister Jenny.

Grace.

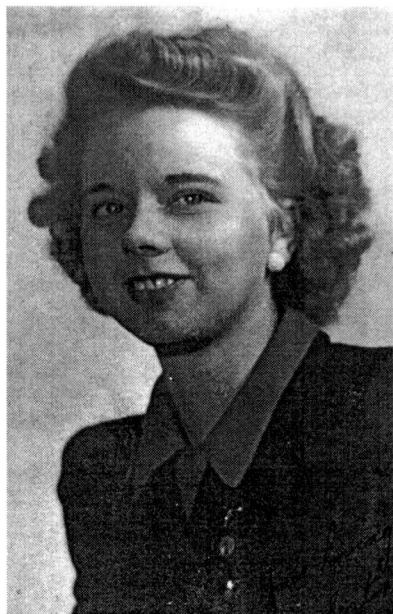

Betty (*Liz*).

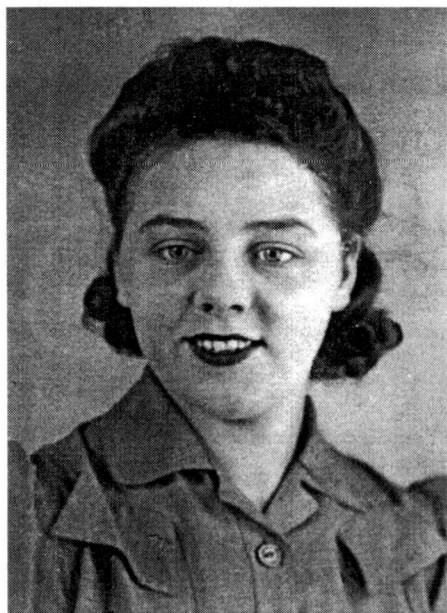

Dot.

Jenny.

Granda Flannigan in his
full R.A.O.B. Regalia.

"Back in your old Backyard"
Ma with her favourite dog 'Midge'.

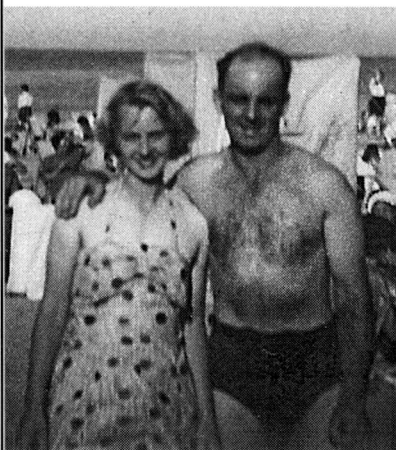
Liz with her husband
George Avison on
Tynemouth beach 1950's.

Jen and Frankie James
on son Ken's wedding day.

Chapter Seven

My return to Cruddas Park School was slightly less than triumphant. The loud fanfare of silence was to say the least a little disappointing. I don't know what I expected, but whatever it was it failed to materialise.

Mr Stephenson was very cool and formal. It was obviously an affront to him that two of his pupils were unable to settle in a school that he had recommended. He said very little, but indicated that he would reserve judgement until he received Mr Green's report.

I was given a place in the top class (it was class, not form in this school). The teacher was Ted Compton, the most respected (and feared) teacher in the whole school. Mr Compton was a no nonsense person, who came to school each day to teach, not to make friends. He had his own methods of maintaining discipline in the shape of a length of thick leather strapping, which had once graced some equine harness. It was about eighteen inches long by just one inch wide but it was as thick as an exercise book. I had experienced a sample of this instrument of torture only once, and once was enough, if 'Mr C' was on duty in the schoolyard for morning assembly you had to be on time. If you weren't you were treated to a sample of the horse's reigns on each hand.

During lessons you listened to what he was saying. His diction was perfect; he pronounced every letter in every word with absolute clarity.

'Tang ang yeeka' would not be chopped down to 'Tanganika'.

There were very few silent letters in 'Ted's' vocabulary. He was extremely proud of the 'British Empire' and took great delight in unrolling the wall atlas, revealing the map of the world, which at that time contained British Empire Pink in every hemisphere.

I had always been in awe of 'Mr C' and expected him to be aloof and unapproachable. I could not have been more mistaken.

During cricket practice I bowled more than sixty balls at Mr Compton. Who proceeded to knock them to all points of the compass. He was so casual and relaxed. I couldn't even get close to his wicket, let alone bowl him out it was more like trying to bowl out Dennis Compton!

"I'll never get you out sir." I moaned.

"Keep going you're bowling very well." He replied.

I didn't know at the time that he was a very talented cricketer and golfer, having represented the county on several occasions. He didn't give praise very often, so to have him say, 'you're bowling very well', was praise indeed.

I got on very well with 'Ted', and found him to be very responsive to good behaviour. He treat me more like an adult than one of his pupils and seemed very impressed at the standard of education I had achieved during my short spell at Pendower.

I knew I would be happier back at my old school. School life had never been so good and it was about to get even better thanks to Mr Compton.

Mr. Stephenson was frowning deeply as he walked towards me.

"Morning Sir."

My manners were improving.

"Ah, Flannigan, yes, good morning. I would like to see you in my office this morning, straight after register."

This could only be one thing, the letter from Mr Green had arrived. It didn't bother me too much, I only hoped I would be allowed to tell my side of the story. I would hate his report to spoil the progress I had made.

He was standing reading the notice board outside of his office as I approached. I stood beside him for a moment until he realised I was there.

"A fine result, yes a fine result. You all played very well and more than a little unlucky not to win, a fine result."

He was referring to the cricket match we had played the previous Saturday.

"You must be the first wicket keeper to bowl out the other side." He said smiling.

What really happened was that our bowlers weren't having much success, so our teacher had told me to get the gloves and pads off and start bowling. I didn't bowl the other side out completely, but I managed to bowl out three of their batsmen before their innings ended. They scored sixty-one from twenty-five overs. We scored forty-seven. A fine result!

I could tell by his expression that the Head had no idea why I was there.

"Did you wish to see me?" He asked.

"Yes Sir, you told me to come to your office straight after register."

He gave me another blank look.

"Ah yes, of course, of course of course."

He hadn't changed much in the last twelve months.

"I have received a letter from Mr Green. He is rather disappointed that you and England (the other boy who had left Pendower with me) decided to return to us. I don't intend to go into details, suffice it to say he is disappointed. I have had a long talk with Mr Compton and this is what we have decided to do."

That was the last time he mentioned the letter, Mr Green or Pendower.

"Now then, according to Mr Compton, you are a fair way ahead of the class work he is currently giving the rest of the pupils, so, you will take charge of all of the sports equipment and the stock room. You will be responsible for the condition of the match balls, the cricket gear and everything else. Anyone who requires the use of any equipment will see you when they book it out and again when they return it. Any defects or shortages will be noted by you and reported to the secretary. Understood?"

"Yes Sir."

"Also we have decided that you should assume the role of

'Senior Boy' in this school from today, and we hope you will set standards for the younger boys to follow."

Senior Boy was always passed on to the best fighter in the school and acknowledged by the pupils for that reason. This was the first time I could remember the title actually being given official recognition.

This was a very proud day in my life. I had just been given a position of responsibility, when all I expected was a telling off.

I had often tried to steal things from the stock room in the past, now I was to have my own key. I could attend whatever lessons I wanted to, or miss them if I had things to attend to in my new job. 'Senior Boy', I liked that. I was already the best fighter in the school but the official title sounded better.

"Of course you will have to attend classes for some lessons, but that will be at the discretion of your teacher.

"So what do you think of that?"

It's amazing how lessons take on a different perspective when you do them by choice. I missed hardly any. I took more notice and found them to be more interesting than I ever thought possible. I believe I learned more in my last year at school than in the previous eight put together.

The teachers became more friendly. They 'asked' me to 'select' a good ball for football practice, or 'would you make sure the pads are nice and white for our match against the Grammar School, they always turn out very smart'. It was a whole new world, and I enjoyed every minute of it. If a fight broke out in the schoolyard Mr Stephenson would say...

"Go down and sort that out would you Flannigan. Tell them we don't allow kissing and cuddling in an all boys school!"

I used to drag the two adversaries apart and say,

"Right you two, the Head can see you from his office window and he sent me down to tell you that the winner has to fight me."

It always worked; I rarely had to use any force.

Our cricket team was pretty weak, but everyone was enthusiastic. I liked the game very much but was desperate to get a win. Our home ground was Forsyth Road playing fields in Gosforth, a thirty-minute bus ride from the school.

We were having quite a good game on one occasion and I thought we were heading for our first victory. The opposing side won the toss and elected to bat first. They were quite good but our bowlers were doing very well. John Daley was a medium pace leg spinner and he was doing most of the damage. At the end of another good over he took up his position in the field, at silly point. It was the position he preferred. I was bowling so I set my field and asked John to move a little closer to the batsman. I bowled a pretty fast first ball but the batsman connected perfectly, albeit with a wild swing. The ball flew towards silly point at about head height. John's hands flew up to protect his face but he was too slow. There was a sickening thud as leather struck bone. John fell forward on his face, completely unconscious. He came around very quickly, in only a few seconds, but he was in no condition to carry on playing. I helped him back to the changing rooms after the teachers abandoned the match. John said he felt as though he was walking up a very steep hill.

Fortunately he suffered no ill effects other than a very bad headache. He didn't bother to have his head X-rayed, or even visit his doctor.

"Me mother rubbed some butter on the bump and that did the trick. It was fine," was all he said.

The game was awarded to the opposing team on the grounds that we had abandoned the match when they were ready to play on. As usual Mr Stephenson found something good to say about our effort and added that we were heading for a certain win, but the injured players health was more important.

"Well done boys, well done, well done!"

During my brief excursion to Pendower I had become more aware of classical music. Mr Garrick had played several pieces on the piano, but he also had a radiogram that belonged to the school for use in music lessons. I was beginning to recognise some of the recordings on 'Two Way Family Favourites' on Sunday mornings. I made up my mind to learn their titles and composers. Listening to that radiogram had spoilt me; it was so different to the old needle and sound box that we possessed. Having no electricity in our house was a big draw back, but I had an idea in my mind that there may be a way to produce that quality of sound another way.

My Idea was to connect an electric 'pick-up arm' to our battery powered radio. We would still use the 'wind-up' mechanism to drive the turntable but the sound would come through a large speaker powered by batteries. It seemed a bit ambitious but I was determined to give it a try. I worked on the project for several months and with help and advice from friends and relatives I finally managed to produce sound as good as electric record players. The volume control was very good but the weight of the pick-up arm was something I could not control. This had an adverse effect on the quality of sound, but at least it did work.

I was so pleased with the result that I sent the idea and the design to a 'reputable' electrical company, with the suggestion that it may be possible to produce a portable record player with electric quality sound without the need of a mains supply. They answered my letter very quickly; saying that they thought it was a very promising idea and had passed on the drawings to their technical department.

After about six months without hearing anything I wrote again, asking them if there had been any progress with my idea. Their response was brief and to the point.

'The Technical Department decided that the idea of a battery powered portable record player would not be viable and we have no desire to pursue the matter any further'.

It was very disappointing at the time, but even more so when six months later they brought out the first battery powered portable radiogram. It was slightly more advanced than my design but the principle was the same. I have never purchased any electrical device made by that company in the whole of my life. It was the only way I could think of getting even with them.

In my new position as Senior Boy at school I was allowed to borrow some of the cricket equipment after a Saturday game. This meant that we had real stumps to bowl at instead of a lamppost, and real pads to protect us against the leather ball. We cleared a section of the derelict land in our street for a wicket, and played for many happy hours. A couple of windows were broken but when we replaced the leather ball with a tennis ball that problem did not arise again.

My Father's stepbrother Nichol and his cronies tried to disrupt our games on several occasions, but eventually they became more interested and watched intently. It was only a short while before they showed an interest in taking part and soon they were as enthusiastic as we were.

As the seasons changed so did our sporting activities. I was the regular goalkeeper for our local Pub, the 'Forge Hammer'. They played in the Sunday morning Business Houses League. I played for them from thirteen years of age until I was sixteen, then I was informed that I had to be eighteen to play in that league, so I was sacked!

We still played marathon football matches in the street. A tennis ball was the match ball and the lamp posts the goals. My pals were all pretty good players and controlled the small grey ball with considerable skill.

One of the most talented players of them all was Eddie Schofield. He was very small in stature, but very clever. His 'strip' for the street matches was a pair of beige satin bloomers belonging to his mother and a pair of her high-heeled shoes. The elastic in the bloomers kept them tight just above his knees, while the shoes gave him an extra couple of inches when heading the ball. His legs were very well developed, possibly due to the high heels, which didn't seem to do him any harm. He played in the school first team for several seasons.

We played a game called 'Doors'. As there were no playing fields around, our streets and lanes became tennis courts, cricket pitches, football fields, netball courts (for the girls), and any other game that required space. 'Doors', almost certainly unique to the Northeast, was a very simple game. The pitch was the back lane and the back-to-back rear entrance doors were the goals. Each player had his own door and the idea was to score as many goals as possible against each other until someone reached a pre-set score against him. This eliminated him from the game. The one who managed to have the least goals scored against him became the winner. It was a good spawning ground for would be footballers and nurtured individual skills in shooting and ball control. The match ball was the obligatory tennis ball that was easily concealed in a trouser pocket if the Police happened to make an appearance.

It wasn't long before my pals and I decided we should have a football team of our own. Not a street team but a team with real football boots, team strips, and a full sized football. We all agreed to put sixpence a week into a fund (or kitty), to pay for our kit. I became treasurer and general organiser by mutual consent and started to get things organised. As I was able to borrow the school footballs it was agreed that our first priority should be a team strip. These were in very short supply, so I had the idea of buying or acquiring some white shirts from friends and relatives and dying them all light blue. Each member of the team supplied one or two shirts so that we ended up with fifteen. We cut the sleeves off and dyed them in our house, so as to ensure that they would all be the same shade of blue. This proved to be very successful and all we had spent was two shillings on dye.

Most of the team players paid their sixpence every week but one or two got a little behind. The main culprit was Brian Bolton who never seemed to have any money on him and I had to constantly chase him for his contribution.

We named the team 'The Elswick Lads' and enjoyed a long run of success against well-established clubs. We bought matching socks, shorts and several pairs of boots for team members who couldn't afford to buy them themselves. The money problem remained a thorn in my side, so a rule was introduced to the effect that anyone who was in arrears with his 'subs', would not be allowed to play for the team until he had cleared the debt. This did not go down to well with Brian and he said he was leaving the team. He demanded his total contributions and threatened to beat me up if he didn't get the money.

I duly gave him what he was entitled to, but on the condition that he picked a day that coming week to 'beat me up'. He chose the next day in the old Elswick Colliery with all the team present to see that it was a fair fight. Eighteen months prior to this I had had a fistfight with Brian and he had hit me twice while I was on my knees then ran away. I had been seething over this since it had happened and was happy to have the chance to put things right.

We assembled at the old colliery at five o'clock. Over twenty of our friends and teammates were present. I was very surprised to see my father's stepbrother had turned up, but I didn't let it bother me.

Brian was quite a good boxer and decided he wanted a 'fair' fight as opposed to what we called 'all-in' or street fighting. I agreed readily and Nichol being the eldest person present said he would be the referee.

Everyone formed a large circle and Nichol said.

"Start when yah ready."

I knew this was going to be a long drawn out thing so I decided that I would let my opponent do all the attacking.

We fought for over fifteen minutes and it was pretty close. I had been defending myself very well and doing very little else. We had to have a short breather once in the 'round' when Brian had hit me full on the nose, which had bled for a couple of minutes. The ground was a little muddy so we moved to a slightly drier place. There wasn't much response from the spectators other than the occasional 'oohs and aahs. No one seemed to be taking sides with either of us.

After almost thirty-five minutes I was beginning to feel more confident. I was landing a lot more blows than my opponent and I could tell that his confidence was wavering. Suddenly he said loudly.

"A'm sick o'this." A'm gan'ah finish it off!"

With that he launched himself at me in a flurry of blows, but I didn't retreat as he expected. I stepped in with a perfect straight left to the bridge of the nose followed by a right cross to the left temple. Brian immediately covered his face with both hands as he had been taught to do but I was on him in a flash. I battered him on the hands, arms, head, shoulders, in fact anywhere I could hit, until he shouted.

"That's it I've had enough!"

We shook hands and my father's brother was the perfect gentleman.

"Well done lads, it was a fair fight and the best man won."

Praise indeed from someone who had caused me so much misery in my life.

It was almost six o'clock and the whole proceedings had taken over an hour. My hands were all swollen around the knuckles, but worst of all, they wouldn't stop shaking. I don't know if it was nerves or damage, but I could barely fasten a shoelace that had come loose during the 'battle'.

Brian's face was in a terrible state. Both of his eyes were swollen into slits and one of them was already black and blue. He was very gracious in defeat and said he had underestimated how much stronger I had grown since our last encounter. I felt rather bad about his injuries and didn't feel any satisfaction in being the victor. Maybe I was beginning to realise how futile violence could be; what did it prove? Yes I could beat one of my best friends, but why? I would rather have his respect than his fear.

Later that night I saw him again, in the back lane sitting on the pavement, looking very forlorn. Two of our friends were standing beside him trying to cheer him up. I could not begin to tell him how sorry I felt for what had happened, and how I would like to make amends. I offered him a 'treat' to the local pictures and I was very happy when he accepted, saying it would give him some time to let the swelling go down. He hadn't been home since the fight and feared he would be in trouble with his parents for fighting.

At around ten o'clock that evening there was a loud knock on our front door. This was quite unusual, as anyone who visited us usually just knocked on the kitchen door and walked right in. My mother answered the knock and shouted to me.

"It's somebody for you."

As I walked down the long passage my heart sank. Standing silhouetted against the night sky was Brian's brother. He was over six feet tall, five or six years older than me, but not heavily built. I approached him with trepidation. 'Should I run back into the house, should I ask him what he wants before I get within striking distance, or should I be my usual self and hit him before he hits me?' All of these things were going through my mind as I reached the front door.

"Did you have a fight with our kid the day?"

I leapt to my own defence.

"It was a fair fight Alan and he said he would give me a good hiding. You can ask the lads, everybody was there!"

"Well he's just had another good hiding off me mother and she sent me down to sort you out. I'm bloody well pleased that somebody has finally shut his big mouth up. He's a cocky little 'get' and he got what he deserved; I just wish I had been there to see it. Don't worry I'll tell me parents what happened and that'll be the end of it."

Much to my relief he was happy not to take the matter any further and even said 'good night' as he walked away.

"What was that all about?"

My mother had heard the conversation with Brian's brother.

"Oh, it was only a little disagreement I had with his brother."

"You're a bloody liar! You've been fighting again! One of these days you'll get what's coming to you. You'll pick on somebody who will give you a bloody good hiding and it will serve you right!"

"I didn't pick on him, he started it and I finished it."

The usual verbal onslaught followed.

"Don't you adopt that attitude with me, for two pins I'd smack you right in the mouth!"

I could never understand what I had said out of place. I always seemed to say the wrong thing to her.

One day, shortly after returning to my old school, I came home while Ma was in the process of making cheese scones. She was rummaging around amongst her cake tins etc. when she asked…

"Do you know where that scone cutter is that you made?"

I had made the cutter for my metalwork project at school and during a recent clearout of my collecting cupboard I had disposed of it.

"You haven't been using that to cut scones have you?" I asked.

"Why" she said with more than a hint of a threat in her demeanour.

"Well it was all rusty. No wonder we've all been getting pains in the stomach. It's just as well I slung it out."

The rolling pin was in her hand in a flash and I was on my way out of the door in a quicker flash. I leaped down the four stairs from the scullery into the kitchen and headed for the door, which fortunately was open. I grabbed the brass doorknob and clashed the door behind me as I made my escape.

A much louder crash and the splintering of timber as the rolling pin hit the right hand panel, splitting it from top to bottom, followed the crash of the door. This was no ordinary rolling pin; this was a piece of hardwood fashioned by my father for killing people!

Phew! That was close. I wonder what I said.

Fortunately Ma had ceased to use, or try to use, physical violence on me since I had warded off one of her wild blows with my left hand, which resulted in my 'almost new' wrist watch being reduced to scrap. It was the first watch I had ever owned. I only had it for a couple of months before it was destroyed.

My mother was having some trouble with her sinuses after a heavy cold. She sent me to the local shop to purchase an ounce of 'Buck Eye' snuff, to see if it would help to relieve the blocked nasal passages. I was unable to get what she wanted, so I went to the local chemist and asked him if he could recommend anything. Mr Hays was more like the local doctor than a chemist. He always seemed to come up with something to solve the problem.

"Tell your mother to try this, it's just new but I'm sure it will help."

He handed me a small circular tin with embossed lettering on the front that read 'Menthol Snuff'. There was no lid; the tin had to be screwed around until a hole appeared in the edge. From this you could tap out whatever quantity you required.

Ma wasn't very impressed, but she said that she would try it. She tapped out a small deposit of snuff onto the back of her hand and sniffed it up into her nostrils. There followed a short bout of sneezing and eye watering.

"Hi, that's pretty good, you can feel the menthol clearing your head."

That was quite a relief to me, hearing her say it was pretty good! She decided she would have another dose and tapped the container onto the back of her hand. Nothing happened. No snuff appeared. She tapped again and a few dust particles fell onto her hand.

"Don't tell me this is finished already, what a bloody swindle. One sniff that's all I've had."

I thought 'here we go again; I'll be sent back to Hays the chemist to demand the money back. Me mother says she's only had one sniff and it's empty already'. It was bound to happen.

She banged the little silver box on the edge of the table, and then tried to look inside, through the tiny hole.

"Here, you can take this back." She said as she sat down in the armchair.

"Tell Mr Hays it must be a faulty tin."

Then she raised the tin to her nose, threw her head back and inhaled loudly and deeply. What followed was obviously painful and very distressing. The entire contents that remained inside the little container shot up my mother's nose. Something had prevented the snuff from coming out of the little hole and the banging on the table must have released it. Her eyes opened with the sudden realisation of what had happened. She screamed in terror as the menthol took effect. Her hands clawed at her face as she threw herself backwards kicking her legs in obvious agony. I didn't know what to do. I grabbed a tea towel and soaked it under the cold tap. Ma snatched it from my hands and buried her face in it. She was sobbing and choking at the same time. I couldn't make out what she was trying to say, but it sounded threatening. Finally the effects started to wear off, but my mother's face was as white as snow. Her eyes were bright red and her nose had dark brown rings around the nostrils. She seemed totally exhausted. Her breathing was still very laboured, and she sounded as though she had a very bad cold when she spoke.

"My God, I'll never do that again." She whispered soberly.

"The snuff must have 'caked' in the tin and I must have loosened it when I tapped it on the table."

Her hands were shaking as she tried to light a cigarette.

"Put the kettle on will you son? I need a cup of tea."

A cup of tea was the answer to all ills. If you broke your leg, the first thing you got for it was 'a nice cup of tea'.

I filled the kettle and put it on the gas ring.

"Bye what a fright I got there." Said Ma.

"So did I, I didn't know what had happened. You said the tin was empty, then two minutes later you were shouting and screaming."

"You would bloody shout and scream as well if you got a box full of snuff up your nose."

Ma was rapidly regaining her composure. There was a slight edge to her voice but I failed to heed the warning.

"That would never have happened if you'd got the 'Buck eye' instead of that bloody tin."

"I know, but Charlotte didn't have any, did she? I thought I was doing you a good turn asking Mr Hays for something."

"You could have tried another shop, Chipsides aren't the only ones who sell snuff."

It was getting a little heated but I had to say my piece.

"If you'd had more patience, instead of deciding it was a swindle, it wouldn't have happened either."

I thought 'should I say any more or should I err on the side of caution', but it just came out, I didn't seem to have control of my mouth.

"That was a really stupid thing to do, put the whole tin up your nose like that."

I was standing beside the tea caddy (soup tureen) when she sprang at me and grabbed my pullover. The first blow just grazed my head as I pulled myself free. The second blow was a 'haymaker', which I easily avoided. I wasn't afraid of her any more but she was still dangerous. I 'ducked' and weaved as she aimed blows at me. Then suddenly my back was against the wall. Ma threw a tremendous right hand, which I blocked with my left. My wristwatch just disintegrated. I didn't know there were so many parts in such a small object. Springs, wheels and glass, the lot just flew in all directions. We both looked at the piece of metal dangling from my wrist by the chrome strap.

"See, that's what you get for your bloody cheek."

I knew it would be my fault.

"If you'd kept your bloody mouth shut, that would never have happened," yelled Ma.

Whatever logic she thought was in that statement escaped me. She broke the watch but it was my fault.

I took advantage of the lull in the proceedings and made for the door.

"Don't you dare go out while I'm talking to you."

What she really meant was, 'don't you dare go out while I'm trying to kill you'!

I ignored her shouts and threats, and cycled away as fast as I could go. She came to the front door and yelled after me.

"You'll have to come back sometime and you'll be in for it."

I just waved my hand and didn't even look back.

That incident was the last time Ma tried physical violence on me. I was often subjected to verbal abuse and the odd missile attack, but she must have decided that I was now too big to beat up. It was a welcome relief and I often looked at my sister and thought, 'I hope you don't have to go through the same process that I've been through'.

One missile attack could have very been very serious indeed

but for my own quick reactions.

Ma was sitting on the arm of one of our armchairs having fish and chips for her dinner. She was using a fork to eat her meal and I said jokingly…

"Mind that's a turn up for the book; fancy using a fork to eat fish and chips; and a proper fish fork as well."

The look she gave me was enough to warn me that I was treading on very thin ice; but I failed to heed the warning.

She carried on eating while she read the Daily Mirror that she had spread over the table to protect the polished top from the hot chips.

"Ah see we've got a new table cloth as well" I quipped.

That did it; Ma's hand moved as quickly as a striking Cobra. The flash of the silver plated fork caught my eye a fraction of a second before it struck. The prongs pierced the skin just below my left eye, bounced off my cheekbone and out through the skin again like skewer, making a total of eight tiny holes in my face. I could have had four cheek rings inserted but body piercing was limited to the ears in those days.

"Oh Jesus what have ah done? You'd make a bloody saint lose tha' temper you; let me see ya' eye."

She thought she had put my eye out so I decided to let her carry on thinking just that. The blood was running down my face and between my fingers but I wouldn't let her look at the damage. I ran out of the house with Ma screaming after me…

"Come back you stupid sod, if you show me up al put more than your bloody eye out."

I have to admit that I was less than respectful on many occasions after that; in fact I was often quite insolent. Most times it was only a brief argument but on the odd occasion she threatened to write to my absent father about my conduct. I don't think she ever did. There were quite a few things I think she would have preferred him not to know about, and I knew what they were! It was a sort of 'stalemate' situation.

I was still having a lot of trouble with tonsillitis. After waiting for what seemed like years to see a consultant, I went back to see our doctor. We had changed doctors after Dr Dove had left our local practice. Our new GP was Dr Henry Moore, a charming little man of Austrian extraction. When he examined my throat he sounded just like S.Z. Sackal, an old film star.

"Sheesh, how are you managing to eat? There is hardly enough rrroom to swallow a pea."

He rolled his Rs more like someone from Northumberland.

"How long have you had a sore thrroat?"

I told him I always had trouble in the cold weather and this one had lasted over two weeks.

"Two veeks, vy have you vaited two veeks to come to see me?"

He could see I was having difficulty speaking, so he said.

"OK, OK, you don't need to talk. Take two of these tablets everry four hours until the svelling goes down, then come back and see me."

He handed me the prescription he had written. It was totally illegible to me. I thanked him and turned to leave.

"In the mean time I vill wrrite to Mr Forsyth, the ENT specialist and trry to get you an appointment."

The Chemist handed me a little brown bottle of tablets. The label read 'Take two tablets every four hours' Penicillin 60 tablets. You never got less than sixty from Dr Moore. He was a great believer in making sure you had enough to get the problem out of your system. It worked very well for me, in less than a week my throat was back to normal and I was able to go back to see him. He was very pleased with the result of the treatment and insisted that I continue taking the tablets until they were all used. I asked him about the consultant but he just smiled.

"My boy, it is now August if you are verry lucky you may get an appointment before Santa Claus comes. But don't vorry, if you feel the symptoms returning come straight back and ve vill put you back on the tablets, OK"

It didn't take as long as the doctor thought. I received my letter from Mr Forsyth in early November. I had to attend the Ear, Nose and Throat Department of Walker Gate Hospital on the Monday after Guy Fawkes' Night. The name 'Walker Gate' conjured up all kinds of foreboding for me, my fathers two half-brothers had been admitted years before, only one of them came out. There was an isolation ward for long- term 'TB' patients and Tuberculosis was almost always terminal before the discovery of Streptomycin, so I didn't fancy going anywhere near this hospital, I was scared.

I'm happy to say Mr Forsyth reassured me that I was in good hands. He didn't explain what he was going to do after the examination, he just said.

"We'll do your tonsils and adenoids at the same time. It's very simple and you will recover very quickly."

That was it, no word of how much it would hurt after the operation, or how sick I would be, or how I wouldn't be able to swallow without pain for nearly three weeks, just simply…

"You will recover very quickly."

This consultation turned out to be the beginning of a very long relationship with this particular surgeon. He performed a total of four operations on my nose and throat in a period of five years. Two of them were quite radical and caused an awful lot of pain and discomfort.

The second of my four operations was the worst. My nasal passages were scraped clean and a lot of polyps removed. Entry to the infected area was through the inside of my mouth above the gums. An incision was made just under the nose and right across to the left side of my mouth, it was about three inches long. Then the bone of my face was scraped clean of all foreign tissue. It must have been quite a severe method as all of my teeth were loose at that side of my mouth after the operation. I think the surgeon may have been a little too vigorous on this occasion. A small fissure appeared in the facial bone above my teeth. I couldn't see it but I could feel a sharp edge with my tongue. I pointed this out to Mr Forsyth at my postoperative examination, but he said it was nothing and would soon heal.

'Nothing' turned out to be a six-month nightmare for me. The fissure started weeping out a dark brown fluid that leaked onto the pillows and sheets during the night. The smell was disgusting; it was just like decaying flesh. My mouth was coated every morning and my handkerchiefs were like sheets of brown paper. My mother stood dishes of disinfectant at my bedside and sprayed perfume around the room from an old cut glass scent bottle with a rubber bulb expeller.

There were no stitches inside my mouth, so the wound healed very slowly. The bone fluid stopped flowing during the day but early mornings remained a nightmare for several months.

Preparation for my tonsillectomy was a pretty crude affair. I walked to the operating theatre and climbed onto the table myself. There was no 'pre-med' to relax me and I was terrified.

As I lay back the anaesthetist approached holding a large black facemask. He placed it over my nose and mouth and said.

"Just breathe in deeply."

The feeling of panic welled up inside of me as the gas started to take effect. I felt as though I was suffocating but I couldn't move my arms to push the mask away. I looked up at the tiles on the theatre wall and they appeared to be melting and running down to the floor. Then total blackness.

The operation was very short and I was back in the recovery ward within an hour. My being over fourteen years of age didn't help me very much, it was considered better for the patient if tonsils were removed at a much earlier age. The healing process took over three weeks. My mother collected me from the Hospital in a taxi of all things. She seemed to be quite worried about my state of health and wanted to know every detail of how I had been looked after. What kind of food they had provided and what had they given me to ease the pain. I was quite impressed; I had never known her to be so concerned about me before. Maybe I'd misjudged her; in fact I know I had. The Old Latin proverb 'we can judge others or we can love others–but we can't do both' certainly rang true.

I was absent from school for three weeks after the operation, so I took the opportunity to catch up on my reading. Mr Compton was a great believer in books, and how much knowledge you could gain from them. With his influence I became an avid reader. During my free periods, instead of writing an essay on the lesson subject, he allowed me to read. I raced through 'The Thirty Nine Steps' by John Buchan, 'The Last of the Mohicans' by James Fenimore Cooper, White Fang, Dog Crusoe, Green Mantel, and Raid on Heligoland. Once I started a book I had to keep reading until it was finished. Sherlock Holmes fascinated me; his application of sound logic and powers of observation revealed the genius of the author, Sir Arthur Conan Doyle. But one man stood way above the others in my opinion. I think he started out working as an apprentice milliner but ended up being one of the world's greatest authors. He was of course H.G. Wells. The vision and foresight he demonstrated in his books was almost beyond belief. 'The Time Machine' and 'The War of the Worlds' were made into very successful films.

I was still reading the boys weekly papers like The Rover, The Adventure, The Wizard and The Hotspur. My favourite was Wilson of the Wizard. He was a supremely fit athlete who was capable of breaking every 'track and field' record. He lived alone somewhere in England and was reputed to be over one hundred years old. In one episode in 1948, he ran a mile in three minutes forty-eight seconds. As it took another six years for Dr Roger Bannister to break the four-minute barrier (three minutes fifty-nine point four seconds) the writers obviously thought that no athlete in the foreseeable future could possibly reach Wilson's standard.

Sadly they were wrong. Seb Coe, Steve Cram and Steve Ovett all beat Wilson's fictitious World Record, on several occasions. But they were in there twenties when they achieved their success Wilson was over one hundred!

Reading became almost an obsession with me. Even during mealtimes I would prop a book up against the milk bottle and read my way through the meal. There are some authors who write the words down and leave you to conjure up the pictures they are trying to portray. They still create excitement and anticipation, but there are others who can paint a vivid panoramic vista with only a few carefully chosen words. I could almost hear Dr Watson's tone of voice as he struggled with the evidence, never understanding how Holmes reached his conclusions.

'Elementary my dear Watson', always seemed to be a bit of a put down for the doctor.

I had magical pictures of Uncas and Chingachook in 'The Last of the Mohicans', and Jack London's 'White Fang' was to me, a real wolf. All of these things I created in my minds eye, encouraged by the authors, until one day many years later I read a book by James A. Michener.

This man was no ordinary writer. This man was a creator. He introduced characters that became real people with personalities that you never forgot. He blended historical facts into fictitious situations rendering them even more credible. Educating whilst entertaining. For me he was the Albert Einstien of the literary world. I wish I had 'met' him much earlier in my life. I have read his 'Centennial' no fewer than six times; a book of over eleven hundred pages, covering millions of years of history. I feel the anticipation building up as 'old friends' are about to emerge, and I learn something new every time I read this encyclopedia of life. All of his books are the same. When you turn the pages you can see the surf in 'Tales of the South Pacific', feel the arrow in between Pasquenelles shoulder blades in 'Centennial' and hear the strange call of the Hoopoe bird in 'The Source'. He was ninety when he died in 1997, but he left a legacy of wonderful stories that will last forever

My period of convalescence ended after my third week away from school. It was a strange feeling actually looking forward to Monday morning. The 'Head' assured me that my sports equipment duties were still intact and had been looked after by another senior boy named Jack Kirkup. I wasn't too keen on Kirkup, as he had indicated in the past that he was capable of taking over as my successor. My first job was to sort this situation out. I 'collared' him in the toilets at morning break and told him I was resuming all my duties as Senior Boy, and he would no longer be required to look after the sports gear. He was very arrogant and told me he had no intention of giving up the job, as the Headmaster had told him he could carry on. I was very surprised to hear that, but I found out later that Mr Stephenson had in fact said that he could carry on, helping me, if I needed him. As I didn't like him very much I had no intention of working with him, so I gave him the option of giving the job up, or fighting me to keep it. I still wasn't one hundred percent fit after my operation, but I wasn't prepared to let this go on any longer. He must have been feeling very confident. He accepted the challenge and we decided to fight it out in the Elswick Park at 'home time'.

I felt a little sick at the prospects of a bruising battle and found myself wondering if I was capable of winning. For the first time in my life I couldn't raise any enthusiasm towards the pending conflict. Maybe this was fear, something I had never experienced in similar situations. I didn't like the feeling, but it turned out to be all for nothing, my challenger failed to turn up. He sent one of his pals to tell me he had decided he didn't want the job anymore so there was no point in fighting over it. His friend also told me he had been worried sick all day at the prospect of facing me.

"Jackie was as white as a ghost when half past four came, he was shit scared!" He said.

'Nice friend', I thought.

I was relieved and promised myself I would shake hands with Kirkup without saying anything about his friend's comments; however he stayed away from school for three days and I didn't see him again till the following Monday. We both laughed about our near confrontation. Jack admitted that he knew he wouldn't be able to beat me and was hoping I would back down. Once again I felt the nagging doubts about achieving anything on the back of violence. I had made another friend that day and it was a nice feeling.

The American humorist Will Rogers once said 'we can get mighty rich, but if we haven't got any friends, we are poorer than a church mouse'.

My duties at school took up most of my time and when 'end of term' exams came along I was wondering how this would affect my marks.

Mr Stephenson sorted that problem out very simply. I would take exams in Maths, Art and Geometry and write essays covering the other subjects. Our class was just coming on to Algebra and Equations, so I was given a separate paper quite a bit more advanced in those subjects. I was quite good at Art and Technical drawing, and did reasonably well in Geometry: mainly because I could draw an Isosceles triangle and had remembered Pythagoras' theorem. The end result was I came second top of the whole school, which was a nice surprise. I had never been so happy at school; it's a pity this was my last term and not my first!

Cruddas Park had a small playground and Bowling Green attached to our school. At the top end of the park there was a building called St. Joseph's Home for Boys. I thought it was an approved school for wayward kids, something like a borstal, but I was wrong. Several residents of the 'home' were pupils at Cruddas Park School. In my position as Senior Boy I came into contact with several of them and was very surprised to find that most of them were at the Home because their parents couldn't manage to keep them at home for economic reasons. Most came from the south of England and had strong 'cockney' or southern accents. I found them to be rather immature for their age and it was a constant problem trying to protect them from some of our 'would be' bullies.

One boy named King told me his mother couldn't afford to keep him as she had just had another baby and her husband had deserted her. I couldn't understand why he had been sent all the way to Newcastle, when his home was in Norfolk. Surely one of his aunts or uncles could have taken him in until his mother got herself sorted out. This situation would never arise in our area! At least that's what I thought. I couldn't imagine any of my family refusing to look after my sister or me if it became necessary.

During the war my mother and father had some marital problems and Ma went down to Bletchley in Buckinghamshire in an effort to patch things up. I stayed with my mother's second eldest sister Jenny and her husband Frank while she was away. It wasn't looked on as any special favour, it just happened. Our Robert stayed with us for a while and we had a great time together.

Frankie used to take us down the Vale in Byker. From there we could walk right through to Jesmond Dene. It was more like being on an extended holiday than being in 'lodgings'. Jenny had a lovely home, everything was brand new and she even had a full size bath under the bench in the scullery. She had only been married a short while and Frankie seemed to be the perfect husband; based on a small boy's observations. He was always joking and larking about, and when he bought me a little white rabbit, I thought he was the greatest. Fancy someone buying something for you without you even asking for it. He even let me keep it in the house, in the spare bedroom. He once heard me swearing at our Robert and didn't even mention it; he just pretended he hadn't heard. His sister Gwenny lived in the same street, Bolingbroke Street in Byker, with her husband Joe. I became very friendly with their son Eric and often stayed at their house all day. They were all lovely people and I was pleased our Jen had found such a nice family.

It was difficult for me to comprehend how any family could

send a son or daughter away from the security of a home. We may be poor in the Northeast in monetary terms but we have untold wealth in the family bond!

At fourteen years of age I began to realise that I would soon be eligible for work so it was time for me to think of a trade or career I could go into. It was 1950 and the signs of the war were disappearing fast. Although another conflict had started in Korea it was far enough away from us not to cause us too much trouble, as yet!

I had a good idea what I would like to do with my life even at this tender age. First of all I needed a job. Preferably something to do with art or design. I had asked the art teacher what he thought my chances were of getting employment in that area and he had been very positive. He said I had a good basic knowledge of art and with training I would probably be able to gain a position in that field.

During my stay at Pendower the art teacher had given us a book cover to design for our art lesson. The name of the book had to correspond with the design on the cover. It all had to be original, no copying from real books. I called my book 'The Ghost of the Lost Canyon'. The front cover was a mountain range with a vivid sunset and the silhouette of a horse in the foreground. Mr Walters seemed very surprised and pleased. I didn't like him very much he was always groping the two boys who sat behind me; I thought he was a queer.

"This is a very fine piece of work. Why haven't you produced something like this in the past?" He enquired.

I was made to stand in front of the class and hold my book cover up for everyone to see.

"You see what can be achieved with a little thought." He said to the class.

"This is very good, what do you want to do when you leave school?"

Well, me being in my anti-Pendower mode, I blurted out:

"I'd like to be a painter and decorator!"

He looked at me in disbelief.

"A what? A painter and decorator? You're in the wrong bloody school son, get back to your desk!"

It was the first time I had heard a teacher swear in front of the whole class. He left the room and didn't return until the bell sounded for the end of the lesson. As we marched towards our next class, Johnny pointed at me whilst talking to another teacher, shaking his head at the same time.

Mr Stephenson had recently introduced a new idea to his staff. One of the teachers was to be responsible for advising pupils on their future after school. He was to be called the Careers Advisor. Whether or not it was a directive from the Education Authority or his own initiative I don't know, but it certainly was a good idea. Two teachers decided to share the job between them, Mr Smith and Mr Carter, the science teacher.

I'd had many confrontations with Mr Smith in the past. He had a foul temper and his favourite punishment was a whack on the backside with a three-foot wooden rule. So being able to talk to him on a subject far removed from schoolwork gave me an insight into what the man was really like. It was like meeting him for the first time, he was so different. He smiled at my naïve questions but took everything seriously. He was like a long lost uncle. I explained to him I would like to do something in the art and design trade and he took an immediate interest.

"There's a company somewhere in Newcastle who are advertising for apprentice silk screen printers. Now I can't remember who they are but I will find out for you and you can ask them what it entails."

True to his word, he gave me the name 'David Allen and Sons Ltd.', the next day. We didn't have private telephones in those days, so I asked Mr Smith if he would phone them and try to get me an interview. I was amazed that he agreed straight away and even seemed enthusiastic. I think he liked my approach.

"You've got a bit of cheek haven't you, but I'll ask Mr Stephenson if I can use the school phone, you get nothing if you don't ask!"

The outcome was that David Allen's were looking for boys who would like to go into the screen- printing trade the following year. Anyone interested had to fill in an application form and when vacancies arose they would be contacted and given an interview. As I still had several months to do at school I was content just to put my name down for the future.

I tried finding out what the trade was and what I would be doing, but no one seemed to know anything about it, so I put Mr Smith on the spot and asked him.

It transpired that the art of silkscreen printing was invented in China over three thousand years ago. The Chinese used the process for printing designs onto silk and other fabrics. From that it had been developed into a major part of the printing industry and was growing more and more popular as new applications were introduced for the medium.

The apprenticeship lasted six years, from fifteen to twenty one but that was reduced to three years some time later. I can say in all honesty that after more than fifty years in the trade I still learn something new almost every day. Anyone who claims to know everything about screen-printing obviously knows an awful lot, but there is still an awful lot yet to come from this fascinating industry. I have seen it grow from printing simple posters for the outdoor advertising market to high tech printed circuits, road signs, wallpaper and even icing sugar in the confectionary business. There is a lot more to come in the future, I hope I live to see it.

Chapter Eight

Since the end of the war my father had been working away at frequent intervals. He had spent several months in Glasgow, Liverpool and the Isle of Man. I don't know if he was earning as much money as he had done in the past, but we seemed to be back in our wartime 'hard up' phase. I was constantly taking his best suits to the local pawnshop and Ma was borrowing money once again. My sister was only just starting school, so my mother decided to get a job again, to ease the strain on the family budget.

I hated going to the pawnshop more than any other chore. It was so embarrassing, and to crown it all, the girl who worked in the shop was the one I decided I was going to marry. It wasn't just a boyhood crush, we had been close friends for years and it just seemed the natural way things would turn out. Her name was Rose Ball, I called her 'Rosie', and when the film of Al Jolson's life story was made 'Rosie you are my Posy' became my favourite song. It was all kids stuff, but at the time I suppose it was quite serious for both of us. I liked being with her, all of her friends and even her family were aware of our friendship. There were no objections to it from any quarter. When I took the suits to her shop she never showed any signs of recognition towards me. I always got a little more money from her, but my red face must have told her how embarrassed I was.

After several trips to the pawnshop, Ma used to have Dad's best suit cleaned. She said it always smelled of mothballs and he would notice that straight away. The dry cleaner was on Scotswood Road just past Park Road, so I took it in on Friday night after school. It was only a ten-minute ride on my bike, so I was there and back before five o'clock. I gave my mother the ticket and told her that the suit would be ready on Monday afternoon. That was fine; Dad would not be coming home until the following weekend, so there was plenty of time. He would find his suit in immaculate condition, never realising that it had been absent from our house as long as he had.

When I came home from school on Monday my mother was in a right mood with herself. She had received a telegram from Dad saying he would be coming home late that night, it read…

'Job finished soon, home Monday, late.'

I thought that was great news and said so.

"That job must have gone really well for him to get home nearly a week sooner."

"Aye, but what about his bloody suit? It's nearly five o'clock now so you'll have to fly to the cleaners straight away."

"Well what difference does it make? He won't mind it being at the cleaners, it's just the pawnshop he doesn't like!"

"Look here's the ticket and the money, get yourself there now and don't bloody argue."

I took the cash and the receipt, jumped on my bike and headed for Glue House Lane. The workers were just coming out of Vickers' subway as I reached the end of our street. As usual there were hundreds of them coming up the bank. I rang my bell as I rode swiftly down towards Scotswood Road, scattering several cloth-capped individuals as I went. This part of the road was still covered in cobblestones, so I slowed a little to negotiate the ninety-degree turn. Looking to my right, it was clear, I turned left still travelling quite fast and ringing my bell. Everything happened in a flash. Two men were crossing the road, one behind the other. If I carried on I couldn't fail to hit them, but I was sure they'd sprint the last couple of yards because they had seen me in time. The first one did just that, but his friend stopped dead and shouted.

"Slow down you mad bastard!"

I slammed on my brakes as I swerved to miss him. The wheels locked almost instantly, but I didn't go over the handlebars, instead the bike skidded sideways over the granite cobbles and into the path of the oncoming traffic.

I was almost into the entrance of the subway when the car hit me. Another second and I would have been safe. I remember the long cream bonnet with the huge chrome radiator screeching towards me, and I even had time to brace myself before the impact. I felt nothing as the car hit me broadside on and my bike disappeared beneath the wheels. I landed back on the other side of the road in front of a red 'United' bus, which the driver managed to stop just as it hit my shoulder. I wasn't hurt too badly, but my pride was in tatters. I tearfully picked up my mangled bike and looked around for the person who had caused this. No one bothered to ask if I was all right, I just had to get out of the way to allow the traffic to continue.

"It serves you right you stupid bugger, you got what you deserved."

It was him; he wasn't content at having me almost killed, he was gloating at what had happened. He was a fully-grown man and I was fourteen but I threw my bike down onto the ground and went for him. I could see his face change colour as I tried to get past the men who were trying to restrain me. My language was disgusting.

"Let the bastard go, I'll teach him a bloody lesson." He said to the other men.

"Let me go and al break his f......g neck." I screamed, totally out of control.

"Ah think ye better gan home Geordie, this fella's really bloody narked ah tell yih, yih shoulda got oot the way and nen o'this would'a happened."

The man decided to take his friend's advice and hurried away up Glue House Lane.

I slung my bike over my shoulder and raced up after him. When I drew level with him I picked up a large piece of broken paving stone and threw it at him as hard as I could. He leaped into the air as the missile crashed at his feet. He was furious and made to come over to my side of the road. I knew he would have half killed me in a man-to-man fight, but the other piece of masonry I had in my hand made him think twice. He shouted a few obscenities at me then hurried on up the bank, anxiously looking back until he was out of range.

I was in remarkably good condition considering I had been run over by a Riley Saloon car and hit, albeit gently, by a 'United' bus. I couldn't say the same about my bike. The car had gone over one of the wheels and the front forks were only about an inch apart, totally ruined.

My mother was quite concerned for several seconds, until she realised I was all right.

"You must have been going far too fast as usual, you're like a bloody lunatic once you get on that bike."

"Ah know I was going fast. I had to didn't ah, to get to the cleaners before they shut!"

"A lot of bloody good that did, you never even got there. Now what am ah going to say to your father?"

"Just tell him the truth for a change. His suit is at the cleaners, you don't have to mention the pawn shop, or even why you were having it cleaned."

She didn't like the bit about 'tell him the truth for a change', but she accepted my suggestion.

It was after midnight when Dad arrived, smiling, rosy cheeked and drunk. I liked to see him when he was under the 'influence'; he was full of carry on and got up to some strange antics. The first thing he did was to strip off to his white singlet and long white underpants. He kept his socks on, held up by little suspenders, and then sat down with a bottle of beer and a bar of chocolate. He would pick up the cat, sling him over his shoulder and bite his tail. Tibby howled and growled until Dad let him go. He called him his 'Geordie Bagpipes'.

The next part of the act was even funnier. The props were all ready to hand: an empty milk bottle a teaspoon and an old mouth organ. The spoon was put into the bottle then Dad stood against the cupboard door and played 'Please Let The Light' using his elbow to drum against the cupboard door and the bottle and spoon as a tambourine. I thought my Dad was really talented. There weren't many people around who could play their own one-man band, the harmonica the milk bottle and the tomcat.

The show went on into the early hours. I was already in my bed settee watching the cabaret in comfort, but it was still a bit of a relief when he finally decided to go to bed. I had told him earlier about my accident and he said he would look for the 'bloody idiot' who got in my way, next day. It was really the beer that was doing the talking. I knew my father was a real tough guy when he was young, and would never run away from trouble, but at the same time he would never go looking for it. He used to say.

"Never go looking for trouble, it has an arful habit of finding you when yah least expecting it."

Dad's Aunt Lizzie once told me a story about an incident that took place when he was just twenty. He worked down Kibblesworth Colliery in Gateshead as a hand putter. That meant he pushed the trucks by hand in the lower seams where there wasn't enough headroom to use horses or ponies. Aunt Lizzie said Dad's sister Hannah had an argument with one of their neighbours and had ended up punching her. The girl's brother, who was thirty, intervened and slapped Hannah several times, marking her face rather badly.

"Well when our Willy came in from work and saw ah face, he just said...

'Who did that?'"

Aunt Lizzie told him what had transpired and said.

"Now listen, it's all over and done with now, let's just forget it."

By this time Dad had stripped off his work shirt, and covered in coal dust he marched out of the house.

"Eee mind ah've never seen owt like it in my life. He went into Sloan's back yard, up the back stairs, opened the scullery door and went straight into the hoose. Two minutes later, oot he comes dragging Edward Sloan with him."

"Is this him Hannah, did he hit yih?"

"Aye Willy he did."

"Mind you Eddie Sloan was a big lad but yah dah battered him from one end of the back lane to the other. Eee, what a mess he made of him. Somebody went and sort the pollis at the finish, they thought wore Willy was ganna kill 'im."

"The Sloans used to be good friends of ours, but by Christ they weren't after that," she said, making the sign of the cross. Lizzie always crossed herself when she was being irreverant.

The police made the two of them shake hands and promise to let the dispute drop.

Lizzie continued...

"Eee, he was a cool customer mind, yah Dah, he just got bath'd in front of the fire and put one o'them operah records on, as though nowt had happened."

During tea on Tuesday Dad said the job at Glasgow was finished and he would be at home for quite some time. There was a large contract in the offing and he was sure he was going to be in charge of it. He would be working in Jarrow, painting the inside of gas pipes. I thought he was joking.

"How do you get inside the pipes, are they that big?"

Dad just laughed.

"No, they're eighteen inches in diameter and you don't have to go inside to paint them. What you do is, place one end of the pipe on a stand with little wheels on, then the other end on a stand about a foot lower, so the pipe is running down at an angle."

"Aye but how do you get the paint right down to the end?"

"Wait a minute and I'll show you."

He looked around the table for something to use as an example and settled on a sausage roll. Placing one end on the sugar bowl and the other on a blue glass cake dish he explained.

"Now this is your length of pipe, about fifteen feet long. You see how it's sloping down? Well all I have to do is heat the 'Bitumastic' up and pour it down the inside from top to bottom, while one of the other men spins the pipe around on the little wheels. That way the paint runs down the full length, coating the inside as it goes. By the time it reaches the bottom it starts to cool and flows much slower. We just leave an empty can to catch the surplus, and then start another one. That's what I've been doing in Glasgow for the last six weeks, but this next job could last for years."

It sounded simple enough, and very effective. Dad said he had made several suggestions on how to speed up the process, and the management had decided that he should take charge of the project.

"Does that mean you get more money?"

Guess who was asking? The lady with the empty purse, Ma!

"If you're in charge, surely that means you get more money."

"Well not always."

Dad seemed to be searching for some way to tell her that he

would just be getting the same wage. If he told her he was getting more money she would expect more from him.

"It works like this on these jobs. If we get a thousand lengths of pipe to do that's a hundred days work for a team, the firm agrees to pay us a wage for the hundred days at say seven pounds a week; now if we work really hard and finish the pipes in less than a hundred days. The firm works out what we would have earned and what we have been paid to date, and we all share the difference between us. So in fact we could earn £140.00 in twenty weeks or £140.00 in only ten weeks. They call it an incentive bonus scheme or something. Seven pounds a week guaranteed would do for me, but the potential for making a lot more money is tremendous."

"Aye but surely if you're responsible for all of them men you must get more money."

Dad sighed deeply.

"You know spending money isn't a talent, it's a sickness. Managing money is a talent. Any silly bugger can go out and spend money like you do, but it takes a special kind of person to spend only what they've got, not what they haven't got!"

It was all light hearted, but I could see my mother bristling.

"What's that supposed to mean?" She retorted.

"Nowt, I was only joking. Of course I'll get the Charge Hand's rate, but I don't know what that will be until 'Squeaker' sets the rate.

'Squeaker' was the site manager employed by Dad's firm, he was responsible for choosing the men and setting the rate of pay for each job. His real name was Billy Morton, but his voice kept breaking when he spoke, so the men had nicknamed him 'Squeaker'. He lived in Clara Street just off Armstrong Road and I was often sent to his house to collect instructions or the 'float' for Dad's jobs. Mr Morton was a very friendly man and he thought very highly of my father. He once confided…

"If your Dad's on one of my sites I never have to worry about it. He makes sure the men do their days work and he does twice as much. But mind don't tell him I said so, 'cause I'll deny it!"

Sometimes I would have to collect Dad's pay packet from Mr Morton, which was always a bit of a ritual.

"Right son, tell yah Dad the time sheets need signing so I'll see him at the South Shields yard on Tuesday, that's all you need to say, and mind be careful with that money."

He handed me a brown envelope with all the figures written on the front. Not a bad week's pay Ma would be pleased; he had earned over six pounds.

I relayed Squeakers message to my father. I thought I had said something funny the way he laughed.

"Did he say what time on Tuesday?"

"No, just that it would be after twelve."

Dad smiled broadly again.

"After twelve, bloody champion."

I knew I was missing something in this conversation, so I asked my Dad.

"What's funny? You seem to be laughing at what Mr. Morton said but I can't see the funny side of it."

Dad held his forefinger up to his lips and pointed to the scullery where mother was preparing the tea.

"Shhh, I'll tell you later." He said with a chuckle in his voice.

After tea Dad said he was going along to see Nichol, his stepfather. He did this about three or four times a week when he was home. Granda Robson had been poorly for quite some time and seemed to be getting thinner by the day. My Dad said...

"I'm sure she's starving the poor man to death."

She being Granny Robson!

As he left the house he motioned for me to follow him. He called to my mother.

"Just come along when you're ready."

"Aye o.k. ah wont be long." Ma replied.

When we got outside he said.

"You know when you go to Squeakers for my pay, you usually get two pay packets at the end of the month, well one of them is my bonus. This month I'm expecting a big bonus, so I didn't want your mother to see it. What Mr Morton meant when he said 'the time sheets need signing' was, that the bonus was through, but he couldn't pay out until Tuesday when he comes to South Shields."

"Oh, so it was all in code, that's what you were laughing at."

"Yeh but the best bit was, he would be coming after twelve, that meant that my bonus is over twelve pounds this month."

Twelve pounds, enough money to buy a three-piece suite or two made-to-measure suits at Jackson's the Tailors. It would pay the rent for six months or feed us for two months. All of this money and we were still poor. I suppose Dad was right when he said.

"Managing money is a talent; not spending it."

When we reached Granny Robson's Dad sent me to the corner shop for a packet of Woodbines.

"Don't give them to me when you get back, slip them to your Granda Robson when your Granny's out of the way."

All this secrecy and intrigue, it was like working for M.I.5.

When I returned from the shop and went into the sitting room, Granda Robson was sitting in his usual chair beside the radio.

"What di ye want." He growled as soon as I entered.

Dad and he both laughed. I was still a little nervous of him but felt less vulnerable when Dad was present. What hair he had left was as white as snow and he looked very thin and weak. Gran was in the scullery boiling potato peelings for the hens, so I took the opportunity to hand over the cigarettes. His face lit up as I pushed the packet into his hand. He had been a heavy smoker for years, but since his illness Granny Robson allowed him only five Woodbines a day, and only one at a time.

"Put them out of the way or she'll have them off you." Dad whispered.

"Aye, yah right Billy, the ones you sent from Glasgow went straight in the bloody drawer."

"What was that you said?" Gran's voice came from the scullery.

"Ah just said there's an arful draught coming from that bloody door."

Being hard of hearing she often missed half of the conversation, fortunately in this case.

"What are you two laughing at?" She said, smiling.

"Yah up to somethin."

"No, ah was just saying to Billy, wouldn't it be nice if some kind little woman was to offer us a cup of tea."

Granda Robson had slipped the contraband into one of the deep pockets in his trousers; the cup of tea ploy was only to cover his hasty movement.

By the time my mother came we were all having a cup of tea and a piece of Gran's home made apple tart.

"Is this what you wanted?" She said to Dad as she handed him a large sheet of white paper.

"Oh aye, ah nearly forgot about that. Here mother, don't say ah never give you anything."

He took the piece of paper and pretended to wipe his backside on it, then crumpled it up and threw it onto the table.

"Eee, what's he like? Did you see what he did? You mucky devil." Gran chided.

She picked up the ball of paper, but instead of opening it up as Dad had expected, she threw it straight into the fire.

"Arrrrr, you silly bugger," Dad yelled, as he dived towards the fireplace.

He managed to rescue the paper ball before the hot coals consumed it. He patted it between his hands, as it had started to smoulder.

"Bye it's a good job that fire was low or else that would have been it."

Dad was gently unrolling the piece of paper as he spoke.

"What's the matter? What is it anyway?" Asked Gran.

"It's a bloody five pound note, that's what it is. The first one ah've ever had in me life and I'll kill Billy Morton for putting it in my pay packet."

"Eee, well ah thought it was just a bit of paper and you were only acting yahself, chucking it on the table after wiping yah arse on it."

Granny Robson hardly ever used profanities, but frequently used the word that described that part of the anatomy. She always maintained it was an old English word that had just gone out of fashion and wasn't considered rude.

"If you ever read that Chaucer book 'Canterbury Tales', you'll see it used in there plenty of times and if it was a real swear word they wouldn't dare print it anyway." Said Granny naively.

The 'fiver' had some yellow marks on the back but fortunately they had not come through to the front. It was only printed on one side and only one colour, black. Nothing like the sophisticated security printing we have today. I could imagine many forgeries circulating before they were replaced in 1957.

I managed to get Dad's good suit from the cleaners before he missed it. My bike was completely useless so I had to go by tram.

I had been down to the Co-op in Newgate Street to look at the new bikes, but that was as far as I had got, just looking. They had a nice red racing model that I loved but it was nearly thirteen pounds. The manager was very helpful and told me about their hire purchase plan, which had just been introduced for Co-op members. You had to put ten percent deposit down then hire the goods until the final payment was reached. This was your 'option to purchase' payment. They maintained title to the goods until that final payment was made. It sounded a bit risky because they could repossess the bike anytime you fell behind with the payments. My mother would have to sign the agreement as I was under age the manager explained. I thought that would be the end of it, she would never agree to do that. He gave me all the figures, deposit, weekly payments, interest etc., and told me to ask my parents adding...

"Your mother will get her 'divi' on it as well."

I looked over the figures twelve pound eighteen shillings and sixpence including purchase tax. That meant nearly twenty-three shillings down and about two and six per week for two years. My pocket money was now three shillings a week, so I was quite prepared to do without that for a few months if it meant having a new bike. I would be working in about six months time when I left school, which would make the payments even easier.

"You're getting no bloody new bike here."

Another little pearl of wisdom and sentiment from my mother.

"I'm not asking you to pay for it, I only want to know if you'll sign for it and I'll pay for it meself."

"Aye and when you can't pay for it, it'll come right back to me. You can go to hell, yah not getting it."

"I'll ask me Da to sign for it then."

"And I'll put you through that bloody wall for yah cheek in a minute!"

Speaking up for yourself or answering an adult back was still considered to be insolence in those days and was usually followed by swift and painful retribution. In this instance it was just an idle threat, which I ignored.

When Dad came in from work he had 'bonus' written all over his face. He took his boiler suit off, washed himself under the cold-water tap and settled down at the table to have his meal.

"Well how much was it this month?"

My Mother knew his bonus was due and his air of well being had obviously given him away.

"Now how do you know if ah've got any bonus at all?"

Dad said smiling broadly.

"Oh aye, ah remember now, one of the lads at the yard said he thought he had seen you flying round the pay office on yah broomstick the day."

The usual pushing and shoving followed and I waited with baited breath for something to go wrong, but it didn't. Dad handed her a brown pay packet that was still sealed and she whooped with delight when she saw the figures on the front.

"Six pound bonus, crickey that's the most you've ever had, six pound."

"Six pound." I said out loud and looked straight at my Dad.

He cringed visibly and his eyes opened wide as he glared in my direction.

I thought, 'right, you've played lots of tricks on me lately, now it's my turn'.

"Let's have a look at that pay packet."

Ma handed me the envelope and Dad looked as though he was about to choke either himself or me!

"Ah can hardly believe this. When ah was up at Mr Morton's the other night he said you were due a bonus off the Glasgow job and it would be well over…"

"What does he know?" Dad interrupted.

"He only sets the rates, the pay office does all the figures," he said through clenched teeth.

"Ah no, that's what ah was going to say, he said the bonus would be well over … err … five pounds, so it just shows you, he was over a pound out!"

Dad's face was a picture. The relief in his eyes could be felt. I just keeled over laughing and then he did the same.

"What's wrong wih you two?" Ma asked.

"Ah think you've all gone bloody mad at the sight of this money."

"You ever do that to me again and ah'll bloody kill you." Dad muttered with his chin pressed into his chest suppressing a smile at the same time

"Ah nearly had a bloody heart attack, ah thought you were going to drop me right in it."

The pay packet was still on the table unopened when we finished our tea. Ma handed it to my Dad and he slit the top open with the bread knife. Before he had time to tip out the contents my mother said:

"Your son's got something to ask you."

I had no idea what she was on about at first and then the penny dropped. I could feel my face turning red. This wasn't the time to ask him for the loan of money. It would look as though I had taken advantage of my knowledge of the bonus.

"No ah haven't, ah've changed me mind, ah can't really afford it."

"You can't afford what?" Dad asked.

"He wants to buy a bike on tick at the Co-op and he needs to borrow a pound for the deposit. Ah told him no, so he said he would ask you. He'll be starting work in a few months time and he could pay you the pound back then."

I couldn't believe it. Here she was asking Dad to let me get the bike that she had been so opposed to only a few hours earlier. I thought, 'I'll never understand her, if I live to be a thousand'.

"A new bike eh, what's it like then, a racer, a roadster or what?"

I described the bike in great detail. How much it was, how many gears, what colour etc.

"Well now, I'll tell you what we'll do, we'll all go down to the Co-op on Saturday and have a look. I'm not promising anything mind, but there's no harm in looking."

I was euphoric. I thought the bike was almost mine. Dad would be sure to loan me the money, I hoped!

Saturday seemed to take forever to come around. Dad had his

best suit on and his trilby hat, he looked just like a 'ticket man'. Ma got my sister dressed and we all made our way to the tram stop.

The Co-op building in Newgate Street was huge. I had been several times to collect my mother's dividend, which was paid out in cash on the top floor.

The little men who support the steel banister on the staircase all the way up the building are still there. I don't know why but they always remind me of the invisible man.

Dad asked the manager several questions about the agreement and I thought he was disagreeing about something, but he was only insisting on having the twelve-month guarantee, in writing. He signed the papers, paid the deposit and said.

"Right, that's it then, you're mobile again."

"Can I take it away the day?" I asked.

"No, I'm sorry son, we have to deliver it to the address on the agreement, it's sort of a check on where you live really, but I'll see if I can get it up to you this afternoon." Explained the manager.

"Here Da, here's the six shillings I've got, that means I owe you seventeen shilling. Ah'll pay that back as soon as ah start work."

"Put your money in your pocket lad. If you can pay it back when you start work then that'll be fine. If you can't, then we'll call it an early Christmas box."

For the first time in my life I wanted to say or do something appropriate to show my appreciation but I could do nothing. I couldn't even say thank you. I felt so embarrassed. I have often wondered what it would have been like to put my arms around my father and give him a hug, but I'll never know. I wish I had of done it when he was alive, now that he is gone I'm filled with regret. Anyway he would probably have thought I was turning queer and punched me on the nose!

My new bike opened up a whole new way of life for me. I didn't care about not having much pocket money; my bike was all I needed. I cycled to places I'd never been to in my life. Places like Felton, Alnwick and Warkworth. I would ride up to Scotswood Bridge and back in about twenty minutes, a trip that would take an hour on the tram.

I went for rides with Rosie on her new bike, but she wasn't allowed to go on the long runs, so I went on my own.

Every other cyclist I encountered became a competitor. If I spotted someone up in front of me it was like a challenge. I would steadily close them down until I was right on their back wheel, then I would stand on the pedals and sprint past them. It was great fun. Some of the other riders would respond and race after me. We raced until one of us had to turn off or give up. They enjoyed it as much as I did and it was always good humoured, never any animosity. It took a long time for me to discover that the aggression shown by runners, cyclists, and swimmers etc., was not directed at their opponents but at themselves. Even boxers, when they loose a fight are more annoyed at themselves, for not having the skill or ability to beat their adversary. Almost without exception, they praise the winner and shake his hand to show they acknowledge his superiority on the night. I had to say 'almost without exception' because I can never forget the night that Brian London fought Dick Richardson in a heavyweight match. I can't recall the exact details of the contest, but I remember clearly Richardson's careless use of his head. He appeared to head-butt London on several occasions, until the referee stopped the proceedings on account of a bad eye injury suffered by London. He was not at all pleased about the stoppage and stormed around the ring cursing and gesticulating about Richardson's actions. You didn't have to be able to lip read to understand what he was saying and some brave, I use the term very loosely, gentleman decided he would take up Richardson's cause.

He jumped into the ring and remonstrated with London, with lots of angry facial expressions and aggressive arm waving. He was only inches away from the defeated boxer when he appeared to aim a blow at him. Whether it landed or not is totally irrelevant, the response was swift and sure. London tapped him with a gentle left jab then lifted him three feet from the canvas with a jolting straight right. The whole thing quickly degenerated into a mass free-for-all. Jack London, Brian's Dad and former British Heavyweight Champion climbed quickly into the ring along with Jack junior, who was also a professional boxer. The three London's proceeded to hand out punishment to anyone who came within range. It was total chaos; bodies were flying in all directions. Some were rolling around the ring in their evening suits and at one point Brian's brother was riding around on someone's back, punching him in the head at the same time.

The London's were natives of the Northeast, hailing from West Hartlepool. The family name was Harper, but the three men in the family took the name of London in their professional careers. Jack junior was a good light heavyweight but didn't do too well in the professional ranks. Jack senior was a professional boxer for eighteen years, winning the British Heavyweight title in 1944. A feat emulated by his son Brian in 1958, a pretty unique achievement for father and son.

Chapter Nine

My friend Henna Andrews had a cousin who lived on Glue House Lane. I thought she was beautiful; her name was Penny Harris. Whenever I saw her I went weak at the knees. She was about five years older than me and I had admired her from afar for a long time. There was no chance of forming any kind of relationship with her but she was always civil and friendly. Whenever she spoke to me I felt as though I had just won the pools. One day Henna and I saw a bike for sale in a local shop window. It was a Raleigh Roadster and the owner wanted ten shillings for it. His mother said she would borrow the money for it for his birthday, so we went to have a look at it, to see what kind of condition it was in. Henna had two shillings to put down as a deposit if he wanted it. I had about four and six left from the six shillings I had offered to my Dad. The seller lived near to Rye Hill so Henna rode on the seat of my bike and I peddled from the cross bar.

The bike was in pretty good condition for the price so Henna decided he would like to have it.

"How much did you want for it again?"

I asked the owner.

"Ten bob, that's all, ah just want it oot the way."

Henna looked at me wondering what I was asking for. We both knew how much he wanted. I shook my head at him in a 'no' gesture and asked the man.

"Would you take five bob for it, 'cause it needs a bit of cleaning and one of the tyres is baldy?"

"Well not really, I did want ten bob but I'll tell you what, if you can give me seven and six now it's yours."

"Will you keep it for is 'till ah gan back yem for the money." Henna asked eagerly.

"Nah, ah think there's another feller coming to look at it eftah and ah might get the whole lot from him."

"How much have you got Hen?" I asked.

"Ninepence of me own and two bob belonging to me mother."

I counted it all up, four and six and two and nine, seven and threepence.

"We've got seven shilling between us, will you take that?"

He hesitated for a few minutes and then he said.

"Aye, gan on then, teck it away."

Henna was over the moon and swerved back and forth as we rode along Westmoreland Road.

"Mind ah would never have asked him to take less for this." He shouted.

"It's worth more than any ten shilling, ah bet ah could get two poond for it off Tommy Chipside."

I got my money back the next day plus a little bonus. Henna told his mother the bike was ten shillings, so he gave me six and kept the rest.

When we got back to my friend's house his cousin Penny was there. She seemed very interested in the bike and said to him.

"You can go for a ride with your cousin now. I can never get anyone to go with me. I've hardly been anywhere on my bike since I got it."

Henna showed no interest whatsoever and told me why later.

"What do I want t' gan for a ride wih hor for? She's a right pain, she's always telling you what t' de, and anyway she'd never keep up with us."

I thought he was mad, I would go with her anytime, to anywhere and I told him so.

"Well tell hor then, she likes you, she would go with yih a'm sure."

I didn't have the nerve to follow it up, but he did. He told Penny I would go with her if she wanted, but he wouldn't.

To my amazement Penny knocked on our door the next night after school. She had her bike with her and she looked a 'picture'.

"Come on then where are we going?"

"Right I'll not be a minute."

I left my tea half eaten and dashed out of the house.

"Where would you like to go?" I said rather nervously.

"Well, not too far, but you just lead and I'll follow."

I was on cloud nine. Here I was cycling along Scotswood Road with a nineteen-year-old woman who was admired by several of my older friends, but had decided to go out with me.

I was very shy, but Penny was very relaxed and talked all the time as we rode side by side. She put me at my ease and very soon my shyness started to melt away.

We crossed over the old chain bridge at Scotswood and turned left to take the riverside paths towards Raynes Steel Works, known as the Delta. The paths were covered with ash from the steel works and were very good for cycling. They were about four feet wide with triangular wooden stake fencing on either side. I rode in front with Penny following close behind. It was quite exhilarating, even at such a slow speed. The fencing flashing past and the sound of the tyres on the ash gave a false impression of how fast we were going. I had obviously picked up the momentum a little without realising, when I glanced behind Penny was about thirty yards adrift. I slowed down and as she caught up I shouted.

"This is great isn't it?"

"Yes. WATCH!" she shouted very loudly.

I turned my head quickly to find I was almost on top of a very tight bend in the path. The wooden fence was only a few feet in front of me. I braked as hard as I could but moisture on my wheel rims prevented the brakes from working properly. I tried in vain to negotiate the bend but instead I hit the fence head on. The bike stood up on the front wheel and I was hurled over the handlebars. I hit the fence with my head and shoulder, finishing up on top of a jumble of wheels, handlebars and steel frame. Every part of my body seemed to be hurting; my head, shoulder, shins, wrists, everything. Penny was no angel of mercy I hasten to add as she stooped to help me up.

"Are you all right?" she asked, her voice breaking several times before she could speak. It wasn't breaking with concern; she was having great difficulty holding her laughter in. Then it just erupted. She laughed hysterically.

"I've never seen anything so funny in my life. You must have gone at least six feet up in the air. Eee, I'm sorry for laughing but it was really funny."

I thought to myself, 'aye it was funny for you, but it didn't half hurt me'. I didn't laugh. I picked up my bike and tried to ride it along the path. It seemed to be ok until I noticed my toe catching the mudguard when I turned the handlebars. I had bent the front forks in towards the frame, making the wheelbase much shorter and the bike much more difficult to handle.

I didn't blame Penny for laughing, but I was disappointed at her lack of concern.

When we got back home I was feeling rather miserable. My bike was damaged, I was aching everywhere and I had made a right idiot of myself in front of the person I admired more than anyone else.

"Tirrah Penny." I said glumly, as we reached her house.

"Tirrah Billy, I hope you didn't hurt yourself too much. Do you fancy going to the Savoy on Saturday. 'The Beast with Five Fingers' is on. It's supposed to be really frightening and I like someone to hold on to!"

I thought 'I'm going to wake up in a minute. I must be dreaming. Is she really asking me to take her to the pictures'? All of my aches and pains were forgotten in an instant. I got that butterfly feeling in my gut and the hairs on the back of my neck stood on end. 'She likes someone to hang on to', I thought, 'that'll do for me'!

"What time on Saturday, first or second house?"

"Oh we'll just go first house, we can stay in and see it again if it's any good."

On Saturday I waited on the street corner for Penny. I didn't want to call at her house and maybe cause her some embarrassment; after all I was a lot younger than she was. But I needn't have worried. She came down Glue House Lane with her mother.

Mrs Harris said to me…

228

"Mind Billy she's terrified of them daft horror pictures, she nearly broke our Arthur's arm last time he took her to see one. Al see you both later, tirrah."

So off we went, apparently with everyone's blessing. I had my Dad's light blue shirt on; his raincoat and his light tan crepe soled shoes. The shoes were miles too big, so I had stuffed newspaper in the toes to stop them from slipping up and down. Penny was wearing a wine coloured full-length coat over a pink jumper and light grey skirt. She looked stunning! Her jet-black hair was perfect and her make-up made her look like Elizabeth Taylor.

"How do you feel after your crash?" She asked.

"Stupid, I just feel really stupid. I didn't realise there was such a sharp bend on that path, and that little drop of rain we had just stopped the brakes from working properly." I replied still feeling embarrassed.

"Eee I felt awful about laughing. Me mother went mad, 'that poor lad could have broke his neck and you just stood there laughing' she said."

"Well it was me own fault anyway and I've only got a little bump on me head."

By this time we were up to St. John's Road just past St. Aidan's Church, when she said.

"I didn't know you had hit your head, let me see."

She put her right hand on my cheek and turned my face towards her.

"Oh I can see it now, it looks quite nasty."

We had stopped walking so she could see the bruise properly. Then she said.

"There, that'll help it to get better."

And she kissed me full on the lips.

I nearly fainted. I would never have tried to do that in a million years. I could feel the blood rushing to my face. I was absolutely dumb struck.

"Oh, what's wrong? Did you not like that? Eee I'm sorry I didn't mean to embarrass you."

I couldn't find the right words to tell her I was the happiest fourteen-year-old in the whole universe. I had dreamed of this moment but that's all it was, a dream: a boyhood fantasy. I thought I had more chance of kissing the Queen than kissing her. At fourteen I was over five feet eight and about six inches taller than Penny. She was still standing in front of me so I pulled her towards me and returned the compliment, with interest.

"Bloody Hell." She exclaimed.

"Fourteen! You're never fourteen. You might have been fourteen when you were born, but you're not fourteen now. Come on, let's get to the picture's!"

Her mother was right; she was terrified of horror movies. The film was about a disembodied hand that walked around on it's own strangling people. It was all supposed to be in the mind of the main actor Peter Lorrie, and it was really his hand doing the strangling. Penny had her two arms linked through my left arm and spent most of the time with her head buried in my shoulder. I didn't mind at all, in fact I was enjoying her company more than the film.

We stayed in through second house and it was just after ten when we left the cinema. She linked me all the way home, I felt very grown up with her on my arm. When we got to her house she asked me in for a cup of tea. I didn't really want to, as her mother and brother would almost surely be in. But she insisted.

"Hello Billy" It was her mother.

"Good picture?" She asked.

"I was petrified," Penny answered for me.

"I'm just off to bed, I've been on my way up there since nine o'clock. Goodnight."

We both said goodnight and Penny poured out two cups of tea. When we finished our tea I said I'd better be going as I was expected to be in by half past ten. It was already after that, she didn't move, I made to stand up but she took my hand and said.

I've always liked you, you know, it's just the age difference. You don't act like a school kid but that's what you are really. If you had of been four or five years older we would have been more than good friends by now. But we can still go cycling together and you can take me to the pictures now and again if you like."

I was bitterly disappointed, but what more could I expect. Deep down I had always known I was not in Penny's league. She was right about the age gap between us but I think I surprised her a little with that kiss.

We did stay friends for years, we went out together occasionally, and we have remained friends. I've thought about her a lot recently when I heard of the untimely death of her husband. I knew him quite well; he was a lovely man. His name was Billy!

The big pipe contract was put on hold for a couple of months. Dad explained that the steel company in Corby could not guarantee delivery of the required number of pipes for another six weeks, so his firm had decided to fit another couple of jobs in before starting.

"Does that mean you'll be going away again?"

Ma enquired.

"No, no I've got a nice little number painting the inside of Vickers' printing machine shop here in Elswick."

That was good news. Dad would be staying at home and I would probably get the 'tea boy' job again. If that were the case, I would have my bike paid for in double quick time.

Dad said his company wanted him to try a new idea for painting large areas, such as the Vickers' factory. The traditional painting by hand was very slow. Rollers had yet to be invented. They had tried spraying, but the problem of maintaining air pressure from the compressors was always a drawback. You could only use one spray per compressor. I'm not too sure of the technicalities involved in this new method of applying paint but I think I'm pretty close. As I understood it each man was given a five-gallon container of paint. This was sealed and pressurised before it was issued. All the painter had to do was squeeze the trigger of the spray gun and the compressed paint was released at a constant pressure until it was all used up. There was no air mixing with the paint or escaping through the nozzle on the gun, so it was very easy to maintain pressure. If the pressure dropped slightly as the level of paint dropped it was easily topped up with a spare air hose that was always at hand.

During one of my visits to the factory Dad showed me how it worked. The paint container was almost half an inch thick. When all of the contents had been used, the inside hardly needed cleaning; the compressed air forced every drop of paint out of the pot. The lid was a bit like the trap door on the conning tower of a submarine. It had a rubber seal and two metal rods, which slotted into two recesses, to prevent the lid flying off when under pressure. It was obviously a very clever idea. The only disadvantage I could see was the container itself. Being made of half inch thick steel and able to hold five gallons of paint, it weighed over nine stones, or one hundred and twenty-six pounds, quite a formidable object to move around by hand along ten inch wide wooden battens, sixty feet up in the air. When I pointed this out to Dad, he bent down, picked the container up by the two handles on the side and carried it along the plank he was working from, as though it was a pot of tea. When I tried I could hardly lift it off the floor.

On Saturday Dad went to work as usual and I played football for Grainger Park Boy's. We were doing very well in the league, second top behind West End Boy's Club. We won our game and it was clear that if we wanted to win the league we had to beat our main rivals. Last time we played them we had drawn. They were only ahead of us on goal average, so the championship was between us.

As I turned the corner into Cannon Street on my bike, Sally Ball, my friend Billy's mam, shouted after me.

"Billy! Ya Dah's had an accident mind, he seems to be alright but the ambulance brought him home from work."

I waved to her in acknowledgement, and sped along to our house. 'What now?' I thought as the memory of Dad's burnt fingers sprang to mind. I left my bike at the door and hurried into the house. He was sitting in the armchair, no bandages, no visible signs of injury, but he looked ashen.

"What happened this time?"

"Don't ask, I think I saw the Grim Reaper the day for the first time. Oh me bloody back's killing me!"

"What are you going to do?"

It sounded like a stupid question but I needed to know.

"I think you better go and ask Dr Moore if he can come and see me. Tell him I fell sixty feet off the scaffolding. I've had an x-ray and nothing seems to be broken but I'm in an awful lot of pain."

'Sixty feet, good God, how is he still alive,' I wondered to myself.

"Yes tell him sixty bloody feet and he walked in here out of the bloody ambulance!"

Ma sounded annoyed, but very concerned. Her voice was charged with emotion.

"Walked? Did they not have a stretcher?"

"Aye they had a stretcher, but he wouldn't get on it, would yih?" she said looking at Dad pointedly.

He wasn't in the mood for arguing he was in pain, so I thought it was more important to get the doctor than to ask any more questions.

The surgery was closed by the time I got there. I knew it would be but I rang the bell. The lady who answered must have been the doctor's wife. She started to tell me in broken English that the surgery was over and the doctor was in the middle of having his tea when Dr Moore's face appeared over her shoulder.

"OK my dear, I vill see to it."

He said while wiping his mouth with a large white napkin.

"Yes my boy, how can I help?"

I told him about Dad's fall, how much pain he was in, and could he come to see if he was all right.

"Sixty feet, he fell sixty feet, goodness, how can he walk? Go, go home right away and I will be only a few minutes behind you. My goodness, my goodness."

He was still talking as he closed the door.

He was less than a few minutes behind me. He passed me in his little black car as I turned down Glue House Lane on my way back home.

The Doctor was already examining Dad as I opened the door.

"Come in, come in and see the man who thought he could fly."

He still had his trilby hat on the back of his head and a chequered scarf around his neck.

"What were you doing sixty feet up in the air? Only the birds are allowed up there."

Dad forced a little smile but the doctor was only joking he wasn't looking for answers. After he had examined him he said.

"You are a very lucky man. No broken bones but you will be very sore for a few days. The shock of the fall will cause your muscles to stiffen up and you should stay in bed until they feel better.

Now if you have a little alcohol in the house I would recommend a small glass for medicinal purposes, or maybe even two. I will prescribe something for the pain but just take them at night before you go to bed, and I will see you again on Monday morning."

This was all spoken in broken English using Vs instead of Ws and rolling his Rs like a Glaswegian.

When the doctor had gone Ma asked Dad what had happened. He didn't seem to mind the questions and he explained what had transpired.

"I had just had a new can of paint sent up on the hoist. I put the empty one on the platform and turned round to pick the full one up when it tipped over. I made a grab for it but it slipped off the planks just as I got hold of one of the handles. So, like a bloody idiot I tried to hang on to it and it just dragged me over with it.

I managed to push it away from me as I was falling and that's all I can remember of the journey down.

I landed on the wooden 'duck boards' in between the line of machines, sort of on the side of my feet. I think me wellies must have absorbed some of the shock of the fall 'cos I didn't feel anything at all. I just got up off the boards and walked down to the ambulance room. The paint pot didn't burst or anything, but it knocked a lump off one of them printing machines."

Ma put a hot oven shelf into their bed to take the chill off it when Dad decided to retire for the night. The shelf was made from cast iron and was used for baking but we heated them up in the winter, wrapped them in old blankets and put them in the bed about an hour before we got in. They were fantastic and stayed hot for quite some time.

Dad limped into the bedroom and I could hear the 'oohs' and 'arrhs' as he got into bed. The Doctor was right; he was stiffening up rather badly.

Next morning I was jolted out of my slumber by loud shouts coming from the bedroom.

"No! No, don't try to help me; I'll have to just ease meself out. Oh! Yah bugger, I can hardly move, its bloody agony!"

The room door opened and this little one hundred and fifty-year-old man, bent double and needing a shave, shuffled slowly forward in his underpants. He looked absolutely pathetic, his face was twisted in pain and he kept saying.

"Jesus, what a bloody state. How the hell am I going to get to the 'back'?"

The 'back' was the toilet, which was situated another fifteen or so yards away at the top of a flight of six stone steps in the back yard. It was going to be quite a formidable task in his present state.

As the day wore on Dad seemed to be moving around a little better. He did manage to get to the 'back', albeit very slowly. Whatever the painkillers contained, they certainly helped to ease his aching body. By teatime he was even talking about going back to work on Monday.

"You can forget that," Ma said angrily.

"Doctor Moore is coming on Monday and if you're at work he'll do his nut. Anyway, there's not one person from your bloody firm been here to see if your dead or alive. Work'll still be there when you're not!"

That was the end of the discussion as far as Ma was concerned. It was true no one had been to see if Dad was OK, but in those days telephones were rare, travel was usually by tram, bus or train, so for someone to come from South Shields to Elswick over a week-end just to say 'How are you?' was not to be expected.

As if to prove us all wrong Mr. Morton turned up about an hour later.

"Christ Bill, when they told me at work what had happened I thought to meself. 'That's him finished!' Ah mean sixty bloody feet, and you got up and walked to the ambulance room. How do you feel now?"

His voice broke about six times before he stopped talking.

"Oh it's not as bad now as it was this morning, I think by tomorrow I should be nearly ready for work."

"Hi now listen, I'm not here to see how long your going to be off work, and I just want you to know I'll be telling the pay office that you will be on full wages until your back."

Well that was a turn up for the book. Full wages without working. There was no sick pay or anything like that then, so this gesture must have been a first. He could have the rest of the week off work after the doctor had been. That would probably help him to get over his fall a lot quicker.

Mr. Morton stayed for quite some time and as he left he said to my mother.

"Mary, keep that bugger in bed for a few days. You know what he's like, he'll be back at work as soon as he can fasten his own shoes."

"Don't worry, I'll be hiding his clothes tomorrow after the doctors been."

Dad wouldn't stay in bed next morning. He was up shuffling about, making tea, obviously still in pain but much better than the day before.

The doctor couldn't believe how quickly Dad was recovering.

"I think maybe you have rubber legs, you should be very sore but here you are out of bed already. I think it would be wise to stay at home for the rest of the week and if you feel OK by next Monday maybe then you could think about going back to work."

I wasn't at school that Monday for some reason so I cycled to my Dad's brother's house in Teams, Gateshead, over the old Redheugh Bridge and down Askew Road into the council estate just behind Gateshead F.C.'s former ground.

Uncle Benny had told Dad that he could get us some coal from one of his friends who worked down the pit, so this was the purpose of my trip.

When I told him about my Dad's accident he was very concerned.

"Hi Alice," he shouted through to his wife in the kitchen.

"Did yih here that? Wore Willie's fell sixty bloody feet and not a bloody bone broken. Us Flannigans must be hard as nails."

"Aye, or as thick as bloody donkeys, one o' the two." She shouted back.

I liked Aunt Alice, she was really friendly and I knew she was only joking. She came out of the kitchen with a big smile on her face carrying a pint pot of tea and smoking a Woodbine.

"Mind he's 'narf been lucky hasn't he. Tell him from me he must have fell on his wallet, that's what saved him. Is he all right now?"

"He must be feeling a lot better now, he was talking about going back to work tomorrow. At least he mentioned it, but me muther nearly jumped down his throat."

"Eee, well ah thought yah muther would be keen to get him back to work as soon as possible 'cause he'll get nowt on the sick."

"No, he's boss was down last night and he said he would be on full pay 'til he was better."

"Full pay, it must a' been their fault yih see, they're just covering tha'sells, paying him when he's off so he won't say owt!"

This was Uncle Benny's conclusions.

"Full pay and the stupid sod's talking about going back to work tomorrow. He must be bloody barmy. If it was me I'd stay off 'til Christmas."

"If it was you? You would be off for good. You were off work six month and you only fell off the chair putting the streamers up."

Aunt Alice retorted scathingly.

They sounded just like my parents, full of compliments for each other!

Uncle Benny filled Dad's old army kit bag with coal from his own coalhouse.

"I'll get some more off me neighbour this week when he gets his load."

I offered him the half crown for the coal but he wouldn't take it.

"Nah it's OK. Yah da can get me a tin of cream paint when he's back at work, and tell him I'll be over at me mother's on Wednesday, so I'll call along and see how he is."

We loaded the bag onto my bike, through the frame, and I started my walk back home. I was able to coast down the hill and over the bridge but once I reached Scotswood Road it was leg power all the way.

Dad went back to work on the Tuesday morning. He was moving very slowly but he managed to dress himself. He had to carry his haversack in his hand, as he was too stiff to sling it over his shoulder. So after only four days, including the day of the fall, he was back at work, having lost only one working day. He said he would come home early if he felt bad, but of course he didn't. He walked the half-mile or so to the machine shop and he walked back home when he finished at five thirty.

When I delivered the hot water next day Dad was back up on the scaffolding, but he was only using a brush to do some finer work after the other men had finished spraying. It looked a lot higher than sixty feet. There's no way they would have got me up there without a parachute.

Uncle Benny was currently employed by a local baking company. He was responsible for issuing the ingredients to the bakers for producing their cakes, scones, rolls etc. This position enabled him to carry on a nice little sideline selling the 'surplus' as he called it, to friends and relatives. Everything was delivered in bulk. Even the eggs came in five-gallon drums, already shelled ready for use.

He regularly brought dried fruit, dried egg and cooking fat, and sometimes even the finished product. As most things were still in short supply he had no problem disposing of this 'surplus'.

When he arrived at our house on Wednesday evening he had with him, powdered chocolate, icing sugar, dried apple rings and a National Food tin full of shelled eggs.

"Now I don't want any money for this stuff or the coal, but if you can get me a couple of tins of cream paint we'll call it 'squits'."

"Well that might be a little difficult." Dad said jokingly.

"Seeing as how the whole of Vickers machine shop is being painted cream from top to bottom, ah think they might miss a couple of tins. You did mean forty-five gallon tins didn't you?"

They both laughed. The paint was delivered in forty-five gallon drums before being transferred to the five gallon compressed containers.

"If you can get two forty-five gallon drums, I can easily get shot of it."

Uncle Benny's eyes lit up excitedly at the thought of all that paint. He knew Dad was kidding him, but he was serious about the prospect of disposing of it!

There were several similar little enterprises in operation at this time and although lots of everyday necessities were either rationed or in short supply they could still be obtained if you had the right connections.

My dad's younger brother Chris worked on the railway in the goods yard. He often had access to a truckload of bananas or oranges or some other scarce commodity, so he and all of the other porters helped themselves. It wasn't done for profit or greed. They knew they wouldn't be able to afford them when they finally reached the shops, so they just took a few samples. Having been deprived of so many things during the war they felt entitled to 'rescue' some if the opportunity arose. It was all put down to 'damaged in transit'. Boxes of bananas were dropped and 'damaged'. Some of the oranges went 'off' and had to be disposed of, and the odd sack of sugar would burst, spilling 'most' of the contents. It was all done 'officially'. The Porter would report the damage to the Station Master, he would make a report out and hand it to the Freight Manager, who in turn would inform the owners of the damage, thus enabling them to make a claim against their insurers. The salvaged part of the goods was distributed amongst the staff and everyone was happy.

Chris often gave us some of the spoils. I remember him bringing bananas once, which he said was part of a consignment intended for an American Air Force base, somewhere down south. Unfortunately, for the Americans, the whole truckload had been confiscated by the War Office and sent to Walker Naval Yard, to be used to lubricate the slipway. They had a ship ready for launching but they had no grease left. As grease was in such short supply the bananas were successfully used in its place, but not before the usual 'damaged in transit' part of the goods had been accounted for.

Shortly after the bad winter of 1942, my Granda Mill's brother Jim decided he had had enough of England. What with rationing, shortages, low standard of living and poor climate he was sure he could make a better life in Australia. He was too old for army service, so he wouldn't have to serve in the Australian Army. Also he was a very experienced fireman and had reached the rank of Station Officer. The emigration authorities assured him that he would be welcomed with open arms in the Australian Fire Service as they were very short of experienced fire officers. So with the prospects of a job, a better climate and a better future, his mind was made up for him. He didn't want to go on an assisted package deal, as there were lots of strings attached to that. He decided to go tourist class, by sea. If he wanted to come back at any time he was free to do so, but on an assisted passage you could only return after a twelve-month trial period.

Uncle Jim was unmarried and lived with his mother, great grandma Mills. He had always been a 'saver' so the cost of sailing to the 'New World' was not a problem to him.

As Station Officer at Elswick Fire Station he had the use of the station car. It was a 1939 Austin, and it was very smart. He didn't use it much as petrol was rationed, but he did drive it to my Nanna's on several occasions.

A couple of weeks before he was due to sail to his new life, the car was stolen. He was furious. He had planned to drive it to Southampton and have it driven back to Newcastle by a close friend. The Police said it would probably be retrieved before he left as there were so few cars around and car theft was very much a rarity.

In spite of the Police optimism the car didn't turn up. Uncle Jim had to travel to Southampton by train, which took over ten hours. Everyone in the family was convinced that he would be back in England within a year. The family were very close and he was used to being looked after by his mother. They were all wrong. He did come back to England several years later, but only for a visit, to show off his new wife and business partner. They had two successful shops in Brisbane and this would be the last time we would ever see them.

I don't know if I heard the stories correctly or whether it was just malicious gossip, but there was some speculation within the family about the disappearing car. I do know I heard it mentioned several times that Uncle Jim had in fact sold it himself and then reported it as stolen. It could have been a joke, but who knows. My Dad said...

"Why do you think it took him so long to come back to England? Because he knew the bloody police were after him. And what was he like when he was here? He was like a scared rabbit! He never stopped looking over his shoulder."

It may have been speculation, but Dad insisted his story was true. In fairness my father wasn't very fond of his 'uncle in law' and always referred to him as 'that bloody little weasel!'

Well that 'weasel' sent food parcels to his family in England for many years, during and after the war. But he only sent them to his three sisters, Jenny, Florence and Elsie. My Grandad never received any but it didn't seem to bother him. His younger brother and he didn't always see eye to eye.

I believe my mother must have inherited her temperament from her father. Granda Mills was fine when he was sober, but once he was under the influence of the demon drink his character changed completely. He wasn't so much violent as abusive. He often threw the whole family out into the street in a drunken stupor, only allowing them to return after he had sobered up. So we frequently had guests on a Sunday afternoon when the pubs closed. They all used to trip along to number 54 and stay with us until the 'all clear' sounded. It happened so often that it was disappointing when he didn't do it. I loved having my Nanna and all the family in with us; it was just like having a party. Everyone laughed and joked about how stupid it was and all had ceased to take it seriously anymore.

I was often sent to see if Granda was still in his mood or if the coast was clear. He always acted as though nothing had happened.

"Tell your Nanna that I'm just going for a lie down and ask her if she'll wake me up at six o'clock."

When I relayed the message to everyone, our Jenny was always the one who had the most to say.

"The two faced sod. I wouldn't wake him at six o'clock. I'd smuther him though, at any time."

"Hi our Jenny, that's enough," chided Nanna.

They all started laughing again, Nanna included!

Another of Granda Mills' eccentricities was the suicide game. It happened one evening when he was in the scullery doing some soldering. We were all in the kitchen listening to 'Itma' on the wireless; everyone was laughing at the antics of Tommy Handley, Sam, Fumf and Mrs Mopp. Just as Mrs Mopp said…

"Can I do you now sir?"

The scullery door was flung open and Granda shouted…

"Good by all!"

He held a bottle of liquid flux up in the air then put it to his mouth as if to drink it. Everyone knew it was poisonous.

He clashed the door and immediately collapsed against it.

"Mind that poison acted quick didn't it? He was dead before he even had time to swallow it."

241

That was our Jen, speaking loud enough for him to hear.

"Where's them bloody policies? He must be worth a few bob more now that he's dead. Do you know where they are mother?"

That was my mother asking her mother.

"Eee shut up you lot," Nanna whispered.

But the ball had started rolling and the comments came thick and fast.

"Do you think we should have him buried or cremated?" Enquired our Liz.

"Oh, I think it will have to be a burial, fire doesn't burn the devil or his cronies." Answered Jenny, with her usual reverence.

After about half an hour of sarcastic banter the scullery door slowly opened. Granda came out with a stupid grin on his face.

"Aye, ah had you all going that time didn't ah? You thought ah'd 'topped' me sell didn't you? Ah could hear you. Ah had you all worried."

Our Jen looked as though she was going to burst out laughing. She said later.

"Worried, he's right mind, he had me worried, worried in case he missed his mouth with that poison!"

In the eyes of a young child my Granda always seemed all right. I couldn't see why there was so much animosity towards him from the rest of the family. I suppose at that time I was too naïve to see his dark side, but I was told all about it when I was older.

Granda Mills ruled the house with a rod of iron. When he shouted jump, everyone said, 'How high'.

No one sat in his chair. No one sat on his stool at the meal table, and no one would dare hang their coat on his nail.

When my aunts reached the age of boyfriends and dancing and socialising they all came to my parents house to get dressed. They were not allowed to wear makeup, and after their night out they returned home via number 54 Cannon Street, to clean theirs all off. I remember the lovely dance frocks they wore, all underskirts and lace in bright cheerful colours; they always looked fantastic to me.

They were all good dancers and when we had a party at our house I was allowed to stay up late and watch them. Harry Roy, Joe Loss and the American bandleader Glenn Miller played the popular music of the day.

The girls used to 'jive' and 'jitterbug', two new American styles of dancing but they were also good at strict tempo.

I wound the old gramophone up continually and one of the adults chose the records to be played.

Everyone seemed to be having a great time and the floor was visibly moving up and down to the rhythm of the dancing.

Then like a bolt out of the blue it all ended. The kitchen door was flung open and the unsteady figure of Granda Mills lurched in.

"So this is where you all are is it. There's not a bloody sole in that house. I want you all along there in two minutes or the door's locked and you're all out on your necks."

He was obviously under the influence of alcohol and leaned heavily against the passage wall as he made his way out of the house.

"What a showing up! Why has he got to make everybody's life a misery?"

Jenny was eighteen and courting Frankie James, her husband to be, who was present at the time.

"Look Jen," Frank said quietly.

"Best get yourself along home and don't upset him. He's had a drink and he'll forget all about it by the morning."

"Aye, that's all well and good, but why has he got to spoil everything. What harm are we doing? He must get his pleasure out of robbing other people of theirs. No wonder me mother's not well, having to put up with him."

"Aye c'mon lasses, Frankie's right, don't give him the satisfaction of locking you all out. He would love that. Think of me mother, she'll have to put up with him all night and if he upsets her again I'll kill him meself."

That was more like it, Ma was on the offensive.

"You as well our Robert, get yourself along home."

Rob looked at his sister in dismay.

"A'm not gannin alang there the neet. If he finds oot a'm not in bed yet he'll gan crackers. Will you tell him a'm sleeping at our Mary's if he asks?"

This request was directed at Grace as they all filed out into the street.

After the girls left, the party fizzled out. Everyone sat around talking and drinking tea. My Dad was really annoyed at Granda's conduct and said so.

"If he comes into this house again with that attitude I'll put him straight out on his bloody neck! He knows we just put up with him for your mothers sake and he plays on that."

"What gets me Billy is he's alright when he's not too drunk. Ah mean, look how he joined in last time, he really enjoyed himself and ah thought his version of 'Ragtime Cowboy Joe' was the best I've ever heard!" Recalled Frankie with a broad grin.

Everyone laughed.

"Well now in my opinion his 'Sleep in the Deep' beats that into fits. In fact I think we should sing that at his funeral." Dad replied.

"When should we have that then? Tomorrow, or should we leave it till after the weekend?" Ma retorted sarcastically.

I once asked my Dad why my Granda Mills always seemed angry when everyone else was enjoying themselves.

"Well, I'm not really sure. He could be angry because of loosing his leg in the war at such an early age, which obviously prevented him from leading a normal life, or it could be the fact that…"

"It could be the fact that he's just a bad sod who can't stand anybody having a good time!" Ma interjected.

"Everybody says, 'ee what a nice man mister Mills is'. He's always clean and tidy and polite. They should have a look in me mother's lav and see the bloody filthy linings (long Johns) hanging beside the cistern after he's shit heself when he's drunk. That's how clean and polite mister Mills is. Nobody knows what he's really like. If he's two soft boiled eggs aren't just right he won't have them. He must have his tea in his moustache pot and he must be able to see the bottom of the cup with not one tealeaf in sight. It must be ready to drink with just the right amount of cold water added. If the dog happens to walk under the table when he's having his meal he kicks it from one end of the kitchen to the other. That's the nice mister Mills. He's a bloody fiend!"

I was to learn more about my Grandad than I ever thought possible. My mother told me about Nellie Black, his 'fancy wife' as she described her. She told me how mean he was to my Nanna and how he kept her short of money for housekeeping.

"But he never knew how I got his little black cash box open. I pinched half a crown for me mother nearly every week out of that box. He never even noticed the way ah stuck the clasp back down with that clear glue. He couldn't remember how much he had in it 'cos he always opened it to put his money in when he came in drunk, and that was the best time to take something out. He counted that money every other day but ah was as crafty as him. He didn't bother with the small change he only counted the half crowns, two shilling pieces and shillings, so I helped meself to the smaller coins."

Granda would often say.

"You know the more I seem to put in that box the less it seems to get."

"Eee well it's always locked Bob, and you're the only one with a key," Nanna reassured him.

Sunday, late August 1943 and we were on our way to the cemetery to put fresh flowers on Nanna's grave. I was dressed in my Sunday best with a brand new white shirt and grey short trousers. It was a beautiful day. The sun was brighter than I could ever remember, a strange unreal brightness that seemed to dazzle you whichever way you looked. Ma was wearing a turquoise blue dress, which I had never seen before, with a hat to match and even a pair of gloves the same colour.

I took great pride in tidying the grave, clearing away the weeds and grass that had invaded the soil since the previous Sunday. I wanted it to be the nicest grave in the whole cemetery.

We took the old flowers out of their vases and I took them down to the rubbish basket beside the fresh water tap. As I was filling my 'pop' bottle with water I noticed a lady coming down the path towards me. She was walking very slowly, almost in slow motion; she smiled as she came closer. Her dress was right down to her feet with long sleeves that ended with a ruff at the wrists. It was very pale ivory in colour but it looked as though it was glowing in the bright sunlight. Her hat was the same colour with a wide brim and white chiffon wound around the crown. She was beautiful. Her big dark eyes seemed to open even wider as she approached. I couldn't believe my eyes. It was my Nanna! She looked much younger but it was her.

"Nanna". I shouted as I ran towards her. "Nanna, how did you get out?"

She was only a few feet away and she smiled as she held her finger to her lips as though to stop me from shouting. I could feel the tears welling up in my eyes as I tried desperately to reach her, but no matter how hard I tried I couldn't get any closer. Something seemed to be holding me back and I shouted again and again.

"Nanna! Nanna! Nanna!"

"Hoy, hoy, what's the matter with you?"

Ma's anxious voice filtered through to me…

She was holding me closely to her like a little baby, as she woke me.

"You must have been having a nightmare, it's alright don't cry, you're alright now."

So it had all been a dream.

I might have known; my new shirt and trousers, Ma's new dress and hat, and especially the gloves it just had to be a dream. But what a dream; it was so real.

When I told my mother about it she was visibly moved and she tearfully told me.

"When you dream of somebody who has passed away, they say the person you are dreaming of is thinking about you."

That short statement was a great comfort to me. I'm not religious and I don't believe in spiritualism, but that dream is as vivid today as it was all those years ago. I get the feeling that my Nanna wanted to see me just once more, as much as I wanted to see her.

Recently, when I chanced upon a photograph of my Nanna with my three-year-old mother sitting on her knee, the beautiful lady in the ivory dress was there in front of my eyes. I had never seen the photograph before in my life, but no one needed to tell me who it was.

Nanna was a real giggler. Her high-pitched laugh was more like a cackle.

Our Jenny and Frankie James were in number fourteen one

night and Frank being his usual self had Nanna in fits of laughter. He had bought a plastic 'dog dirt' at some joke shop. There was always a white enamel jug on the table full of water and on the pretence of pouring himself a drink from it Frankie peered into the jug.

"Good God, how did he get that in there? Jack! Come here" he shouted sternly at the family pet.

"Are you responsible for this?" he said as he pushed the jug under Jack's nose.

"Ee mind Mrs Mills, ah thought you would teach your dog better manners than this…look what he's done in this jug."

As Nanna looked cautiously into the receptacle she shrieked with laughter at what she saw. The plastic 'dog dirt' was sitting at the bottom of the half-filled jug.

She slumped back into her Queen Anne chair and laughed till she cried.

"Ee stop! Stop! Jenny, send him home will you, a've nearly wet meself with his daft carry on," Nanna cried, trying to look serious.

"Aye come on Frank, we'd better go before Happy Harry comes in." Jenny said, referring to Granda Mills.

"If he comes in and catches us all laughing he's liable to do another good-by all!"

"Either that or he'll chuck you all out and I'll end up with my usual six lodgers, and I've got to be up at five o'clock in the morning for work," said my mother.

She was working at the Co-op dairy in Cowgate and the early shift started at five thirty in the morning. I often woke up in the morning to an empty house until one of my aunts turned up to get me ready for school.

Living in Cannon Street was more like living in a small village. Once you turned the corner at either end of the street you were home. You knew every individual; who you could turn to for help if you needed it; who to avoid and when to avoid them. The 'Bookie' the 'Criminal' the 'Prostitute' the 'Shirker' the 'Worker' the 'Queer' the 'Religious' the 'Agnostic' the 'Alcoholic' the 'Sex Offender' the 'Suicidal', we had them all.

Starting on the odd numbers of the houses from the Glue

House Lane end, number three was the first house, or houses. There were five flats in number three, occupied by five different families.

Mrs Holliday lived in one flat and her son 'Dapper' lived opposite to her on the same landing. Her two daughters Sally and Phyllis lived on the 'even' side of the street. They had married two brothers Billy and George Ball. They used to live at number three with their parents, who we called, 'Old Mr and Mrs Ball'. On the opposite side of the passage they lived in one flat and their youngest son 'Dickie' lived next door with his wife Annie. When the old Ball's passed away their daughter Polly took over their house with her daughter Kitty and son Richard. Downstairs at the back end of a long stone passage there was a one roomed house, which was occupied by Mr. and Mrs. Kelly and a huge black dog. Three toilets were provided for all of these people and they were situated in the back yard. Two very steep stone staircases away.

Next door, number five, was another one roomed house formerly occupied by my Granda Mills who moved into number fourteen as his family increased. This was now rented to 'Grandma Riley' a one armed lady whose brother lived next door at number seven with his wife and daughter. Number nine was another three-house address. The Petersons, Jackie, Janie, daughter Pat and son Brian lived upstairs on one side of the landing and the Georges, Norman, Rose, Owen, Mary, Kathleen and Veronica lived opposite.

Ginny Bartlett and her daughters Maureen and Eva occupied the downstairs flat. Mr Bartlett was killed in a pit accident several years previous and Mrs. Bartlett eventually re-married Ned Ramsgate who lived with his mother and sister three doors away, at number fifteen. Some of the flats had basements below them, but they were known as Back Cannon Street, even though they shared the same house number as the people above them. The Clifford family lived below the Bartlett's at number nine Mr and Mrs Clifford, daughter Doris and son Richard. Mr. Clifford was the most tattooed person I had ever seen. The crucifix on his chest went right up to his neck and the cross extended to both of his arms. A large Indian head and headdress covered his back, below that a pack of hounds were chasing after a fox, which could just be seen disappearing down some convenient orifice!

Number eleven was home to Mr Forester in the street level flat,

Mary and Charlie an elderly couple lived in the basement flat and the Andrews upstairs. One of the flats upstairs was in a pretty bad state, so the Andrews' lived in the more habitable two-roomed flat opposite. Mr Forester's son Jack lived in the one-roomed house at number thirteen with his wife and two children.

As the basement houses were below street level the one bedroom had a window, which was six feet below the pavement. A metal grill covered the 'pit' that had been constructed to allow the occupants to have access to the window for cleaning. Needless to say these 'pits' became filled with all sorts of rubbish that was dropped from above. As the only access was through the actual window many of the tenants gave up trying to keep them clean.

The next house was very posh indeed. Number fifteen was the home of the Ramsgate's. They seemed to be very well off and there was a rumour going round that they owned their house and their daughters flat upstairs. They were the only family in the street who spoke with posh Geordie accents (that means they said 'Yes' instead of 'Why Aye'). The mother was quite old even when I was a child, but she was still around when they pulled all of the houses down many years later. She had two daughters and one son. The eldest daughter lived in the flat opposite to my father's brother, Christopher, at number seventeen. Her other daughter Doris, also had a daughter but I can't remember a husband being present. Ned was the only son and he wasn't very popular. He once threw half of a house brick at me, probably for cheek, and when I told my Granda Mills he went and knocked on his door, but he wouldn't come out. Granda shouted at him through the window.

"Come out you big brave man, let's see you throw a brick at me."

He had taken his shirt off and all you could see was his straps holding his wooden leg in place.

Ned was quite a big man but he didn't seem too keen to face the one-legged Mr. Mills.

Four families occupied number nineteen. An old man just known as Frankie lived in the basement flat. George Morgan lived in the street level flat and Johnna Currin and his wife lived in one of the upstairs flats with Jermima Lesley and her son Barry on the opposite side of the landing.

The Thorburns lived in number twenty-one, a one-roomed house. At one time there were eight people living in that one room, Lizzie, her boy friend her father and brother, two sons, and two daughters. I don't know where they all slept but they only had one double bed.

The next three or four properties were derelict; in fact there were only two or three of the next fifteen flats habitable. One of them, number twenty-seven, was home to Mrs Green, a very old lady who dressed in Victorian clothes. Her son Ralph and his family lived further along the street at number fifty-nine. The Morrisons and their daughter Mary occupied number thirty-three. Their home was in the middle of all of the derelict flats, which we used as an adventure playground. I was in this block one day pulling some wooden lats from the dividing wall in one of the rooms, when I heard a door shut and footsteps of someone going down the wooden stairs. I remained perfectly still 'til they were gone then I crept nervously towards the landing door listening intently in case anyone else was around. It was all quiet so I opened the door. As I was about to leave by the wooden staircase, I thought I would have a look in the flat opposite. There was a sink on the landing that had been shared by the previous occupants and strangely enough they had left a plate and two cups on the draining board.

I pressed the sneck down with my thumb and pushed the apple green door open. I almost died of fright. The house was completely furnished. There was no one home, but the fire was on, the kettle was still hot and the table was set for three people. Mrs. Morrison was supposed to have left weeks before, but obviously still lived there. I closed the door and quickly vacated the premises. I had no intention of being accused of housebreaking!

After the empty buildings the next occupied house was number thirty-nine where my mother's cousin Chrissie Trainor lived with her family. As far as I recall the rest of the properties were unoccupied until number fifty-three. This was directly opposite to our house and was occupied my friend John Hodson's grandparents. Their son John lived on our side of the street at number forty-two. Number fifty-five was empty and uninhabitable. It was the birthplace of 'Seaman'

Tommy Watson, the famous boxer.

Number fifty-seven was the Flynn's, fifty-nine the Green's, sixty-one the Astons, sixty-three Granny Day and sixty-five Alice Brown's, the last house still standing. The rest of the odd numbered houses had been demolished many years previously, leaving a large plot of land that was never re-developed.

The 'even' side of the street was fully occupied. The houses were slightly larger and in much better condition than those opposite. The numbers started at four, the first house from the Glue House Lane end. The Bucktons were the tenants, Mrs. Buckton and her two daughters and grandson Billy. Billy's name was Haines but he was always known as 'Billy Buck'. His grandmother was a frosty old lady who didn't seem to like anybody. She would rush out to see what they were up to if anyone even walked past her window.

I spent a lot of time in the next house, number six. It was the home of my life long friend Billy Ball. Billy's Granda used to bring live mussels and winkles (known as willicks) from the North Shields fish quay and we would roast them over the open fire on an old shovel. Their house was the only one in the street to have a living room downstairs and two bedrooms upstairs. At one time there were eight members of the family living there. I often wondered what it would look like with fitted carpets and nice furniture. Their pet jackdaw would have made a right mess of that.

Number eight was an upstairs flat with three bedrooms, a sitting room come dining room and large scullery. The family consisted of Mr. and Mrs. Hope and their eight children. The two eldest members of the family were daughter Ginny Bartlett of number nine Cannon Street and son Jimmy who lived in number sixty-six. The house below the Hopes was home to the fourth Ball family. George and wife Phyllis, daughters Rose and Connie and son George jnr. Rose was my childhood sweetheart for many years.

Number twelve was the Morgan's residence. Mr. and Mrs. Morgan, daughters Peggy and Bella, sons Joe, Johnny, and Alec. Eldest daughter Janie and son George lived opposite with their families.

The next family lived at number fourteen most of the time, but frequently migrated to number fifty-four, largely depending on the mood of the patriarch. They were of course the Mills bunch.

At number sixteen Mrs Soper, her daughter and son Tom were hosts to our local bookmaker, James Parks or 'Cocky' as we all knew him. He used the Soper's back yard and washhouse as his office and frequently escaped from police raids through the house and out into the front street. Then disappearing into his own house at number eighteen, where he lived with his wife and daughter. Cocky was a very fine sprinter in his youth and I was told that his nickname came from the confidence he showed as an athlete. He was a member of Benwell Harriers, which sadly ceased to exist in the 1960's. In the early '50's his bookmaking business took a bad beating and he was forced to work again for his living. He ended up labouring on the buildings and delivering newspapers.

Two very nice ladies lived at number twenty, I only ever knew them as Jane Ellen and her mother. Jane Ellen was a spinster who looked after her ageing mother. She was a very fragile lady and seemed to be a little slow. I think they were quite well off, as they were very well dressed, and their house was always immaculate. They lived above my Granny Robson at number twenty-two, and she often invited them down for tea, so the family got to know them very well and always included them in any family party or celebration.

The Porter's lived at number twenty-four, above my great uncle Billy Trainor, at twenty-six. Uncle Billy's wife was my Nanna's sister Lizzie but she died when she was only 34 years of age and sad to say I have no memories of her at all. They had three daughters, Chrissie, Jenny and Sadie. Chrissie married Ronnie Kirk a Londoner and they had three children, Ronnie, Jean and Billy. Ronnie snr. was tragically killed falling from a ladder while working in London. Chrissie had moved to London with the two eldest children, Jean and Ronnie, leaving the youngest, Billy, with her sisters and dad, and there he stayed. He was supposed to join the rest of the family once they got themselves established, but he never did. His grandfather and Aunt Jenny brought him up and to this day he acknowledges her as his mother; and to his children she is Grandma. Sadie, the youngest, moved to Birmingham and sadly died of cancer when she was very young. Her two sisters survived her into old age.

Uncle Billy's sister Jane lived at number thirty, below the Dodd family in number twenty-eight. Her married name was Collins. There was never a Mr. Collins around in my lifetime, just Sammy her son, and two daughters. The Anderson's lived in number thirty-two, the Taylor's in number thirty-four, in number thirty-six an old couple who never used their front door.

The Sharpes lived at number thirty-eight. They had a dog, Prince and I was terrified of it. It wasn't very big but it barked at everyone who walked by. It chased me right to my front door one day, probably because I ran away more than anything. When I turned around to see where it was it was coming straight at me. I held my hands out in front of me as it tried to stop and one of my hands went into its mouth as it skidded to a halt. It didn't bite me, but it scared me half to death. My father went to the Sharpe's house and complained about the dog. He said he got very little response from the owner so he decided that the next time it was running loose in the street and I needed to pass it to reach home I was to go to my Nanna's and get Jack, their bull terrier to protect me. The opportunity came along a couple of days later. I was on an errand to the corner shop and when I passed my Nanna's house Jack was sitting on the front step. I made a fuss of him as usual and he made as if to follow me as I walked away but I told him to stay and he lay down in the sunshine in front of the bedroom window. When I reached my granny's house Sharpe's dog bounded out of their door. It spotted me at once and ran towards me barking loudly. I was petrified and shouted.

"Jack!" as loud as I could.

Jack was up in a flash and I could hear his claws hitting the pavement as he hurtled towards me. Prince saw him at the same time and turned tail and headed back to the sanctuary of his home. He reached his door and shot through as fast as his legs would carry him. Not to be denied, Jack followed him at speed right into the house and dragged him savagely back outside.

My Granda Mills eventually managed to pull Jack off his prey. Poor Prince was badly mauled and sustained a broken back leg, which never healed properly. Needless to say the Sharpe family never forgave us for the attack. I believe the youngest son held a grudge for many years after that incident.

The Sothertons were next in number forty. They were in the upstairs flat above the Hodsons, who lived in number forty-two. Mr.

and Mrs. Hodson, with two sons John and Allan. John was the same age as me and we were friends for many years as school kids. We don't see each other very often now but I still consider him a close friend and it's always a joy whenever we meet.

I remember a game that John made up when we were kids. As we had very few toys we were always searching for some new game to play other than marbles. John's game required three small stones, a lolly stick and a goal drawn on the wall about six inches by four. He made up all of the rules based on the game of football and I'm still convinced that some game manufacturer could develop it into a very popular board game along the lines of subuteo.

Joe Parks jnr. lived at forty-four above the Jobsons, a very poor family but they always seemed to be happy. Benny snr. Lilly snr. Benny jnr. Lilly jnr. Annie and Robert. I bought my first gramophone from Benny jnr. sometime in 1951, I paid him four pounds for it and he included his Nat 'King' Cole record collection in the deal. The Jobson's house was a favourite gambling den where we played Brag and Pontoon and several other card games. We only played for pennies, but a session would often last for anything up to ten hours. There were one or two who tried to cheat but we usually caught them and threw them out. One of their favourite tricks was to pretend to put their penny into the 'pot' by placing their hand over the table near the money and 'snapping' a penny against the underside of the table with the other hand, declaring loudly.

"A'm in!"

It worked sometimes, but when it failed retribution was swift and painful.

Number forty-eight was a door I never saw opened. It was sometimes more convenient for elderly people to use their back door to avoid using the very steep staircase down to the front door. I think the couple were called Reeves, but I'm not sure. I am sure about the next family in number fifty. Freddy Daws with his wife and daughter. Freddy ran the Forge Hammer football team for a number of years; he had some form of skin complaint and had to have his hands permanently bandaged.

The Hutchins lived above us in number fifty-two. 'Totty' the father, Jean snr. son Jack and daughter Jean. They were a very nice family, but the father was very frail and died when I was very young. Daughter Jean married someone local and moved into Glue Terrace. Jack studied to become a chemist.

Number fifty-four was Flannigans door. The Bedfords at number fifty-six, occupied a three bed-roomed upstairs flat; Jimmy and Alice with daughters Doris, Margaret and Joyce; Mrs. Bedford's father Mr. Martin and her brother George.

The McGargills lived at fifty-eight. Mrs. McGargill was my Uncle Billy Trainor's other sister; she was married to Charlie McGargill. Sons Charlie, John and Jimmy and daughter Kitty all lived at home, but John left home after he married in about 1950.

Joe Parks senior and his wife lived in number sixty, above the James' in sixty-two. The James' eventually bought several houses in the street and became our landlords. After number sixty-two there was a row of flats or tenements known as 'The Barracks'.

The tenements had been used during the 1914-18 war to house soldiers during their training, after that they were always called 'The Barracks'. The name persisted until they were demolished during re-development in 1956.

The house numbers followed in sequence but some of them had five or six different families living at one address.

The first passage had three families in residence at any one time and the tenant's seemed to change at regular intervals. Number sixty-four didn't seem to be very popular.

Number sixty-six was a different story altogether. Jimmy Hope lived on the ground floor with his wife Betty and children. The second floor housed two families, the Peters, Mary, Robin Knight (her live-in partner), Michael and Jean, her children, occupied the flat on the left of the wooden staircase and the Merriks, Mr. and Mrs. and sons John, Frank and Patrick were on the right. The Casey's lived above the Peters on the third floor and Teddy and Mary Hold above the Merriks. I believe John Merrik was my Granda Mills' cousin.

Teddy Hold was in the Navy during the war and served on the submarines. It was reported on the wireless that his sub had gone missing, presumed lost with all hands. His mother and brothers were all devastated at the news but fortunately it was wrong. Although they were missing for several weeks the submarine finally limped back to port and Ted got his photograph on the front page of the Daily Mirror. The whole crew received a hero's welcome.

There were only three flats that were habitable at number sixty-eight. The top floor belonged to Ted and Annie Kettle, daughters Mary, Nancy and Catherine, and sons Ted, Danny and Michael. Ted snr. used to say about his three sons and daughters.

"Six Kettles, three wih spoots and three withoot."

Below them the Philips lived for many years, but when they moved back to Carlisle the Davids took over their accommodation. On the ground floor Tom Calloway and his wife occupied the remaining one roomed flat. Tom had been in trouble with the law for many years, but was now suffering from what turned out to be terminal tuberculosis. His wife was a well-known prostitute but had the good sense not to bring her clients home.

On to number seventy where Tom's sister in law Sylvia lived with her mother and young daughter on the ground floor. The second floor was the home of the Medley family and the top floor housed Peggy Casey and her husband. He was a very nice man, but a bit of a curiosity, being the first person we had ever seen without hair in any of the usual places.

The Brownlees dominated number seventy–two. Cecil with his wife and family on the ground floor, Cecil's brother Bobby on the second floor and Bobby's son on the opposite side of the passage with his wife.

Various families occupied number seventy-four over the years. John and Peggy McGargill, Jimmy Hold, Freddie Hold, Mrs. Hold, the Storers, Freddie Leak, Jessie Small and Hughie. He was a strange man who lived with his wife and family. They seemed to be a little backward and lived in abject poverty.

The last tenement in the block seemed to be a bachelor haven. The two well-known drunks Don and Slasher occupied the two ground floor flats. They were very friendly but seemed to be permanently inebriated. Upstairs housed Tommy who was badly disabled after a polio attack, and his friend John, who sang hymns all day. Then there was Richard. He was unemployed but always very clean and tidy, but he refused to wear trousers, instead he wore ladies skirts. Not a kilt, which he could have worn without anyone commenting, but ladies skirts with pleats and fancy designs. In those days he was considered very strange and given a wide berth by most of the locals.

Several other characters passed through these flats over the years, too many to name or recall, but I do remember two brothers who lived in number seventy-four for a few years. They were twins and went everywhere together. One day they climbed up an electricity pylon and very foolishly touched the main cable. They were both electrocuted and so badly burned that one of them lost an arm and a leg and the other lost a leg. That was the first tragedy involving electricity in the 'Barracks'.

The second was only a few years' later and again involved two brothers. They were Joe and John Philips. They played the same ridiculous game as the previous two, they both climbed a pylon near Stella Power Station, but only the elder of the two Joe, touched the wire. He was thrown from the top of the pylon by the force of the current but survived both the fall and the shock, only to die in hospital the next day.

The younger brother John escaped unhurt but it didn't teach him anything, several weeks later he fell from the top of a lamppost and broke his jaw.

We had several incidents, major and minor to contend with over the years.

Mr. Harris, Penny's father, fell down the pit shaft while on a site seeing visit to the coal face accompanied by Mr. Grantham the Deputy responsible for the redundant colliery, and was killed.

Frank Newman, who lived in Richard Street cut his own throat in the back yard toilet in an attempted suicide, but survived.

The person, who tried to break my sledge, shot and killed an innocent lady thinking she was someone else. He got life in prison and was out in seven years.

Another member of our community, although I use the word member very loosely, raped his young niece and made her pregnant. When he came out of prison he impregnated his girlfriend whom he married. He then proceeded to rape his wife's underage sister and another girl who was a friend of hers. Both of them got pregnant and both had babies. He paid dearly for his folly, but it never taught him a lesson.

Tom Calloway deserted from the army during the war and when the M.P.'s came to arrest him he threatened to shoot them if they came anywhere near him. After a stand off lasting several hours he gave himself up. He was discharged shortly after for health reasons. When he married Peggy Gibbons the 'wedding party' of Tom, Peggy and Dickie Ball came rolling along Cannon Street, paralytic drunk. They were laughing and shouting (and swearing) oblivious to anyone else. Peggy stood on her hands against the wall then went right over in the 'crab' and walked away on all fours. Unfortunately she had somehow forgot to put her knickers on that day and we kids were treated to an anatomical extravaganza.

My friend Henna commented rather loudly.

"Cor ah didn't kna she had a pet hedgehog!"

"Oh ah did, but ah didn't kna' she kept it up there." I retorted.

We all laughed but kept a safe distance from Peggy. She was, to say the least, slightly unpredictable and not averse to giving you a clout.

Chapter Ten

In the midst of sorrow

Bella Morgan died very young. Ronnie Robson, my cousin died at only five. Vera Sharpe of number thirty-eight died in her teens. My Nanna died aged forty-seven. Charlie McGargill died suddenly. Ralphy Green died of heart failure. Billy Ball's young brother Lenny died of leukaemia. Elswick cemetery was filling up rapidly.

When I was in the junior school at Cruddas Park I was in Miss Chaffer's class for over a year. She was a very tall stern lady but I got on extremely well with her. She always chose me to act in her many plays and concerts, I felt as though I was one of her favourites. I sat next to John Eden in the third desk from the front. Michael Old and Leonard David sat in front of us. There were about twenty-four pupils in our class, boys and girls.

Leonard David was one of the nicest, quietest, friendliest boys I had ever met. He was from a very big family, who would eventually end up living at number sixty-eight Cannon Street.

One Monday morning Miss Chaffer called the register as usual. Leonard had been absent from school for a couple of days with a large boil on his neck, so it was no surprise that he was still off. Miss Chaffer closed the register and slowly walked to the front of the class, her hands clasped in front of her in a sort of double fist.

"Children. I would like you all to pay attention for a moment please."

She sounded very melancholy.

"I have to tell you something that I have never had to tell a class of mine before. I cannot explain how awful this is to deal with, but you have to know and I have to be the one to tell you."

She was struggling to maintain her composure and as she looked up to the ceiling I thought I detected a tear in her eyes.

"You all know Leonard David has been absent over the past week with that very painful boil. Well on Friday he was taken into hospital when it burst. Unfortunately septicaemia set in and Leonard died of blood poisoning."

Her voice faded away into a whisper and I only heard 'died'. Several of the girls started to cry and Miss Chaffer dabbed at her eyes with the handkerchief she had taken from the sleeve of her cardigan.

I could not believe what I had just been told. I'd had loads of boils, as had almost every other pupil in the class. Boils were just part of growing up, they appeared in every area of the body, but they just came, burst, and went. You didn't die with them. They were always painful, but never fatal.

I met Leonard's mother when the family settled in Cannon Street a few years later and was amazed to discover that she had been in the same class as my mother when they were at school. They became very good friends and only lost touch after they married.

In the midst of all this tragedy and anguish, there was always something to smile about. This was never truer than when the local cinema, 'The Crown', decided to host a talent contest. They advertised on the screen for anyone who aspired to join the world of showbusiness. Anyone who thought they had a gift or talent they would like to perform, had to sign up for the forthcoming event. The response was tremendous. They turned up in droves. Young boys and girls, ex-servicemen, miners, butchers, bakers, and I'm sure at least a couple of candlestick makers! They were all local people; all hoping to break away from the poverty that we all lived in, via a career in showbusiness.

All of the contestants were serious in their bid to become 1940's Pop Stars, but sadly their talent fell far short of their enthusiasm.

We had a young girl singing 'Greensleeves', a song reputed to have been written by Henry the eighth over four hundred years earlier. A real show stopper! Then there was 'Torna Surriento' by Poncielli, a mere hundred years old, all chart topping stuff! My particular favourite was performed by one of my father's half brother Nichol's friend, Ken Willis. Performed is maybe a mite too generous in this instance; 'massacred' is probably a better description. The song was called 'Chickery Chick' and as far as I can recall the first verse went something like this:

Chickery Chick, Cha-lah, Cha-lah
Chickle la roamy in a bannonicker
Walicker Walicker can't you see
Chickery chick is me!

I had never heard anything so ridiculous in my entire life. Not then and not since. The singer did the song real justice. He was even worse that the lyrics. He had a stupid grin fixed to his face for the entire song and his voice sounded like a bad ventriloquist trying to throw it to the other end of the stage without moving his lips. He should have tried throwing it into the Tyne before he entered the competition.

When he finished singing most people just started to laugh. They thought he was about to start telling jokes and 'Chickery Chick' was his introduction. I had known Ken all my life; I also knew he couldn't sing, I only wish he had known.

Despite the corny meaningless song and the voice to match Ken received a tumultuous reception from the audience, orchestrated by Nichol Robson and about a dozen of his followers. They clapped, stamped and whistled as loud as they could, and unbelievably Ken Willis and 'Chickery Chick' went through to the next round.

The contest went on for over two weeks and on the night of the final Patrick Roony sang superbly. His 'Come back to Sorrento' easily won him first place and first prize. The prize was a contract with the organisers to tour the UK as a support act for stars like Tommy Trinder and Max Bygraves etc.

I was very friendly with Pat and got to know him quite well. I was able to ask him what he'd been up to during his brief encounter with showbusiness.

He said he was paid ten pounds a week out of which he had to pay his own and his mother's accommodation, he had to be accompanied by an adult as he was still under age. He paid all his own travel expenses and at the end of the day his mother had to use her own money to make ends meet. They stayed with the company for one season but when they returned to Newcastle they both agreed that they had had enough. Pat had a fine voice but he decided to use it to support Newcastle United F.C. rather than himself.

'Chickery Chick' came nowhere. Ken Willis had entered as a joke; his mates had dared him to do it.

Little 'Greensleeves' sang a different song in the final and her voice sounded much better, she came third.

As my fifteenth birthday approached, my mother agreed to let me have a few friends to tea to celebrate. It was to be the first time I would have a birthday party and as it turned out it was also the last. I invited equal numbers of boys and girls and happily they all turned up on the day. For some reason I was very nervous. I knew everyone; they were all my friends, male and female, but I couldn't help feeling apprehensive.

They all arrived while I was getting ready in the only bedroom, I felt as though I had made a mistake inviting them. I wanted to just run away.

Then I spotted the bottle of QC Sherry on the gas meter cupboard. I had seen characters in films have a shot of 'Dutch Courage' from a whisky bottle so I decided to do the same, only with sherry. I wasn't too keen on alcohol at that time but sherry was quite sweet, so I took a swift mouthful straight from the bottle. It was lovely and warm and didn't burn your throat, so I had another go.

The affect was immediate, my shyness and anxiety just fell away. I tried another mouthful and to my amazement the bottle was empty. I looked on the floor to see if I had spilled any but it was dry. I had drunk the lot. I replaced the screw cap and put the empty bottle back on the gas meter cupboard. I was about to join my friends when my mother came into the room.

"What's the matter with you?" She asked.

"You're bright red."

"I've just been bending down fastening my shoes." I replied.

"That's why me face is red."

My eyes seemed incapable of focusing on Ma's face and I'm sure my speech was slurred. So was she.

"Have you been drinking? If ah thought you'd been drinking…
you'd better get in there with yah bloody friends quick, it's not the
last you'll hear of this a'm telling you."

I didn't care! I had a lovely warm glow about me and I just
didn't care. My friends cheered loudly as I opened the sitting room
door. Most of them were already sitting at the table waiting for me,
anxious to start eating.

My mother poured the teas out for everyone and then she took
my sister along to our Lizzie's house, saying she would be back at
nine. So she had kept her promise, leaving us alone to make our own
entertainment.

Her parting words were loud and clear…

"And keep out of that bedroom!"

The sherry had gone straight to my head and I found myself
laughing loudly at anything even remotely funny. All of my guests
recognised the symptoms. I was drunk! We had a good time listening
to records and talking about our impending entry into the world of
commerce (getting a job). Brian Bolton worked in the coalmines.
Tony Canning and his cousin John Hodson were both working for
Vickers Armstrong as apprentice pattern makers and Kenny Flynn
had been accepted in the same trade, starting when he left school
later in the year.

I told my friends about my prospects as a silk-screen-printer
and this seemed to impress everyone.

"Does that mean you'll be doing paintings on pure silk?"
Someone asked.

"Yeah, I think so, but it will take a long time to get to that stage,
the apprenticeship lasts six years." I replied.

I didn't know what I was talking about but the sherry made me
feel full of confidence.

As the night wore on the effects of the alcohol wore off, leaving
me with quite a headache. I also realised that the empty sherry bottle
would cause quite a stir, so I had to do something to avoid getting
another 'ear bashing' from my mother. The only 'off license' that was
open in the vicinity was owned by the family of one of my guests,
so I had to ask her if she would persuade them to let me have a half
bottle of sherry. It was illegal then as now for anyone under the age

of eighteen to purchase alcoholic drinks.

Mrs. Henderson allowed me to buy the sherry and I was able to replace what I had consumed. Her daughter Doreen and I became good friends and soon we were going out together quite regularly. I got on well with the rest of the family, Doreen's sister Jean and brother's Wilf and Fred.

The Henderson's came from Bishop Auckland originally when they took over the management of the Forge Hammer pub on Scotswood Road. Their full title was Mr. and Mrs. Bishop-Henderson, which raised quite a few eyebrows. Doreen was the same age as me and Jean was about two years older. Their father suffered a nervous breakdown shortly after they arrived and was tragically drowned. Mrs. Henderson was a very stalwart lady and with the help of her two sons managed to continue running the pub successfully until she decided to try the 'off license' business. She lived and worked in Benwell for many years finally choosing to end her days in a retirement home. She died aged ninety-nine.

My friend Jimmy James had turned up for my fifteenth birthday party much to my surprise, we had drifted apart since we went to different schools and hadn't seen much of each other socially. Jimmy wasn't a sportsman so we didn't even meet on the football field. We reminisced during the party about how we used to play together in the old Elswick Colliery, and the camping and swimming in the Tyne at Wylam. It all seemed like a lifetime away.

"Look, our Annie's been given two 'away day' train tickets by somebody who works on the railway. You can travel anywhere you like, as many times as you like, within the week, all on the same ticket."

Jimmy said excitedly.

"She's not interested, so she's given them to me. Do you fancy?"

"Do ah fancy what?" I replied.

"Do you fancy having a couple of days travelling up and down the West Coast line for nowt?" He said impatiently.

"We could go to Carlisle or somewhere like that, or Corbridge, or Hexham, or even just up to Wylam, it's years since we were there."

I looked at him through an alcoholic haze. He was still bad tempered. He had a look on his face that was saying, 'if you don't answer me quickly I'll punch you right in the mouth'.

He had tried that once when we were kids and if his grandmother hadn't dragged me off him by the neck of my jersey, I would have killed him. He didn't fight like other kids. He kicked, nipped, bit, clawed and gauged, so when I got him on the ground I sat on his chest and punched him in the face several times. My neck was covered in deep scratches and his gran nearly choked me with my own jumper.

We got over that very quickly but old Mrs. James never forgave me. Whenever I called for Jimmy I could hear her saying...

"What are you playing with him for? He was punching yah face in only last week."

I wasn't too bothered what she said; I didn't like her either.

So I eventually agreed to go with him. The train tickets were valid for six months but the weeks travelling time started when the ticket was first 'punched'.

We travelled to Hexham first, and then on to Brampton Junction, a place I had never even heard of, then back on the return train to Newcastle. It took a whole day and we both enjoyed every minute. On the way back we decided to get off at Wylam just to see if there had been any changes since we were last there.

The train stopped at South Wylam so we just stayed on that side of the river. We walked along the riverbank as far as the old sewage pump house and threw a few pebbles into the water. The tide was quite high but still had some way to go before it covered the sewage pipes. We climbed down to the concrete landing and Jimmy walked onto the huge black pipes that stretched out into the river.

"You know, this is where we should have fished from when we used to come camping. We could have thrown our lines right out into the river from the end of this pipe."

I was about ten feet from him as he made a throwing guesture as though he was casting his 'dead line' and the next second he was toppling off balance into the river. He half turned as he slipped and grabbed hold of the pipe with both hands as his legs went under. His arms were wrapped around the thick metal but there was nothing to hold on to and his flat hands started to slip around the pipe as the force of the current sucked him under. Jimmy screamed in terror.

"Am gannin under."

I ran towards him and grabbed his jersey but he just kept on going down. I sat astride the black pipe, which was about three feet in diameter, and stretched down far enough to grab the belt holding his trousers up. That did the trick; he stopped sliding away from me and started to haul himself up using his flat hands to gain some purchase on the pipe. Once he managed to get his right leg up over the pipe he was safe, wet but safe. He was really grateful, I don't think.

"I suppose you'll be telling everybody how you saved me life when we get home," he said sarcastically as he wrung out his trousers.

"Ah would ih been alreat anyway, ah could of got me sell oot but you had to be a hero!"

I thought 'you ungrateful sod, I've a good mind to chuck you back in'.

The river was very dangerous at this point and I wouldn't fancy anyone's chances of surviving in that current.

Well, James William James was wrong. I never told anyone about the incident and this is the first account of that near fatal day of over fifty years ago. I never looked on my actions as saving his life, but as preventing his drowning!

There was something about water that seemed to fascinate Jamesy. When we were seven or eight we were playing in Elswick Colliery near the old water pit that was used to hold excess water pumped up from the sump at the bottom of the shaft. We had been warned on several occasions, to keep away from the pond, as it was very deep and full of rubbish beneath the surface. Jimmy in his usual attitude towards water decided he would build a raft and sail over it.

Whilst in the act of retrieving some logs that were floating on the surface he slipped and fell in. I wasn't there at the time of the incident. I had chosen not to be part of the venture but I was told later what had transpired. Jimmy was submerged for several seconds beneath the slimy water and almost drowned. Someone living in the colliery cottages nearby dragged him out and Charlotte Chipside phoned for an ambulance from her shop.

I'm sure he would have 'got oot hesell' if no one had interfered.

The pollution in the water was more of a hazard than the water itself and James junior was treated to a carbolic bath, and a good hiding from his granny.

In spite of the minor mishap we still enjoyed our day on the trains. It was quite a novelty travelling legitimately rather than hiding in the toilets until the ticket collector was out of sight and dashing out quickly to board the train before it left the station.

The train back to Newcastle didn't stop at Elswick so we would have to walk from the Central Station back to home. Jimmy wasn't too happy about this, as his trousers were still a little damp, so he produced a shilling from his pocket, which he swore earlier he didn't have, and we caught the next tram home.

On the way he said he could get two tickets for a 'trade showing' of a new film just out called 'Destination Moon' in Technicolor. It sounded great to me so we decided to go the next day. It was long before any suggestion of space travel or flights to the moon but it was very close to what has been achieved since. As no one knew at that time how to control re-entry into the earth's atmosphere everyone on the fictitious space ship perished as it burned up with the tremendous heat caused by friction. I suppose it was the only way to end the story at this particular time, it was over fifteen years before re-entry was achieved successfully on a manned space flight.

Getting into the pictures for free was something we'd often done, but getting in through the front entrance for free was something special. Our usual means of entry was slightly more complicated and fraught with danger. One of us would pay for our ticket and as soon as the picture started he'd go to the toilet, open the fire exit door and let us in. So, one person went into the loo and two came out. This went on until everyone was safely in a seat. It wasn't a bad deal really, fourpence, for six or seven people to go to the pictures. The dangerous part of the exercise was being caught. One of the ticket collectors was a bit of a bully and if he caught you 'dodging' in he threw you out bodily along with several hard slaps and a parting kick up the rear. Assault, bullying or abuse was for the future, at this time it was just accepted as normal. You took your chance and if you were caught you paid the price!

Picture houses were often referred to as 'flea pits'. It was true you often came out carrying more 'friends' than you had when you went in. I was in the Crown one evening watching 'Nannook of the North', a documentary about the life of an Eskimo and his family. At that time I found it totally boring, preferring Cowboys and Indians. I was almost falling asleep when I felt a cold spot on my leg. I pulled up my trouser leg and to my horror found the biggest cockroach I had ever seen. It had climbed above my sock and seemed to be settling down for the night. I pulled it off and threw it over the heads of the people in front near the orchestra pit. I hastily vacated my seat and headed for the exit. It was most annoying leaving before the film was finished, especially when I had paid to get in on this occasion. I complained loudly to the usherette who cringed as I told her what had happened.

"Just a minute pet, don't go, I'll tell the manager about this," she said shakily, and she disappeared up the stairs to his office.

When she returned she said the manager was very upset about the incident and intended to have the whole cinema fumigated on the following Sunday. She also handed me two tickets for the next picture starting on Monday, in the best seats upstairs in the circle. I was delighted but my devious mind began to work overtime as I pondered how many times the same story would work in the future.

The free tickets took my friend Jimmy James and me to see 'The Jolson Story', the Hollywood version of the life of the world's greatest entertainer Al Jolson. I was absolutely captivated by this film. The singing was marvellous and the miming performed by Larry Parks, who portrayed the great man, was faultless. I became an instant fan of Jolson, as did my friend Jamesy. He and I scoured all of the music shops in Newcastle trying to find old photographs or any literature on the true story of his life. I have collected every version of his recordings since that day, from old 78 shellac records to the latest compact discs. I never tire of his voice and still take great pleasure in watching his impersonators, good and not so good.

Jimmy and I used to kid ourselves that we could sing like him and we often tried our impression of 'My Mammy' in the privacy of Jim's fathers house, which was always available. I never knew Jim's mother but his father worked in the family coal business. Apparently his parents had parted company when he was very young and his grandmother had brought him up. In those days most offspring were named after their father or mother and in the James' family there were three Jimmy's, all living in the same house. They had two huge

Clydesdale horses each pulling a four-wheeled cart loaded with bags of coal. It was amazing to see them haul their massive loads up Glue House Lane. Their strength was incredible.

According to my friends calculations each cart was capable of carrying forty bags of coal. That represented a weight of over two tons, plus the weight of the cart and scales etc. I can recall one occasion when the James's bought a new horse. It was the largest animal I had ever seen; so large in fact that it wouldn't fit into the stable. Freddie James, Jimmy's uncle, took the animal down to their third stable in Back Cannon Street, which they used to store feed and bedding and removed the loft flooring so that the horse could stand up with his head between the joists. These were well over eight feet from the ground, so this was no Shetland pony. He was a very handsome beast, as black as ebony with a pure white diamond shaped flash on his forehead. Unfortunately his size was his 'biggest' problem. He was very docile and easy to handle but getting him in and out of the stable was a major problem, so the Jones' were forced into selling him.

When the sequel to the 'Jolson Story' was released it was as big a success as its predecessor. It was a wonderful insight into how both films were made. Once again Larry Parks was superb in the major role and after 'Jolson Sings Again' we all waited anxiously for the sequel to the sequel. There was speculation about the title of the third Jolson film, 'Jolson Broadcasts', 'Jolson Sings On' and several other suggestions, but they never materialised. Larry Parks was in trouble with the McCarthy Investigative Committee who accused him of being a member of the communist party. He pleaded the Fifth Amendment of the American Constitution and refused to testify. In Senator McCarthy's eyes this was tantamount to an admission and after making one more film, 'The Master of Ballantrae', Larry Parks' acting career came to an abrupt end. He appeared in small parts in low budget movies some years later, but the star of the two Jolson epics never reached that high plateau again. In the meantime Al Jolson himself had passed away. It was the end of an era. All I can say is thank goodness for Thomas Alva Eddison's invention of sound recording, and thank heaven for the wonderful films of this great entertainer's life and talent.

The success of the Jolson films seemed to inspire a number of would be Al Jolson's. Max Bygraves did a reasonable impersonation of him for a BBC Radio Documentary on his life. Then there was the Canadian singer Norman Brooks who sounded very close to the original, and even portrayed Jolson in the film made about De Silvas, Brown and Henderson the famous song-writing trio. It was called 'The Best Things in Life are Free'. They wrote 'Sonny Boy' for Jolson as a joke, thinking he would either throw it out, or it would prove to be a huge flop. How wrong can anyone be? 'Sonny Boy' was one of the most successful ballads ever written and heralded the revival of Jolson's flagging career.

We had our share of would be Al Jolson's locally, but one stood out head and shoulders above the rest. His name was Norman Bolt.

Sunday evening live shows were still very popular at the local cinemas and were usually a sell out, but on every other Sunday the Westgate Picture House at the bottom of Westgate Road was packed out long before the show started. The reason, Norman Bolt! His impression of the world's greatest entertainer was superb. When Freddy Stebbings struck up the 'Mammy' introduction the whole place erupted. Norman walked onto the stage dressed in evening suit and white kid gloves and just held out his hands. Every person in the cinema just stood up and applauded. He would sing maybe three or four of the most popular Jolson songs then say goodnight, kissing his hands and waving goodbye. There was no way he was ever going to get away with that. Back he came for his encore, not once or even twice but on most occasions six or eight times. They wouldn't let him go. At the finish Freddy Stebbings had to get his band to play the national anthem before the crowd would stop shouting 'more!'

I saw Norman perform on several occasions and he just seemed to get better and better. By a strange quirk of fate I found myself working for the same company as Norman several years later. He still had a very fine voice but he said the money was no good anymore on the 'Club circuit', so he had started his own sign writing business and carried on in that until his death in the 1990's.

Variety shows were still very popular in the early 1950's and some impresario's had the courage to import big stars from America.

We had the Palace Theatre, the Empire, the Grande, the Theatre

Royal and the City Hall, all still producing regular shows.

The big 'names' of the day were Billy Daniels, Guy Mitchell, Frankie Lane, Al Martino, Louis Armstrong, Johnny Ray, The Four Aces, Mario Lanza and many others. They all appeared in Newcastle.

Of course we had our own crop of popular entertainers, but television was beginning to gain in popularity and many of them were making the transition to this medium. Some of our singers made it to the 'big time' and one of them; Frankie Vaughn even went to Hollywood and made a film with Marilyn Monroe.

Steve Cochran, Dennis Lotus, Dickie Valentine, David Whitfield all made a good living in the UK but one of our best singers of all time, Steve Lawrence, tried his luck in the U.S. He had a wonderful tenor voice but lacked the 'following' in this country. He made many good recordings but never seemed to gain the popularity that he deserved.

In desperation he moved to America in an effort to 'kick-start' his career, but he seemed to vanish altogether from the 'Pop' music scene. I always thought he would be a big star. He was handsome, well built, and his voice was good enough to sing opera. But it was never to be; shortly after moving to the States he was tragically killed in a car crash. I have several of his recordings and I think the world lost a huge talent the day he died.

During the late 1940's and early 1950's the cinema was enjoying something of a 'boom time'. Almost every new movie that came out was in Technicolor. Up until that time films were only made in black and white. Colour brought more realism to the screen and even the advent of Television failed to affect the takings at the box office. A night at the pictures usually meant a long wait in a queue until seats became available. As everyone was used to queuing for trams, groceries, meat, new ration books etc. it was no hardship to wait a couple of hours to get into the pictures. On some occasions it was even better outside than inside the cinema. By this I mean the free entertainment. There were buskers by the score. One of these was a regular in town. He lived in the Salvation Army Hostel somewhere in Newcastle and I watched his act on numerous occasions over the years. The first time I ever saw him was in my own street when I was about five or six. At that time he had a partner who sang through a metal funnel, rather like a loud hailer. I'll call my busker 'Walter'

271

because it seems to fit.

When Walter's friend finished his rendition of 'Mother Kelly's Doorstep' it was then his turn to perform. He placed a square of plywood on the pavement and proceeded to jump up and down on it in the pretence of tap dancing. The timber clattered about quite a lot and I suppose it could have been mistaken for tap dancing. They had no music, and Walter's partner clapped vigorously to his footwork. The next step was the collection. Both men knocked on every door in Cannon Street and just held out their doffed caps hoping to receive some reward. Almost everyone in the street was as poor as the two entertainers; but some kindly soles managed to spare a copper or two and they seemed to go on their way happy!

Walter was a familiar character in Newcastle for over fifty years. His long grey overcoat and trilby hat were instantly recognisable. He sat on a seat in Northumberland Street squeezing an old Horner accordion in and out for hours on end. No identifiable tune ever came from his playing but the sympathetic warm-hearted people of Tyneside always subscribed to Walter's efforts, especially in his twilight years.

On one occasion in the early 1950's I queued outside the Odeon for over an hour to see the latest development in cinematography. It was called 'Cinema scope'. The film was 'The Robe' with Richard Burton and Victor Mature. The screen appeared to be a hundred feet wide and when the lions roared in the arena they seemed to be in the auditorium with you.

During the wait to get in, the assembled crowd was treated to a brief sample of Walter's talent. It was a mouth organ on this occasion and he gave his usual classic performance. He sucked and blew his way from the front of the queue to the back, then back up to the front. That was it. Performance over. The playing was even worse than his accordion playing. The harmonica was badly strained and hopelessly out of tune, which made it sound very like my Dad biting the cat's tail on a Sunday night. Walter was freezing cold and obviously anxious to get back to the Salvation Army Hostel, so he whipped his trilby off and scuttled down to the back end of the queue and made his way backwards saying.

"Thank you, thank you."

As he pushed his hat in front of each person he passed.

When he came to the front of the waiting patrons he stood looking down the line of people then into his hat, then he placed one hand behind his back, closed his eyes and started, what I thought was going to be a song.

"Well, you must be the stingiest lot of buggers in Newcastle!" he cried.

"Not one bloody penny, not one bloody penny did ah get off any of yih! You lot of tight sods. Ah hope yih divent get in, ah hope there's nee seats for yihs, anyway ah've seen the bloody picture and it stinks. It stinks worse than ye tight buggers!"

He turned and walked away, still looking into his empty hat.

I felt really sorry for Walter and wished I had put something into his trilby. The rebuff didn't deter him in any way, he was back in Northumberland Street the following Saturday but I never saw him 'perform' in front of a cinema queue again.

In October 1992 I saw him sitting alone outside of Eldon Square. It was cold and Walter was very pale. His eyes looked like two little black buttons sewn into their sockets. His nose was wet but he didn't seem to notice. I looked at him for a long time and I could sense it would be the last time I would see him. I felt very sad for this old man whose life could not have been easy. He had nothing. He had no one. But worst of all no body seemed to care.

My mind flashed back to that night outside of the Odeon and as I brushed past him I pressed a five-pound note into his hand. He gazed at the money and turned to see where it had come from but I was already in Marks and Spencers. I watched him through the window as he slowly rose to his feet and looked around slightly bewildered; I never saw him again!

꘎

As technology surged ahead in the 'Motion Picture' industry we were treated to such delights as 'Stereophonic Sound', 'Vistavision', '3D', and 'Cinerama'. All fantastic inventions and all geared to keep the crowds coming to the cinema. Some companies even experimented with smell, but that seemed to fizzle out. Three-dimensional films were very clever even though everyone in the audience had to wear a pair of cardboard spectacles, provided by the cinema, to achieve the 3D effect. People screamed and ducked below the seats as rocks hurtled towards them after an explosion or landslide. It was very difficult not to react; the rocks really seemed to be about to burst out of the screen.

Television production was gaining momentum even though the receivers were as big and as ugly as the back of a 'double decker' bus. The screens were still very small and transmissions limited, but their popularity was increasing rapidly, at least for those who could afford them. Even at this early stage in their development the 'Movie' Companies were painfully aware of the intense competition that would eventually come from television. Competition that they would not be able to cope with, that would lead to a rapid decline in their industry.

All of this was still a few years away and new and exciting developments still managed to draw the crowds. A night at the pictures was a popular form of entertainment and in many cases still the only place courting couples could express their undying love for each other, on the plush double seats in the back row of the Haymarket.

The gimmicks continued to pour out of Hollywood, things like 'Surround Sound', with loudspeakers all over the theatre. Cinerama with a huge screen, which seemed to wrap itself around you: it was so big it was possible to watch one side of the screen and ignore the other side. They used three projectors and although it was very effective you could see the overlap of each projection. I saw the film 'The Life of the Brothers Grimm' in 'Cinerama' and although it was very well done I enjoyed it much more on the ordinary flat screen.

Along with all of these new developments came the epics. Mostly on a religious theme these productions were made on a massive scale. Thousands of 'extras' filled the screen, the great plague and the parting of the waters in 'Moses', was achieved with unbelievable realism. Samson destroying the temple, 'Buddy' Bear's battle with the bull in the arena in 'The Robe' and Victor Matures' encounter with two fully grown tigers in 'Demetrius and the Gladiators'. All of these were 'small beer' by today's standards but they were all made without the benefit of computers and at that time were the eighth wonders of the world.

Chapter Eleven

A new start. A new life?

As the end of my final term at school approached I still hadn't heard from David Allen's with regard to possible employment. They said originally that they would contact me nearer to my leaving date and I would get an interview. So rather than just wait for something to happen I decided to contact them and let them know I was available.

I didn't fancy using the telephone so I took a bus to Marlborough Crescent and walked from there to the head office in Bath Lane.

The lady behind the frosted glass window in reception was Miss Younger and she was most helpful.

"Yes my dear, this is David Allen and Son's, but this is the Bill Posting section of the company. The Screen-Printing is in the 'Old Infirmary Buildings', just opposite Marlborough Crescent."

She listened patiently as I told her of my desire to be a screen-printer, and how I had been waiting anxiously to hear from that branch of the company.

"Listen, I'll tell you what I'll do. I'll phone Mr. Johns and tell him you're here and we'll see what he has to say."

Mr. Johns was the manager of the Screen Printing section and obviously the man I should be talking to.

I could hear her clearly as she made her phone call.

"Hello, Johnnie? Hello, this is Margaret Younger. I have a young man over here who put his name down earlier this year for a screen printing apprenticeship; as he hasn't heard from us since then he has come here on his own initiative to see if there are any vacancies."

There was quite a long pause and then she spoke again.

"Yes, yes, OK Yes I'll do that with pleasure. Cheerio."

She re-appeared at the frosted window.

"Now then Mr. Flannigan, here's what you have to do. Go back to Marlborough Crescent. Do you know where the railway canteen is?"

"Yes, just next to the goods station, two of my aunts used to work there."

"Good. The Old Infirmary Building is just behind there. Mr. Johns' office is right on the top floor and the company name is on the door. He said he will see you at two o'clock."

I suddenly felt butterflies fluttering round in my stomach. Suppose I get the job, will I be able to do it? Will I make a fool of myself? Will everyone think I'm a bit thick if I make a mistake? The nagging doubts in my mind made me feel sick. I wanted to jump on a bus and just go home. Who wanted to be a silkscreen- printer anyway? I would be much better off working at the Delta Steel Works or painting and decorating or something!

All of these thoughts ran through my head as I made my way along Clayton Street and over Neville Street towards the railway canteen.

When I reached the Old Infirmary I couldn't believe what I saw. This ancient grey sandstone building blackened with soot and industrial grime looked totally derelict. There were no windows in the long corridors or stone staircases. Each habitable section of the building had some glass in the windows but most of them were simply boarded up to keep out the cold. When it was a hospital, in the distant past, it had been used as a de-lousing clinic for soldiers coming home after the 1914-18 World War. It was an absolute tip.

As I made my way up the staircase I was quite surprised to hear machinery in operation in various sections that had been partitioned off.

I found the David Allen sign on a door, which was about four feet wide and only about five feet six high. It read 'David Allen & Son's Ltd – Poster Room'.

I knocked on the door but no one answered. I turned the brass doorknob and pushed, but that didn't work, it was a pull open door.

The door slowly opened as I pulled and as I stepped into the room it quickly closed and pushed me forward like some giant hand.

"You want to watch that door son, it's bloody lethal, it's killed two rent collectors already this year."

A gentleman in a green warehouse coat issued this warning without looking up from the cinema poster that he was working on.

The room was about thirty feet long by about twenty feet wide, two sloping benches, almost as long as the room itself, were being used by six or seven people in various stages of production. Some were signwriting posters; others were doing what looked like intricate artwork.

A quiet voice to my left said.

"Yes, can I help you?"

The owner of the voice was quite a small man with a much larger head than he should have had. He was standing at his desk with a large watercolour brush in his hand. The painting he was working on was a scene of a beach with holidaymakers lying about on the sand and paddling in the sea, I could just make out 'South Shields' in the sky.

I could feel my face turning red as I answered him.

"Err, Miss Younger said I had to come at two o'clock to see Mr. Johns."

"Oh, so it's you who couldn't wait to be a screen printer."

He said with only a suggestion of a smile.

I handed him my school report, and assumed that he was Mr. Johns, as he hadn't admitted that fact.

He told me how these premises were only temporary and the firm was busy looking for a new factory. They occupied six large sections of this building on three of the four floors. The hours of work were forty-four hours a week but this was shortly to be reduced to forty-two and a half, and the starting wage was twenty-seven shillings and eleven pence a week, which was just about three and a bit pence an hour in decimal money.

"Now don't think you can just come in here and do as you like, this is not school, this business has to make money to pay all of our wages and you will be expected to play your part. Any nonsense and your out, understand?"

'You'll be expected to play your part' I thought. Does that mean I've got the job? It must do. Surely he wouldn't say that unless he was going to give me a try.

"Right, now, when do you leave school?" He asked.

"Err, next Friday sir" I replied nervously.

"Next Friday eh? Well how's about starting the week after that? That will give you a week's holiday before you settle in to full time employment; oh and by the way you don't have to call me sir, my knighthood isn't due till the New Year." Everyone in the room laughed, but me, I thought he meant it.

Well that's how it all started. I got my own job at fifteen years of age and that's the way it would always be. I would never ask anyone for help again in my life. I made my own decisions and had to stand or fall by them.

My Headmaster was delighted that David Allen's had accepted me as an apprentice screen-printer.

"Well done, well done, well done Flannigan. I'm sure you will do well. It is nice to see someone determined to start on a new phase in their life with a career in mind. Your last school report was excellent and if you maintain that standard of dedication you can't fail to do well."

I can still hear his voice today when I look at that old piece of paper, signed by him, Mr I.E. Compton and my mother, and dated July 1951.

I said my goodbyes to the teachers, Mr Scottie who did such a wonderful job reading my poem, Mr Nelson the games teacher, Mr Hunt, art, Mr Carter, science, Mr Kennie, Mr Smith, Mr Taylor, woodwork Mr Compton and last of all Mr Stephenson. I also took the time to say goodbye to Miss Chaffer my former teacher in the Junior School, who was now my sister's teacher.

The old adage, 'School days are the best days of your life' proved to be one of the truest maxims I've ever heard. It was not so apparent on my first few days in the work environment, but I soon began to realise what a dirty world we live in. I couldn't believe how workmates 'stabbed each other in the back'. How they tried to make themselves out to be conscientious and hard working by telling tales about how lazy or inept other members of the staff were. It was mainly the older members of the workforce who indulged in these practices and in most cases it was to cover up for their own inadequacies.

It was a great shock to me. I had always been brought up to believe you never 'squealed' on your friends or acquaintances.

Everyone in the firm was friendly and courteous to each other and yet at the 'drop of a hat' many of them would condemn or criticise their colleagues remorselessly. I very quickly spotted the danger zones and stayed away from them. I listened to the individuals who criticised but made no comment in either direction.

The 'Old Infirmary' was a fascinating place, honeycombed with passages and staircases like some old fortress. Many of the rooms were derelict and not in use, so they were a haven for rats! The whole building was infested with them; some of them were as big as Tomcats. There was one in particular that was really huge; everyone had seen it at one time or another. It didn't bother to run away because whoever came face to face with it swiftly turned and ran in the opposite direction.

On many occasions during our dinner breaks three or four younger rats would come around where we were eating and pick up any crumbs that were on the floor.

When the council pest controller was called in he laid three-foot squares of plywood, covered with a very sticky substance, under each set of storage racks. He then sprinkled some kind of bait onto the glue to attract the vermin. Next morning we were amazed to find over thirty rats had stuck themselves onto the glue traps.

It was horrific to see this heaving mass of live creatures desperately trying to extricate themselves from their plight, but the more they struggled the more they became enveloped in the adhesive.

The old cleaner collected the boards and burned them on his rubbish fire that he started every day in the yard. To his credit he killed the rats before he incinerated them, saying…

"It doesn't say you have to be cruel and burn them alive just because they're vermin."

The thirty-rat cull didn't seem to make much difference to the overall population; they were still in abundance throughout the building. With the railway canteen and the Marlborough slaughterhouse in close proximity it was pretty obvious that they would never be completely eradicated.

My first week at work was quite eventful. I was put onto a workbench with another screen-printer called Ian Hardcastle. He had a very coarse nickname, so I won't say what it was, but it was very apt! We were printing some posters for the 1951 South Shields Flower Show and when we completed the first run Hardcastle left me to clean the screen while he organised the second colour.

The stencil was made from paper and was attached to the silk with large dots of an adhesive called Sillphil. The method of cleaning was very primitive and I only had to be shown once before I was able to do it alone. I was very keen to do the job quickly and efficiently so I set about it with great gusto! The screen mesh was made from pure silk and was very delicate. I soaked the hardened glue with hot water then rubbed both sides of the silk at the same time as I had been shown. The Sillphil softened very quickly; I had the screen cleaned and ready for the next stencil before the printer returned. Suddenly a small hole in the mesh started to expand and I could hear a 'click-click' coming from that area. I asked one of the other printers if he knew what was happening. By the time he came to have a look the half-inch hole had become a four-inch split, and it was still spreading.

"Oh God, don't tell me you've split the screen on your first day here."

Hardcastle had a stupid wide grin on his face and he seemed to be enjoying the colour change in my complexion.

"You'll have to go and tell Mr. Johns, he'll go spare."

I could feel my knees trembling. My first day at work and I had committed a cardinal sin. What was I going to say? I had been very careful and I had no idea how it had happened.

"Hardcastle!"

It was Les, the foreman.

"You can get yourself down to the poster room and tell Mr. Johns yourself about the screen. You had no call to leave the new lad to 'clean off' on his own. He had no idea that silk stretches when it's wet and anyway that hole should have been patched before you started work this morning. Les was of Norwegian decent and used quite a lot of foreign sounding words to emphasize his directive to the luckless printer.

"Aye, OK Les, I was only joking anyway, to get the new lad going. I had no intention of sending him to see Johnnie (Mr. Johns' nickname was Johnnie, but only to senior staff).

It was normal practice to take a rise out of new apprentices, in fact it was expected. Usually they were sent on fictitious errands for things like 'a tin of rainbow coloured ink' or a 'left handed screwdriver.' I was very relieved to hear Hardcastle was playing a joke on me.

Playing jokes and pranks on each other was the main source of entertainment: the printers being the instigators and the apprentices the victims.

There were two 'pot-bellied' stoves in the main screen room and these had to be lit every morning. Not only did they heat the place (very badly), but also they were used to help dry the posters and heat up our pies or pasties for dinnertime.

One of the staff brought two Dickman's pies for his lunch every other day. He put them on top of the stove to warm up in time for the dinner break. On one occasion, he took a bite out of one of them and a look of dismay and disbelief spread over his face.

"Some bastards pinched me meat!" He exclaimed loudly.

"Look, there's not a bit in either bloody pie!"

Everyone in the place just fell about laughing. It was so funny to see this very large person standing there with two empty pies in his hands. Someone had cut the top off the pastry, eaten the meat and placed the top back onto each of the empty pies.

"Well, the doctor said you had to lose weight Frank so that's a good way to start!"

"If ah find out who it was they'll lose weight as well, 'cos ah'l tear their bloody head off!" Frank retorted, as he glared menacingly at each of us youngsters.

He was a very big lad was Frank, but there was a medical reason for his size. He had thyroid or gland trouble, or something like that and although he wasn't a very big eater he weighed eighteen stone at eighteen years of age.

His nickname was inevitably; 'Tubby' and he hated it. I never used that name simply because I wanted to see my sixteenth birthday!

Another member of the workforce was Norman Starkey. Norman was about the same age as me, he had a steel brace on his leg to enable him to walk after it was infected and permanently weakened by T.B.   He was given the nickname of Benny for some obscure reason, so Norman Starkey became Benny Starkey, and Benny he stayed to this day.

Benny was the subject of the most elaborate hoax ever played on anyone at David Allen's. Everyone was in on it, and even Mr. Johns lent his support to carry it off.

Starkey had been boasting about how he picked up two girls on the previous Sunday evening, and how well he had got on with them. Being a bit of a 'Walter Mitty' no one believed him, so they decided to play a joke on him to teach him a lesson.

The main poster room had a Redifusion receiver that had been installed by the previous occupants. The programmes were piped direct to the speaker without any need of power or receiver. An extension had been taken from this speaker to the other poster room on the floor below.

Dave Ellington was an artist who had very special talents. He created moving models to advertise forthcoming attractions at the local cinemas and was a wizard with electrical devices. He rigged up a microphone that could be switched into the Redifusion speakers and used by the staff upstairs to pass messages to their colleagues below.

"Benny, I want you to go down to the bottom poster room and trim these showcards on the small guillotine". The foreman Les handed Starkey a pile of cards.

"Oh, can you not send somebody else, ah'm not used to that guillotine and I hate trimming", he whined as he looked at the cards in dismay.

"Look, just get yourself moving and get the bloody job done, it'll only take you half an hour, now go'on move yourself!"

Benny picked up the showcards and moved off reluctantly in the direction of the main corridor. When he was out of sight Les dashed down to the poster room to let everyone know that everything was in place for the sting!

"Hello Benny, what are you doing in this part of the world?" Dave Ellington greeted him in his usual cheery manner.

"That bloody Les sent me down here to trim these bloody showcards and he knows I hate using this bloody guillotine."

'Bloody guillotine' was a very apt description of this hand operated machine, several people had bloodied themselves whilst operating it.

The other members of staff bowed their heads over their jobs and mumbled their condolences, desperately trying not to laugh.

The radio was playing requests on the very popular programme 'Housewife's Choice' and Benny whistled along in his usual tuneless fashion as he prepared to cut his job down to size.

As the music died away a voice suddenly made this announcement:

"Good morning ladies and gentlemen, we interrupt this programme for a police message.

On Sunday evening two young girls were accosted by an unknown male as they left the Westgate Cinema in Newcastle upon Tyne. They were last seen, accompanied by the man walking towards Marlborough Crescent Bus Station. The gentleman in question was dressed in a blue blazer and light grey flannels and seemed to be walking with an injured leg or foot. Eyewitnesses say they thought the girls were trying to get rid of him but he insisted on walking them to the bus station. These two girls have not been seen since and their parents are very worried. If the gentleman in question could contact the police at Market Street Station or any police officer he may be able to help them with their enquiries."

Benny continued with his whistling. He wasn't cutting the showcards; he was just standing there looking at them. He said nothing. He put his pencil back into his warehouse coat pocket and walked out of the room, still whistling.

"Have you got that job cut down yet Starkey?"

Les inquired as Benny came back into the screen room.

"Aye, it'll not be long ah've just got to go to the gents across at Marlborough," he replied as he hung his overall up.

Everyone in the place was in hysterics as he left the building, heading for Market Street and not the gents toilets.

When he was out of the building the foreman sent someone to tell him it was all a joke and he had to come back to work; but he wouldn't believe them, saying:

"Don't be stupid, how could it be a joke? It came over the radio; they even stopped the programme to make the announcement. Ah'm gannin to Market Street or else ah'll be gannin to jail."

It took the boss himself to convince Benny that it had all been an elaborate hoax and I got the feeling that Mr. Johns had thought it had gone a little too far.

Starkey laughed as much as we did, when it finally dawned on him, but judging by the names he called everyone I don't think he found it that funny.

Two more apprentices were employed by the company about three or four weeks after myself so I was no longer the new boy. I was amazed to find out how much I had learned in such a short space of time and how I was able to show the other two how certain things had to be done.

That brought the total number of apprentices to five and the rivalry between us was quite intense. It was all very friendly and light-hearted but we all wanted to be the best and it was a 'feather in our caps' if any of the other printers asked for one of us in particular, to assist them. We all got on very well and still do to this day. The others were Joe Paine, Tom Mansel, Gordon Clegg and 'Benny' Starkey.

Cleggy's nickname was 'Ooby', courtesy of Mr Jim Bennison.

The reason for the unusual pseudonym was Gordon's tendency to sing 'oo-dooby-dooby' to the strains of Ted Heath's 'Blacksmith's Blues', in preference to the original words.

Several other youngsters passed through David Allen's over the years but the aforementioned stayed to become fully trained screen-printers.

Joe Paine and I became very good friends and worked as a team for several months. He was slightly more experienced than I was so he was in charge of our jobs. We worked very well together and were even praised for our efforts by Mr Johns, which was very rare indeed.

Of course we made sure we had plenty of spare time to explore the old infirmary and to play tricks on our workmates.

The roof of the old building was flat in places and Joe and I often took our lunch break up there. The view was marvellous. We could see the river Tyne and most of the bridges. The cattle market on Scotswood Road, the 'Slaughter House', Marlborough Crescent Bus Station and Barclays Bank with its famous clock tower.

The air raid shelters, left over from the war were still standing and were frequented by 'dossers' and tramps. The canvas bunk beds were often a welcome resting-place for these unfortunate people. On many occasions during the day the local prostitutes also used the shelters to 'entertain' their clients. 'Peggy' who lived in Cannon Street, was a regular and we shouted her name everytime we saw her. She couldn't see where the shouting was coming from, so she just gave the two-fingered salute in the general direction of the building.

During one of our explorations Joe and I stumbled on an old access to another part of the roof. It was well away from the occupied area of the building and it was covered with lead, over a quarter of an inch thick. Lead was still in short supply and highly prized by scrap dealers. It was just like striking gold and converting lead into cash was something I was quite good at. It took us over three weeks to strip off the precious metal and another week to melt it down into ingots.

From the proceeds Joe bought himself a set of alloy racing wheels for his bike and I paid my Dad his money back and cleared the balance of the H.P. left on my bike.

As winter approached and the dark nights started to creep in life in the Old Infirmary took on a more sinister dimension. All of the workrooms were well lit but the hallways and stone staircases were in total darkness. Needless to say the pranks became more and more frequent. The Ink store was on the second floor, so any ink or turps had to be carried up three flights of stairs. Everyone was terrified to leave the sanctity of the well-illuminated screen room and we youngsters tried to go around in pairs. We weren't so much afraid of intruders; it was more the fear of being scared witless by our workmates. If the room suddenly went quiet it was a sure sign that someone was up to something.

One night during overtime everyone left the screen room at the same time, except Benny Starkey, he was finishing off cleaning his screen. We all met in the corridor and crept back towards were Benny was working. He was whistling nervously in his usual tuneless fashion near the pot-bellied stove. Noel Dobson, one of the senior staff, indicated that we should all stay at the door while he flitted silently from one hiding place to another carrying an old galvanised bucket that was used to carry away the ash from the fires. When he was only ten feet away from Starkey he threw the bucket up into the air. The noise of it landing on the parquet floor was deafening but the noise of Benny's screams surpassed that by several decibels. He shouted in a fluent 'Foul' dialect for what seemed like ten minutes, cursing, swearing and vowing revenge. He was shaking from head to toe, and he managed to smoke about five cigarettes in as many minutes.

"You stupid bastards, you could o' give me a f......g heart attack." Benny cursed.

"You should have more sense Dobson, ah nearly shit me bloody pants!"

It all fell on deaf ears, Noel was crying with laughter, as was everyone else. 'Poor Benny,' I thought, 'that's two shocks he's had in no time at all'.

Albert Capes was in charge of the stores and packing. He had just joined the firm having taken over from an old character called Charlie Bell. Old Charlie was sacked for continually arguing with his right shoe, which he affectionately named 'Johnnie.'

For some unknown reason Albert took an instant dislike to Joe Paine, and vice versa. He was really horrible to him on several occasions so Joe made up his mind to play a trick on Mr Capes, or several if the opportunities arose.

In the 1950's screen-printing inks were very crude and in the very early stages of development, thinning or cleaning had to be done with turpentine, which was delivered in five-gallon containers. When the containers were empty Albert stored them in an old corridor behind the room that Joe and I worked in. There must have been over a hundred cans piled up on top of each other. The wall between was well over four feet thick but Joe had discovered a hole at the bottom of the skirting on our side of the wall that went right through to the 'can store'. It must have been to house an old gas or water pipe in the distant past.

His plan was to thread a length of string through the hole and

286

then through the handle of one of the five-gallon cans at the bottom of the pile, pull it out of position, causing the rest to crash to the floor. It would only cause minor inconvenience for Mr Capes, but knowing him he would blow it up into a major incident.

Threading the string through the hole was a little tricky but I managed it by pushing a length of wire through with the string attached. Looping it around the handle of one container and passing it back through to Joe. When everything was in place we waited until it started to get dark. Albert was in and out of the passage all day clattering and moving the cans around, so when it was quiet and darkness had fallen Joe pulled on the string. There was an almighty crash as the metal cans tumbled to the floor followed by the cries of Mr Capes who unknown to us was still in the passage. We quickly released one end of the string and pulled it back through the hole disposing of it in the rubbish bag. Joe suggested that we should go through to next door to see if 'Capesy' was all right, but I disagreed.

"As soon as he sees us he'll automatically think we were responsible. He can't be hurt anyway they're only empty cans."

"Aye your right," answered Joe.

"And if we start laughing, he'll know for sure it was us."

So we decided to leave well alone and got on with our work.

Mr. Capes wasn't hurt at all. He reported the matter to Mr Johns who came down to see for himself. His conclusion was that there were too many cans in the passage and they should have been returned to the ink company long before now. He suggested that they had been disturbed by the rat population and admonished Mr Capes for stacking them badly. No one even hinted that they could have been moved deliberately, even Les could only speculate....

"I'm sure you sods had something to do with it. Them containers have been in that passage for years and they've never moved until you two started to work down there."

Saturday mornings were quite a bit more easy going than weekdays. We worked from eight thirty in the morning until twelve thirty in the afternoon, but most of the time we just prepared our jobs for Monday or finished off any trimming or packing that needed to be done.

Joe and I had finished a batch of sixteen sheet posters for a company called 'Strikes Seeds'. They were printed in brown, yellow and green. It had taken us most of the week to finish them. This Saturday we sorted the spoils from the good prints, guillotined them down to size and took them to Mr Capes for packing. By the time we were finished it was after twelve o'clock so we just tidied our bench area in preparation for our next job.

"Bill, just nip through to next door and see if Capesys in his little ducket."

Joe said with more than a hint of mischief in his eyes.

"What for?" I asked.

"Never mind what for just now, I'll tell you shortly," he replied.

I crept through to Albert's packing room and sure enough he was in his 'little ducket' as Joe called it.

"Aye, he's in their Joe, what are you up to?"

Joe waved a finger in the direction I had just come from and we both tiptoed through.

The door to the little room was only about an inch ajar; Joe closed it very slowly so as not to alert Mr Capes. Then he pulled the hasp and clasp into the closed position and popped a piece of wood through where the padlock normally went.

"Gotcha," Joe whispered as we tiptoed, very quickly, back to the screen room.

"That'll keep that bugger quiet for a bit."

Joe laughed.

I said...

"Wouldn't it be funny if he was in there the whole week-end?"

"Nah, Johnnie always does his 'tour' when everybody has clocked off at half past twelve. He'll let him out when he checks the downstairs poster room, before he locks up." He replied confidently.

When we left the building Les said he was meeting Johnnie in the 'King's Head' at Marlborough Crescent for a drink, which they often did on a Saturday. What we didn't know was that Mr Johns was already in the pub, as some of the poster writers were working all day, he was having his lunch there as well.

The outcome was Albert tried in vain to attract someone's attention by banging on the door, which was below 'Nicky's' joinery business. Mr Johns left the 'King's Head' at three o'clock and eventually let Mr Capes out of his prison at three thirty when he finally locked up. He assured him that he would fully investigate and root out the perpetrators on Monday.

Albert tried to claim overtime for his three-hour lock up but Johnnie would have none of it and told him he had a good mind to charge him board and lodgings.

There was never any investigation and we learned, via Les, that Mr J thought it was hilarious.

Working at David Allen and Sons wasn't all fun and games. The serious side was as Mr Johns had informed me on my first interview, we all had to pay our way by producing good quality posters that the clients were happy with.

The company was originally a 'bill posting' company. They owned or leased a number of sites and hoardings that they rented to companies to advertise their products. As the business prospered the owner, Mr Sam Allen decided they should start producing their own posters, which would automatically increase their chances of renting more sites. This proved to be the case and in a very short space of time the printing overtook the billposting and became one of the biggest screen-printing companies in the country.

Mr Allen treated this part of the business as a hobby. He lived in London but visited Newcastle at least once a year. He was heard to say, that as long as he owned David Allen and Sons the screen business would always be safe, whether it made money or not.

Every time a visit was imminent the word went round the Old Infirmary, 'Sam's coming'.

A major cleanup operation ensued. All of the usual rubbish that accumulated in this very messy industry had to be disposed of. We stored old posters and spoils to be used for packing and washing off screens. Paper was still in very short supply and nothing was wasted. A very large rack in the main screen room housed all of this paper, which was referred to as 'gash sheets'. To cover its untidy appearance for Sam's inspection Les had the brilliant idea of covering it with large sheets of brown wrapping paper. It worked perfectly and looked really smart. Everyone's bench space was marked with two inch white lines and each area had a brand new rubbish sack hanging from a six-inch nail.

The younger members of staff were dispatched to the staircase to remove the very rude illustrations of male and female body parts from the red ochred walls. They were only drawn with chalk but were of gigantic proportions.

Sam's Rolls Royce slowly crunched its way over the rough ash track and stopped outside what had been the original entrance to the old hospital. As this was no longer in use Mr Johns went scurrying 'round the corner to greet the entourage.

It was strange to see this little man dressed in his 'Sunday best' walking in front of the three cars as he directed them to the entrance. It was reminiscent of the introduction of the first speed limit, when drivers had to employ a person carrying a red flag, to walk in front of their vehicle to alert pedestrians of their approach.

The inspection went very well and Mr Allen seemed to be a very charming man.

Arthur Day, the managing director, his secretary and several other white-collar workers flanked Sam as he came into the main screen room. He didn't seem to be too interested in the guided tour he was being subjected to, but once he reached the benches everything changed. He was fascinated by the process and looked on in wonder as the prints came off the screen. We had several large posters arranged around the room and he commented favourably on every one.

As the party moved towards the exit Sam stopped at the brown paper mausoleum and burst out laughing. He pointed to the middle of the heap and Mrs Allen looked and laughed as well. Arthur Day's face turned purple and poor Mr Johns just went a deathly white.

When they left we all went up to the 'gash' rack to see what had tickled Mr and Mrs Allen.

"Oh no." Les exclaimed.

"Who the hell did that? Somebody's gonna get their ball's chewed off."

I thought he was going to burst into tears.

"What is it Les?" I asked.

"If you don't already know go and have a shuffty!"

On the middle sheet of brown paper so neatly festooned to the 'gash rack' was this little inscription:

This heap of shite was constructed in preparation
For Sam Allen's annual visit!

I knew who the culprit was immediately. It was Hardcastle; he was the only one in the place who pronounced the offending four-letter word with the addition of an 'E'.

I thought, 'he's dead; he may as well go now. Johnnie'll know it was him'.

Mr Johns did have a good idea who the guilty party was but he couldn't prove it. He bullied and threatened all to no avail. Hardcastle denied all knowledge of the deed and in any case Mr Allen insisted there should be no witch-hunt, although Arthur Day and Roland Johns would have preferred to have had the culprit burnt at the stake, or hung drawn and quartered.

After the visit, the giant genitalia returned to the walls of the staircase. It was a welcome sight coming in to work to familiar, dare I say faces, yes faces would be correct. Many of them had curious facial expressions. I thought the phantom cartoonist was Joe Paine, but he refused to take credit for them.

"I'm more of a poet than an artist."

Joe said as he recited his latest work.

I wish I were a caterpillar
What a blooming farce
I'd climb up all the rhubarb trees
And slide down on my … Hands and Knees.

I always suspected he was a little mad, but that poem and his favourite song sung by Frank Sinatra. 'Grab a mip-map-mop and a brim-bram-broom and clim-clam-clean up the rim-ram-room, 'cos your bim- bam-baby's coming home tonight', completely convinced me. He was mad!

As we got deeper into my first winter at work the Old Infirmary got colder and colder. We had a delivery of coke every couple of weeks to keep the 'pot-belly' stoves going, but they were totally inadequate. Everyone in the screen room wore fingerless gloves and scarves in an effort to keep warm. The old enamel dish that we used for hot water, was frozen solid every morning. Even the milk left over from the previous days tea break, turned into ice overnight.

It was a very strange sight to see people clearing snow from the corridors inside of the building.

The first task every morning was to get the fires going. We foraged around the building searching for anything we could use as kindling, like laths and pieces of old timber from the derelict areas of the buildings and any offcuts from next door, which housed a 'lollypop-stick' manufacturer.

Once the fires were lit we banked them up with coke and just left them, hoping that they would be well away by the ten o'clock tea break.

One morning the fire beside the foreman's bench didn't seem to be working very well. There was more smoke than usual and the bottom of the grate wasn't burning all that brightly. Les poked at the base to remove any ash or shingle but it didn't seem to make much difference. He lifted the cast iron lid from the top and peered inside.

"There must be a blockage inside the fire." He said.

"The coke isn't even red."

He poked a steel rod into the top of the stove and pushed down hard. The rod stopped, obviously on the blockage. Les pulled it out and thrust it down again with some force. There was an almighty bang and he was engulfed in a plume of smoke and flames. Hot ash shot up into the air and what was left of the glass in the windows rattled loudly.

Les's eyebrows were completely burnt off. The front of his combed back ginger hair was a mass of tiny copper coloured curls and his face was bright red. He looked shocked and bewildered.

"What the bloody hell happened?" He gasped, with a look of terror on his face. The question was obviously rhetorical. No one knew anyway, except maybe the person who lit the fire that morning.

"What did you light that fire with this morning?"
Les asked his apprentice, Brian.

"Err, just some sticks and a drop of turps. Oh aye, ah put the skin off that tin of vermilion in as well." Brian replied.

This was quite normal, burning old turps and the skin off the inks, but there was a right way and a wrong way to do it. Brian had chosen the wrong way.

He soaked the sticks with the old turps and lit them. When they were burning properly he put two or three shovels full of coke on top of them. As the coke was heated and glowed red he banked the stove up to the halfway mark. Then he spotted the waxed membrane covered with dried ink from a twenty-eight pound tin of vermilion. He put this on top of the fire then covered it with more coke. The result was the membrane stopped the air from circulating so the fire burned very slowly. As it did so it heated the ink, which created a build up of gas in the top of the stove. When Les penetrated the dead part of the fire the hot coals below ignited the gas, causing the explosion and his perm! He was furious with Brian. Les was very vain about his hair and it would be quite some time before it returned to normal.

Brian Watson was a very nice person. It was his intention to become a commercial artist sometime in the future and he was only working as a screen-printer to gain some knowledge of the trade. It was only a short while after the explosion when he was again messing about with the same stove. He raked out the ash from the bottom of the fire but there was some clinker jammed in between the bars. Using the large metal rod that Les had previously used, he levered the obstruction out of the front of the fire; at the last minute it shot out rather quickly and ended up under a rack full of posters. The rack being made of wood and filled with one hundred posters, immediately burst into flames. In seconds it was a raging inferno.

Frank Gold grabbed a fire extinguisher and shouted across the screen room for me to get another one. We both reached the blaze at the same time and I was amazed to see the foreman grab his coat and run out of the building.

I was on one side of the fire and Frank was on the other; between us we managed to put it out surprisingly quickly. Unfortunately Frank sprayed right through the flames and covered me from head to foot in foam.

The whole incident lasted only a few minutes yet everyone but Frank Gold and yours truly, was outside in the yard.

The rack was completely ruined but at least no one was hurt. Mr Johns and the rest of the staff returned to the screen room and a full inquiry was started right away. Brian explained to the boss what had happened. It was just an unfortunate accident.

Frank and I got a telling off for cleaning ourselves up in the firm's time and Brian Watson was transferred to the poster room.

While Les was making out his report for head office I heard him saying to Mr Johns that 'Brian Watson and I quickly brought the blaze under control using the available fire extinguishers'.

I thought that was a real cheek. Les was out of the building so quickly he didn't even have time to see who had put the fire out let alone do it himself. He was just a blur as he passed me! When someone commented on the report he said it always looked better for insurance purposes if the person in charge was seen to take control of the situation, whether he actually did or not.

Chapter Eleven

Life can be cruel

In 1951 I joined three Boy's Clubs. I became a member of Grainger Park Boy's Club, St. Aidan's Youth Club and St. Michael's Catholic Boy's Club.

I was very keen on boxing at this time and Grainger Park was the most successful club in that field. They had several local champions and a couple of national champions. St. Michael's had a good football team but badly needed a goalkeeper so I applied for the job and got it. I wasn't too keen on joining a Catholic Club as I had heard that Father Cranley visited the club on several occasions and he had quite a reputation for 'press-ganging' members into attending church services.

I have to say that religion has never been my strong point.

St. Aidan's was a Methodist Club and the main attraction was girls. It was the only mixed club in the area; this made it very popular. It was also the haunt of Penny Harris, which made it even more attractive to me. I was still very fond of her but that was all to change in the not too distant future.

The Club Leader at St. Aidan's was Mr Ben Trewitt. He seemed too nice a person for our area and his accent was pure BBC. His main function was opening and closing the club; apart from that he didn't seem to take too much interest in what was going on. On the good side he was a fully trained masseur, which was a tremendous asset when treating football injuries, but I concluded after a couple of treatment sessions that he concentrated far too long on area's of the anatomy that were extremely sensitive. So on the down side I was convinced he was a puff and my visits to his 'treatment sessions' came to an abrupt end. For a joke I took one of my boxing friends to Mr Trewitt's massage parlour for a complete body massage. When he came out I thought he was going to kill me. His face was bright red and his clothes looked as though they had been thrown on.

"Hi, that bugger kept touching me up," he said as he tucked his shirttail into his trousers, he gave me a long enquiring stare, then he said.

"You knew, yih swine, you knew he was a queer. You deliberately set me up. Well it nearly misfired 'cos at the finish I told him…If you touch me there once more, I'll tear your bloody arm off and shove it down your throat!"

"What did he say to that?"

I enquired, trying to stifle my laughter.

"Oh, he said, c'mon now Ronnie there's no need to be like that."

Being a homosexual in the 1950's was against the law and punishable by imprisonment, which happened to a number of public figures. In Elswick it was also very dangerous. Any queer making unwanted advances to anyone was liable to be severely beaten up Naturally.

Now they have all 'come out' as they call it, and the sooner they all go back in the better. I feel no pity for their problems with Aids; I only feel anger at the way that they have infected half of the human race with their disease. The only way I could ever accept homosexuality would be if one man could make another man pregnant. Delivery would have to be natural, no Caesarean, and I would have to be present at the birth. I think if that happened, the homosexual population would move into rapid decline.

Ben Trewitt was moved to another Boy's Club after only a couple of years at St. Aidan's and eventually ended up in an administrative job still within the youth movement.

These people never seem to be dismissed or exposed, they just appear to be moved around from place to place, protected by their peers and colleagues. I think they should be ostracised and a lot more!

The war in Korea was beginning to look like World War Three. The North Koreans assisted by several hundred thousand Chinese communist soldiers had the Americans in complete disarray. Their forces were pushed further and further south until it seemed they would be driven over the edge and into the sea. It all seemed so far away from home that it didn't concern us, until the British and Commonwealth Governments decided to send troops to support the Americans.

National Service was still in force in the U.K., so thousands of young conscripts were sent to Korea.

My Dad's half brother Nichol was due to serve his two years National Service and he indicated that he was very keen to do his bit. Unfortunately his father (Granda Robson) was seriously ill with cancer and Nichol was granted leave from induction on compassionate grounds.

It was so sad to see this mountain of a man slowly disappearing from the face of the earth. He was able to walk around for several months but his weight just fell off him. I would estimate him to have been about sixteen stones in his prime and well over six feet tall. The last time I saw him he was lying on his back in a single bed with just a blanket covering him. There seemed to be no one under the blanket, it looked as though only his head was there, he couldn't have weighed more than six stone.

Nichol was sitting on a chair at the side of the bed with his hands clasped between his knees as though he was praying. His eyes were red rimmed and he smiled as he looked up.

"I just wanted to see him once more" I said to him as I peeped round the door.

"Come in Billy, it's alright, he can't hear anything, he's had some morphine."

Granda Robson's breathing was very laboured and his mouth was wide open. The noise coming from his throat sounded very much like snoring. My Dad told me later that it was called the 'death rattle'.

It was very strange standing there looking at this dying man. Why had I been so intimidated by him in the past, he was only a human being, not the monster I thought or imagined he was. I pictured him standing at the top of the three stairs in their passage roaring.

"Wha di ye want?"

His hair was almost gone and his once ginger moustache was white and grey with only a hint of its former colour. He died that day.

Once the funeral and everything was out of the way Nichol reported to the authorities that he was now available to serve his two years National Service. Strangely enough they informed him that being his mother's only means of support he could apply for exemption from military service. Granny Robson was delighted but Nichol would have none of it, he was determined to do his National Service. He even talked about staying in the Army and making a career of it. Most of his friends were now in uniform and I got the impression that his enthusiasm for army life was just bravado to show everyone that he could do it as well as they could. I never believed that he was as keen as he made out. I think he was driven by his ego.

Our Robert was also doing his National Service. He was posted to Malaya along with his friend 'Jocka'. They must have enjoyed army life because they both signed on as 'regulars' and served five years with the colours and seven years in the reserve.

I was quite thrilled to learn that Nichol would be out of circulation for a couple of years. We both tolerated each other but there was never any love lost between us. He had been a thorn in my side on numerous occasions and although I didn't see him that often the spectre of his presence was always there.

I'd had several bad experiences with my father's half brother but there had also been some good times in the relationship. He had allowed me to drive his delivery van when I was only twelve, which had sparked off a lifelong interest in cars. He was the architect of my first sexual experience at thirteen (which sparked off a lifelong interest in cars!). He also taught me never to trust anyone completely, and especially not him.

When he came home on his first leave I was amazed at the change in his attitude. Nichol seemed to be much more conciliatory, even a little subdued. He liked the army, or so he said, but he had learned that he was to be posted to Korea and he wasn't too pleased about that.

The going away party was the usual get together. Lots of old friends and neighbours came to wish Nichol 'bon voyage' and assure him that the Korean War was almost under control and he would be home in no time at all.

The United Nations were trying very hard to get the two factions to agree to separate and divide the country into North and South Korea with a buffer zone at the thirty-eighth parallel to be manned by a Multi-National force under the auspices of the UN. But this was early days and agreement was way into the future.

I had said a lot about Nichol's conceit and bullying in the past but I felt sorry for him as he tearfully boarded the tram to the Central Station. Several members of the family accompanied him to see him safely onto his train and help him with his luggage. It was to be the last time we would ever see him.

The story in the Evening Chronicle some months later read:

Local National Serviceman Nicholas Robson was tragically killed in a freak accident in Korea. Private Robson, son of Widow Mrs Alice Robson of 22 Cannon Street, Elswick was exchanging arms while on guard when a bullet was accidentally discharged killing him instantly, he was nineteen. His mother and family members are devastated. A family spokesman said:
"This is a double tragedy for us coming so soon after his fathers death."

My Granda Mills handed me the newspaper as I walked up Glue House Lane. It was folded over at the page where the story was written. Nichol's photograph at the top of the column made him look about fifteen, he was in his army uniform and smiling broadly.

"Here, take this home. Nichol's been killed," was all he said.

The memorial service for Nichol was very moving. There was no coffin or remains; they had been interred in Korea. One of his former girlfriends, who was a professional singer sang 'The Old Rugged Cross' as a solo. St. Aidan's Church was very large and dwarfed the tiny congregation of mourners. We sang 'Abide with Me', 'Rock of Ages' and the sailors hymn, 'For Those in Peril on the Sea.

The vicar paid tribute to the ultimate sacrifice made by this brave young soldier who gave his life so that others could have their 'freedom'. A fine tribute; but not true.

The official cause of death was accidental, but the letter from the War Office that came with his few meagre belongings read:

'Private Robson took his own life whilst on guard duty! His colleagues and friends said he had been very depressed and lived in terror of being captured by the Chinese'.

My father had intercepted the letter before it reached his mother and he made sure she never saw it or learned of its contents. So my Granny Robson lost the whole of her second family. Ronnie died when he was only five, Nichol died at nineteen and Granda Robson shortly before him. She still had her three sons and two daughters from her previous marriage but her whole new family had been wiped out.

The death of my father's half brother was a shock to everyone including myself, but not many people were aware of his true character and at fifteen years of age I wasn't very generous when it came to forgiving.

It was a tragedy for someone to take his own life and especially at such a tender age, but sad to say I wasn't in deep mourning at his passing.

Funerals are very emotive occasions and I have great difficulty in handling the sadness that they evoke. But I have to say my feelings go out more to the people who are left behind than to the deceased. After all they are totally out of it. The pain of bereavement and sense of loss are for the living. These are the people I shed my tears for.

After the service the collection plate was strategically placed at the exit. Everyone filed past, placing his or her offering noisily on the silver tray. Granny Robson opened her black handbag and fumbled amongst the contents with her handkerchief in one hand, ready to stem the ever-flowing tide of tears. She placed a five-pound note on top of the collection of silver coins and as she turned towards the door my father picked the 'fiver' back up and replaced it with two half-crowns.

"She'll be looking for that bloody fiver in a day or two," he muttered.

He realised she was too upset to appreciate what she was doing, five pounds was more than a week's wages and she couldn't really afford to be that generous. He said he would give it back to her later when she calmed down. My Uncle Benny was furious and said so.

"Five bloody quid, what's she trying to dee, buy him a bloody place in heaven. Here wor Willy gi' me that fiver, if she can afford to put five poond on the bloody collection plate, she can afford to pay for the drinks the'sefternoon!"

We all walked back to my Gran's house, where she had prepared sandwiches and the usual selection of homemade cakes etc. The men carried on down Glue House Lane to the 'Crooked Billet' on Scotswood Road. They stayed there until they were thrown out at three o'clock.

Weddings and funerals seem to be the only times families' get together in any great numbers. It was a sad day but it was nice to see people you rarely saw. Aunt Edie was there with Hughie her second husband, her son's Matty and Willy Martin and her daughter Edith from her first marriage. Dad's brother's Chris and Benny with their wives Anne and Alice. My mother and father, my sister and myself. The usual gathering of friends and neighbours, and of course Jane Ellen and her mother.

The men were all drunk when they returned from the pub and the sombre atmosphere was transformed into more of a party atmosphere. It was nice to see how they tried to make the mood more of a celebration than a mourning, they even succeeded in making my Granny smile occasionally, albeit through the tears.

My Mother's brother Robert rarely wrote letters home from Malaya but during his stay in hospital he managed to bring us up to date with what he was up to.

The reason for his hospitalisation had nothing to do with the

301

war against the communists; it had more to do with his consumption of large amounts of alcohol.

He and his friend 'Jocka' were in a Nightclub in Kuala Lumpur drinking very heavily. Rob was fine when he was tipsy; he would sing and carry on like the life and sole of the party that he was. He was friendly, generous and full of fun, but once he reached the 'drunk' stage his character changed dramatically. The fun became stupid, the friendly became loud and boisterous and the generosity turned to nuisance. He wasn't looking for trouble but inevitably it found him, on several occasions. On this occasion it found him once again. In the ensuing fracas Robert was hit on the jaw with a gin bottle. His jaw was badly broken and he had to have it wired up for several weeks. One of his teeth was pushed up into the upper jaw resulting in the loss of that one and the one above it. He wrote:

'This is my second time in hospital in only four weeks. Last month I was on my way back to my tent, slightly the 'worse-for-wear', when I tripped over a length of rope with little red tags attached. These were printed with 'Danger Restricted Area'. I fell into a deep trench but landed in a very soft mud-like substance (these are not the exact words he used to describe the incident or the mud). 'I sank deeper into the mire, fortunately feet first, and then the smell and the realisation of where I was suddenly hit me. I had fallen into a disused cesspit!'

As there were very few flush toilets in overseas army camps deep cesspits were dug and wooden seats provided. They were commonly known as dry toilets or thunder boxes. They were perfectly adequate but as the residue was never flushed away they gradually filled up. Once they had reached a certain level they were abandoned. The wooden seats were re-located over another hole and the old pit was roped off and covered with sand until it settled down, then it was concreted over.

Private Robert Mills of the Green Howards was in it up to his neck!

"I shouted as loud as I could" he wrote.

"Two of my friends came to the rescue, but only from the safe distance afforded by a six foot length of tow rope. I chucked all of my clothes back into the pit and my two mates borrowed a hosepipe from the vehicle bay and hosed off most of the filth. I finished the job in the showers, then I had to report to the M.O. (Medical Officer), who insisted that I spend the night in the Military Hospital, where I was subjected to a Carbolic bath and a very large anti Tetanus injection."

The Green Howards, now disbanded, served in Malaya for several years fighting the communists. It was mostly jungle warfare and the inexperienced British soldiers were supported by a large contingent of Gurkas. These loyal little men were fearless fighters and more than a match for the communist guerrilla's. They were ferocious in battle and ruthless in their efforts to defeat the enemy. Rob once told me he witnessed a hand-to-hand skirmish involving several outnumbered Gurkas. One of them drew his legendary kukri and cut both arms off one of the attacking enemy before decapitating him. They seemed to resent taking prisoners and would rather die than be captured. Obviously they thought the enemy should be the same.

Robert's regiment was posted to Germany after four years in Malaya. He spent his last twelve months in the army driving T.C.V.'s (Troop carrying vehicles), which he later recalled.

'It was the cushiest time I ever had, apart from the time I nearly followed the truck in front into the Rhine'. On that occasion several soldiers were drowned when their vehicle plunged into the river whilst on a training exercise. The exercise went on for six weeks and yet another five servicemen were killed when a tank they were sleeping under moved during the night.

'Still, Rob said. "That was way below the five percent of casualties that they allowed for."

As we moved into the second half of the twentieth century the war was just a distant memory.

Rationing was still in force, but several scarce items began to creep back into the shops: bananas, tangerines, oranges and even coconuts on the odd occasion. Our local mobile fruiterer even had pineapples, but you needed a bank loan before you could afford to buy one!

The pubs were open longer and rarely ran out of beer.

Mary Bennett opened an 'Off Licence' on Scotswood Road next door to her sister Lizzie's General Dealers. Bella Lookup still had a good business with her 'second hand' shop and Katie's 'Penny Dips' was doing very well selling white 'baps' dipped in thick savoury onion gravy.

White flour was once again available and the bakers had a fantastic display of scones, cakes and tarts in their window.

The Fish and Chip shop, which had only opened occasionally during the war, opened every day except Sunday. Although fish and chips were one of few things not rationed, the fat needed to cook them was. Our local 'Chippy' had been taken over by a southern family who introduced many new ideas, which caught on very quickly. They started selling battered sausages, pies, Spam-fritters, pickled gherkins and soft drinks like Tizer and Lemonade. They even put the chips into a spin drier to retrieve the precious cooking fat, which was still in very short supply.

The newspapers were full of the 'Festival of Britain'. This was the Governments way of trying to get the economy back into some kind of order. Hundreds of companies were desperately trying to get their businesses back into full production and the festival was going to help. It was to be an exhibition of British technology and expertise, the like of which had not been seen in this country for over a hundred years. The only trouble was, it was in London and as far as the Northeast of England was concerned it might as well have been on the moon.

Most people in the south of England think the north starts at Luton and ends at Northampton. I believe the Romans are largely responsible for this attitude.

In 208AD Septimius Severus, the Emperor of Rome, divided Britain into two separate provinces. One based in the south, which he named, Britannia Superior, with London as its capital. The other in the north with York as it capital, Britannia Inferior!

Need I say more?

The newsreels in the cinemas showed the preparation of the stands and exhibits. A huge cigar shaped object known as the Skylon, was to feature as the symbol of the event.

I failed to detect any sign of enthusiasm, or even any interest in what was happening hundreds of miles away. London was like another country. It took almost eight hours to get there by road and these were in a dreadful condition. The number of car owners in Newcastle in 1951 could be counted in tens, not hundreds. In modern terminology it is referred to as the North-South divide. Fifty years earlier London was England and the rest of us were the poor relations (not much has changed). We all wore cloth caps and mufflers, boozed away our dole money, went home and beat the wife (after throwing our dinner on the back of the fire), staggered into bed and slept, until the pubs opened again.

My own interest in the festival was limited to the new set of coins that were issued by the Royal Mint. Plus the fact that Charlie Tate our County Welterweight Boxing Champion was in the final of the A.B.A. National Championships. Charlie boxed for Grainger Park Boy's Club, and this was the most successful bid we had ever made to gain a national title. He stood only five feet six inches in his stocking feet but he was solid muscle and bone. I watched Charlie sparring on several occasions and I thought his boxing skills were very limited but when he launched an attack very few of his opponents survived.

The last Great Exhibition was held in Crystal Palace in 1851. Queen Victoria had been on the throne for fourteen years and she still had another fifty years to go. So this 'Festival' as it was called took place in similar circumstances. George VI had taken over the throne after his brother David who abdicated in 1936 and it was fourteen years after his coronation in 1937 that the Festival of Britain opened. Sadly King George VI didn't have another fifty years to live; in fact he had less than a year.

The King was known by his family as 'Bertie', which in historical terms could be regarded as slightly unfortunate. His Grandfather Edward VII (also known as Bertie) waited most of his life to be crowned King and died only nine years into his reign. Prince Albert, Queen

Victoria's husband and George's Great Grandfather (also Bertie) died in 1861 only ten years after he masterminded the Great Exhibition of 1851. I think the Royal family could be forgiven for leaving 'Bertie' out of their name selections for our future monarchs.

The ups and downs of 1951 were many. Most of the deep mines still had reserves of coal for several years ahead but the cost of bringing it to the surface was making them uneconomical. In some cases it was costing more per ton to mine the coal than it could be sold for. It was the beginning of the end for the once mighty coal industry.

I remember once in 1949 I was reserve goalkeeper for the Forge Hammer football team. We were playing against a pub team in Sunderland called The Aquatic Arms. After the match (which we lost) the opposing team invited us back to their local for a 'pie and a pint' as they described it, as a good will gesture. One of the players, a coalminer, shouted to the barman.

"Here Freddie, get these lads a drink," as the three underage followers, myself included, entered the pub.

He pulled out a roll of pound notes as big as my fist, peeled one off and handed it to me.

"Here son, pay the barman for your drinks and bring me the change."

I discovered during the friendly banter that followed, that he worked at Easington Colliery, he had his own house and was thinking of buying a car, all from coal.

Two years later on the 29th of May 1951, eighty-one miners were killed in an underground explosion at Easington Colliery. A subdued Durham Miners Gala stood silent for two minutes in reverence to their dead comrades...it was a very sad time in County Durham, I often wonder if he survived!

The British Aviation Company De Haviland in 1951 was running the final tests on the world's first passenger jet airliner, the 'Comet'. The jet engine invented by Frank Whittle (later Sir Frank) would be used in the future in almost every aeroplane in service, but the Comet was a world first... This British invention was a masterpiece of aeronautical engineering and design. Its sleek lines and shiny metallic finish and the absence of propellers made it look like something out of a science fiction 'movie'. The whole world queued up to buy it. They were not to know that this was one of the most dangerous aeroplanes ever to take to the skies. The wing design was flawed and some vital areas of construction were questionable. The outcome was several fatal crashes, the loss of one hundred and ten passengers and crew and the scrap heap for what was thought to be the most advanced flying machine in the world.

On the lighter side Newcastle United won the F.A. Cup in 1951 with the help of the legendary Jackie Milburn, or as he is affectionately known 'Wor Jackie'. Milburn was the uncle of the two world famous Charlton brothers, Bobby and Jack.

I listened to the match on our 'Redifusion' which we had just had installed. We paid two shillings a week for 'piped' programs with no interference, batteries, or accumulators to worry about. My Aunt Grace listened with me and I remember her leaping into the air shouting 'We've scored' when Newcastle took the lead. 'Howay the lads' could be clearly heard over the radio from the fanatical Geordie supporters. As the final whistle blew, the 'Blaydon Races' Tyneside's National Anthem rose to a crescendo, completely drowning out every other sound in the great Wembley Stadium.

Another local hero in 1951 was Gosforth Harrier Bert Hemsley. Bert won the Morpeth to Newcastle road race again that year for the third time. No mean feat when taking into consideration that the race took place on the morning after the New Year celebrations. In that same year he won the Sheffield Marathon for the second time in succession at the age of 43.

Juan Fangio of Argentina was crowned World Driving Champion in 1951 and went on to win it three times in that decade.

One of the sporting highlights of that memorable year was 'Jersey' Joe Walcott's successful bid to become the World Heavyweight Boxing Champion. At thirty-seven years of age Joe was and still is the oldest boxer ever to win the title. He had been a professional since he was fifteen, lying about his age, and after two epic battles with the 'Brown Bomber' Joe Louis, which he lost, I was happy to see him crowned champion. He didn't reign long; less than a year later he succumbed to the 'Brockton Blockbuster' Rocky Marciano. Walcott floored Marciano in the fourth round but failed to do what every other opponent failed to do, beat the 'Rock'. When he finally retired Marciano was the only heavyweight champion in boxing history to retire undefeated. Forty-nine fights, forty-nine wins.

It seemed strange in 1951, six years after the war, that most things were still rationed. You could only buy a pound of steak every three weeks by saving your allowance and the bacon ration had been reduced even further, to only three ounces a week. By this time Germany had ended food rationing altogether, it made you wonder who had won and who had lost the war.

News filtered through to the Northeast that some shop-owner in London had opened a new type of store. It was called self-service shopping. All you had to do was help yourself to anything in the shop, pop it into a basket and take it to the cashier and pay for it. There was no need to ask how much it was, everything was clearly labelled and priced. I couldn't believe anyone could be so stupid. Fancy allowing customers to help themselves; this was asking for trouble. Surely ninety percent of their goods would just be stolen; it would be far too much of a temptation, especially to people who were dishonest at the best of times.

I really thought that Mr Sainsbury, whoever he was, was certainly short of a few brain cells. He would soon learn his lesson!

The Co-op in Alnwick, Northumberland had a similar idea. They converted one of their stores into half self-service, but maintained the old assisted service in the other half of the shop, just in case the idea didn't catch on. Very wise I thought!

Well, I was wrong, very wrong! Fifty years after the first self-service stores opened there is upwards of fifteen thousand dotted around the country. They are now called Supermarkets or Superstores, turning over billions of pounds in an industry that changed our whole way of thinking when buying food. Once rationing ended many of the old traditional corner shops went out of business, unable to compete with the supermarket giants. Shopping became more of a social event than a chore. Families would shop together in the safe traffic free stores, have their tea or evening meal in the restaurant and go home to settle down for a night in front of the new family pastime, television.

308

The huge wooden box, reminiscent of our old Cossor wireless, housed the tiny ten inch screen that was soon to become the nation's favourite source of entertainment, but at the present time Radio was still king.

I was listening to the Light Programme one evening in 1951 to Twenty Questions or Brain of Britain, or some other programme, I can't quite recall; when there was a brief period of silence at the end of the show. There was no announcement for what followed, only a lot of strange noises, a maniacal scream and a splash of water. Then the announcer said:

'Ladies and Gentlemen, the 'Goon Show', with Spike Milligan, Peter Sellers, Michael Bentine and Harry Secombe'.

The next thirty minutes was total mayhem. The characters, Bluebottle, Eckles, Neddy Seagoon, Moriarty, Min and Henry Crun, were either drowned, blown up, shot or sent to work down a Welsh sock mine. It was totally ridiculous, but hilarious.

It took a little while to grasp the non-existent plot, but once you realised how outlandish it was it just became funnier and funnier. No one had come across this brand of humour before and at first there was some opposition to the show, but this rapidly faded away and 'The Goons' became one of the most listened to programmes on the radio.

We were all used to straight situation comedies like 'Ray's a Laugh', 'Take it from Here', 'Life with the Lyons', and the ever popular 'A Life of Bliss', but the 'Goon Show' was nothing like these, or anything else for that matter. They just transcended all conventional ideas of comedy. 'Spike' Milligan, who also provided several of the voices, wrote the scripts. The other three, Secombe, Sellers and Bentine provided the voices of the other characters. Michael Bentine was the first to leave the show to pursue a solo career in radio and television. Peter Sellers became an international film star and Harry Secombe starred in films, T.V. and stage shows, notably in musicals where he used his very fine tenor voice to much acclaim. Terence 'Spike' Milligan carried on writing scripts and starred in several mad T.V. shows. His books on his experiences in the army are so funny they take twice as long to read as anything else, you have to stop to wipe away the tears of laughter so often.

One fine Spring Sunday morning I was helping my Dad to decorate our living room. Wallpaper was almost unobtainable so we were using the stippling method to create a pattern similar to wallpaper. Dad had painted a background colour onto the four walls and he and I were dabbing colours onto it with a piece of old lace curtain. It was quite effective sometimes but I had seen some awful results in the past.

The Redifusion was going full blast and Dad was humming or singing along to the records on 'Two Way Family Favourites'. I was waiting patiently in the hope of hearing Jussi Bjorling or Caruso being requested, just as I did every Sunday. After half of the programme went by I thought I was going to be disappointed this time.

I heard Jean Metcalf say something about a new 'American sensation', but I wasn't able to make out the name. When the record started I could feel the hairs on the back of my neck stand on end. It was Mario Lanza singing 'Be My Love'. My Dad was mesmerised. We both just stood on our ladders, not moving until the final strains of that top 'C' faded away.

"Bloody hell, who was that?" Dad exclaimed.

"What a bloody voice. I've never heard anything like that since Caruso. What was his name?"

The question was aimed at me but I couldn't reply. I could feel the lump of emotion in my throat. What a voice. He would be able to sing anything. OK I loved Jussi Bjorling, Caruso, John McCormack and several other tenors, but this voice was new, young, and sensational. Then Cliff Michelmore said...

"Well that was for Lance Corporal Roberts of the Royal Green Jackets from his fiancée Brenda. Mario Lanza singing 'Be My Love'. Now who could fail to respond to that?"

"How much would that record cost then?" Dad enquired.

"About six bob." I replied.

"Bloody hell, six bob, they're not getting any cheaper are they?" Dad remonstrated.

Later in the programme one of the presenters read out a request for someone who had just lost his girlfriend. He wanted her to know how he felt when he realised he know longer had a sweetheart. The record was 'Cry', sung by Johnnie Ray.

I thought it was quite nice. Johnny didn't have much of a voice but he put the song over very well. Dad had his own views!

"Did you ever hear such a load of bloody rubbish in your life? How the hell can they put records on like that after that other bloke? 'Cry', yih bugger, he should cry, wih bloody shame. Who the hell told him he could sing anyway?"

Dad never sat on the fence. Once he had made up his mind about something it wasn't an opinion anymore it was hard fact. He used to call the very popular Alma Cogan, whom he hated, 'The Black Minorca' and Judy Garland 'couldn't sing to save her bloody soul!'

I always thought my father was by tradition a Labour supporter until I heard him describe Michael Foot as...

"That bloody clown', I'll never know how he gets past Guy Fawkes Night;" and Neil Kinnoch as a ginger haired 'Welsh Rarebit'. In his humble opinion all MP's were only out for one thing, to make life easier for themselves.

"What do they do as soon as they get into power? Gih tha'sells a bloody big rise and buy a bloody big house in London." He questioned and answered himself.

I think he would have preferred a form of 'Liberalised Labourised Conservatism' to cover his political ideals! Maybe tinged with a hint of Communism.

He loved the World War Two 'Winnie' as he called Churchill, but abhored his harsh treatment and 'Jack Boot' handling of the miners strike before the war; but that was all in the past. Churchill had ousted Clem Attlee's Labour party and became Prime Minister for the second time.

My Dad, as contrary as ever, was delighted at Churchill's victory and said so.

"Well if it hadn't been for him during the war this country would be part of Germany by now. That bloody idiot Chamberlain thought he could stop Hitler with a piece of bloody paper. Churchill's a hard man but at least he's not frightened to make tough decisions. He'll get the country back on its feet again and the Unions'll not tell him what to do neither."

The Trade Unions had been growing in strength and

membership since the end of the war and the Labour party's close relationship with them was no secret. They donated large sums of money to the party funds and they obviously wanted some support for their movement in return.

My father thought it was unhealthy for any political party to be too closely associated either with Unions or private companies.

"It might not always be the case but corruption is never far from people's minds when politicians have outside interests in business or anything else."

In 1951 David Allen's and Sons wouldn't even allow a Union representative to come into the building. We all joined the Sign and Display Trade Union, but in my opinion it was a waste of time. They did manage to negotiate a shorter working week for us, but I think it was only because industry in general was gradually coming to terms with the inevitability of a five-day week. Otherwise they achieved nothing of note in all the years I was a member.

I kept my membership going for many years until I discovered that our representative was a silent partner in another screen-printing company. For someone who advocated state ownership for almost everything, to be a partner in a private business was totally hypocritical in my view.

The General Election had generated a great deal of extra work for our firm and we had been working a lot of overtime. A new ink, developed in America, proved very popular with election candidates. It was called Day-Glo and as it's name implied, it glowed in daylight.

There were only four colours available originally, Fire Orange, Saturn Yellow, Arc Chrome and Signal Green. As it was so new no one knew much about it in our company we just followed the manufacturers recommendations with varying results. Most of the work was for very large posters simply saying, Vote Conservative, or Labour (I can't even recall any other parties at that time). We printed the Day-Glo first then over printed it with a dark background of Navy blue or Black. The result was stunning bright wording which definitely caught the eye. David Allen's owned hundreds of advertising sites and our billposter's were working flat out with the Election work. After the first hectic week someone noticed that the posters, which had been printed with Saturn Yellow were beginning to fade slightly. This didn't cause too much concern, as the colour would probably last long enough to cover the Election campaign. That is, until it rained!

On my way to work I passed a large hoarding site attached to the Cattle Market. The 'forty-eight-sheet' poster printed in Fire Orange red and black was now very pale pink and black, after a night of severe rain. By the time I got into work there was already an inquiry going on.

'How much thinners did you use for the Day-Glow? What mesh count did you use for the Day-Glo? Did you use a hard or soft rubber to print the Day-Glo?'

After speaking to the British Agents for Day-Glo, Mr Johns issued new instructions for printing their inks. Thinning had not too exceed 20%. Mixing had to be carried out with an electric mixer, not by hand, and care had to be taken to ensure that all of the pigment was stirred in thoroughly from the bottom of each tin. Only when all of this was carried out to the letter, could we start printing. Then as a further precaution to avoid fading, each print had to be 'pulled' twice to obtain a heavier deposit of ink.

As each printer was expected to produce at least six hundred prints a day, this meant an increase to twelve hundred per day in one fell swoop. There was lots of moaning about the extra work 'for the same money', but it soon became apparent that everyone was capable of achieving it.

The extra effort needed to reach higher production figures was quickly forgotten when other facts about the new ink started to emerge. First of all there was the smell. The reducer was very strong and when you washed off your screen or squee-gee the skin started to come off your hands like dandruff. If you were using yellow, your skin took on a yellow appearance and when you took a drink of water, it tasted of solvent. Passing water was quite funny; mine was often bright red and smelled like Tomcats. Today the Health and Safety Authority would have a field day with Day-Glo, but in 1951 it was a case of 'anything goes'. On the positive side, you were always sure of having a seat to yourself on the bus. No one would sit beside you because of the smell! It was even worse in the hot weather; everyone working with Day-Glo sweated pale green or pink, depending on the colour they were printing.

The makers very quickly realised the shortcomings of their new product and quickly revised the formula, enabling thinning to be done with turpentine or white spirit. This reduced the strong odour and prolonged the outdoor life considerably; it also required only 'single pulls'.

It's strange to look back on those pioneering days of screen-printing. A day's production in 1951 now takes less than one hour. Exposing a photo stencil took anything up to two hours; it now takes two and a half minutes. Most companies have UV inks, which are dried by passing the print through a tunnel housing a very powerful ultra-violet light source. We had to 'hand rack' everything we printed and drying could take hours, or in some cases days. A hand cut positive or stencil could take anything up to eight hours to prepare, depending on how intricate it was, now the most complicated 'hand' cutting can be done on a computer driven machine in less time than it takes to boil an egg. That's progress, but it's not as much fun!

Once the Festival got under way the whole nation was bombarded with events, shows, exhibitions, gifts, memorabilia and souvenirs. The exhibition ship 'The Campania' visited the Tyne, but the queues were so long to get on board that I couldn't be bothered to wait. Now I wish I had been more patient.

The Captain of 'The Compania', Captain Frank Thornton, hailed from Whitley Bay. An honour indeed for someone from the Northeast (no relation to Summer Wine Frank Thornton)

There were flower shows, marches, festival illuminations, festival rock, festival concerts, but there wasn't much in evidence along Scotswood Road. All we seemed to have was festival apathy!

I suppose it must have been a success of some kind. Over eight and a half million people visited the site at South Bank in London. The Dome of Discovery got very good reviews but it was still too far away to make much difference to us in Newcastle.

Chapter Twelve

GHOSTS AND GOULIES

One of my school friends, Tommy Daken, known to everyone as 'Dinky' was also our local 'paper boy'. He had the loudest voice I have ever heard in my life. His cries of 'Chronicaall' or 'Footbaall Finaall' could be heard from about a mile away.

On Friday nights I used to accompany him on his rounds delivering the Evening Chronicle and collecting the money for the previous weeks supply of papers. Tom was no great scholar and ranged about the middle of the class academically, but at fiddling his paper money he was just short of being a genius. I tried on several occasions to fathom out how he did it, but in the days of no computers or calculators it was way beyond me.

He collected the money from each client and entered the payment in his little notebook. Then he re-entered the transactions into another book but changed the amount they had paid to slightly less than they owed. This gave him a surplus over the amount of cash he had to hand over to his boss. As I pointed out to him, he would have to pay that surplus in eventually to balance the books, but he just smiled and said...

"Yeah, I know, but I never have to get everyone's account up to date. They always owe for last week's papers so I just keep deducting a few pence from here and a few pence from there and at Christmas, when everyone gives me my Christmas tip, I pay it off their arrears. No one ever queries what I do and the boss thinks I'm the best 'paper lad' he's had, since me Da packed it in."

Tom gave his week's wages to his mother, but his permanent source of 'fiddle' money kept him in pocket money for the rest of the week.

After we had handed in the 'takings' our next stop was Mary Bennett's Off License. Tom bought a two-pint bottle of cider and we sat in the derelict building next door drinking it between us. The sweet gassy apple juice was delicious and it went down a treat. I wasn't aware at the time that cider was alcoholic, there was no indication on the bottle in those days and no one objected to us youngsters buying it. Lots of kids drank it, but not by the pint. In no time at all both Tom and I were 'stoned' out of our minds. We both stood up and started to giggle. There was still quite a bit left in the bottle but we couldn't stop laughing long enough to drink it. The effects didn't last long and left us both with thumping headaches. One of the older lads later told us it was the gas in the cider that caused us to be affected so quickly, he explained…

"It's just like Champagne that the rich people drink, it's full of gas and that takes the alcohol to the brain much quicker than beer. So instead of drinking a lot of beer or spirits they can drink a few glasses of watery looking fizz and very quickly get blottowed!"

I didn't know if he was right but it sounded feasible.

I remember one Friday night it was particularly cold for the time of year so Tom and I decided we would have a fire in one of the old buildings and drink our cider in comfort.

We occupied number forty-seven, an upstairs flat, still in good condition, habitable, but destined for demolition. There was an abundance of wood from floorboards etc., so we soon had a roaring fire going in what had been the front room, or living room. The services had all been disconnected but the fireplaces and chimneys still worked efficiently. There were no toilets inside any of the houses, even when they were occupied, but a gap in the floorboards provided us with adequate facilities.

We shared our cider in the usual way and poked slivers of wood through the potatoes that were roasting on the open fire.

Suddenly Tom gripped my arm and nodded towards the door at the top of the stairs. It was slowly opening. There was no grating of rusty hinges or ghostly creaking, it was just opening very very slowly.

I could feel my skin going tight and the hair on the back of my head standing to attention. My mouth was drying rapidly and I was finding it difficult to swallow. The pressure on my arm increased to the point of actual pain and the fingers on my left hand started to go numb.

My friend's eyes were like two large organ stops fully extended, more white than coloured. Neither of us could move. We weren't afraid of being caught by the Police or anyone in authority; it was the unknown that scared us.

The sharp intake of oxygen rushing to replenish our starved lungs sounded like some over-worked vacuum cleaner as a face appeared round the cream and green door.

"Aye yah buggers, yih thought it was 'Sandshoe Dick' didn't yih?" Said the face.

"Ah bet yih both nearly shit yah pants. Ooh, can ah have a tatty?"

It was Jimmy Walters. He was about four years older than us but we were good friends. We both played the mouth organ and frequently played duets together.

"Hi man Jimmy, could you not whistle or something coming up them stairs, instead of creeping about like that?"

Jimmy had a very nasal laugh and he sniggered away to himself as he retrieved a potato from the fire.

"Ah knew it was you two up here, so ah thought ah would just have a bit o' fun, especially with this place being haunted!"

"Haunted, who said that like?" Dinky asked, his eyes still popping out of his head.

"Who said it was haunted? Ah've niver hord o' that before."

"Well it's not exactly haunted, but something very strange happened when owld Mr Aston lived here, years ago."

Jimmy's voice trailed away as he stared into the fire.

"It all started in the 'Forge Hammer' one Saturday night. Four young'uns were playing darts beside the snug. Mr Aston, Don, Slasher and owld 'Baggy' Hope were playing dominoes. The Flynns were playing three-card brag just next to them on another table and all the usual 'regulars' were sitting in their favourite seats. It was just like any other Saturday, except for one very unusual incident; a stranger came into the pub.

Scotswood Road had a reputation for being a rough area, unjustified I might add, but we didn't get a lot of strangers, at least not like this bloke. He wasn't very tall but he was well built. His face was bright red, like most of the other boozers, but his clothes were very strange. His belly stuck out of his coat revealing a bright-embroidered waistcoat, and his light coloured trousers looked more like tights. The hat was the best of all. It looked like a top hat that had been crushed under the forge hammer at Armstrong's factory and it seemed to be made out of blue Astrakhan.

The date was 1927 and most of the locals were sampling the new beer from Newcastle Breweries, it was called 'Newcastle Brown Ale', later to gain a worldwide reputation for its potency.

The stranger ordered a pint of Bass and asked the barman if he could have it in a tankard. It wasn't an unusual request but not one you would expect from a stranger. He seemed to be familiar with the pub and smiled and nodded to everyone as though he frequented the place on a regular basis.

"Dih yih mind if ah sit here hinny?"

He asked no one in particular as he eased himself into a seat next to the domino players.

"Aye, shove alang a bit Dennis so this fella can get both cheeks on the seat," said 'Baggy' to his friend.

Mr Aston shuffled himself further along the leather bench seat until there was enough space to accommodate the stranger.

"Mind you ah like a good game of dominoes. I've been watching you fellas and I can tell you're all good at this game," he commented.

"Well we don't usually play dominoes on a Saturday, cards is our game but the Flynns got here before us the neet and there's only one pack of cards," grumbled Slasher, "and them young'uns got the darts so we had to be content wi'h dominoes."

"Would you rather play cards like?" Enquired the stranger.

"I've got a pack of cards that hasn't even been opened yet. If you want you can borrow them."

He produced a pack of playing cards from his pocket. They were in a black ebony box only slightly larger than the cards. The design on the box was bright red and looked like a Chinese dragon.

"Mind them's fancy cards," remarked Mr Aston, as the owner tipped them out of the container and laid them on the table.

The backs were covered with a tiny red diamond pattern and the edges were gold, just like the pages of an expensive Bible.

"Aye they're nice aren't they? Me mother gave me them a few years ago. She was a funny old bugger; she used to read them Tarot cards and all that rubbish. She told me these cards would be lucky for me some day. She even used to call me Lucky, though my name's really Luke. But I've never been a card player so I've never been able to find out if they're lucky or not," the stranger explained.

"Well now Luke, why don't you watch us play a few 'hands' of brag and see if you can pick it up. Then if you feel like it later on you can join in," suggested Don, winking at the others.

So the four friends Don, Dennis Aston, 'Baggy' Hope and Slasher, rubbed their hands at the prospects of teaching a total novice how to play three-card brag. It could turn out to be a pretty expensive evening for the stranger.

He watched the four intently. He watched them 'blind brag', he watched them 'bluff', he observed the lack of expression on all four faces, never giving any clue as to what kind of a hand they had and he was impressed. He learned that one two three 'stotting' was ace, two three of the same suit. He learned that although three aces were unbeatable in some 'card schools', in Elswick they could be beaten by three three's, which was known locally as a 'prile of priles'.

When he thought he was ready to take part in the game Luke said...

"Deal me in next hand will you? Let's see if I've got the hang of it."

When the landlord of the Forge Hammer called 'last orders' Luke was loosing quite heavily, but he didn't seem to mind.

"Never mind lads, I might get lucky next time. So much for me mothers lucky cards."

"Just a minute there Luke," said Baggy.

"We usually go straight from here to Aston's hoose and play cards for another couple of hours if you're interested. That's OK isn't it Dennis?"

He winked in the direction of his three friends. Mr Hope had no intention of letting this idiot, with more money than sense; get away from them while he still had some money in his pocket.

The five of them left the pub together and lurched across Back Cannon Street, up the short but very steep cobbled back lane and along Cannon Street proper. They were all a little under the weather and Don and Slasher supported each other as they sang 'If you were the only Girl in the World'.

They were both slightly off balance due to the bottles of Newcastle Brown Ale in each of their jacket pockets.

As the party settled in around the dining room table the gaslight threw an eerie glow over the scene. The flickering of the coal fire created an ensemble of dancing shadows and although it wasn't a really cold night there seemed to be a chill in the air.

"I think we could shut that window lads," said Mr Hope.

"It's always been a cowld hoose this."

"Don't worry, it'll soon warm up," replied Luke laughing loudly.

They all looked at him in surprise. Not at his comment, but at his laugh. His deep basso profundo voice echoed round the room, sounding as though he was laughing through the horn of an old phonograph.

"C'mon then lads, let's get started, I'm anxious to win my money back with me mother's lucky cards," he joked.

But it was no joke. Luke the novice card player was transformed into, Luke the 'Las Vegas' dealer. The cards flew from his hands with astonishing dexterity. He bluffed, he bragged, he blinded, and every time he won! The stakes were very small, they only bet in pennies and ha'pennies, but in 1927 tuppence could buy you a fish and chip supper.

"Well, that's me skint," sighed Slasher, "I'll just watch and see if anybody's cheating," he joked, as he unscrewed the cork and poured his second bottle of 'Newcastle Brown' into a pint pot.

By midnight the pennies and ha'pennies were stacked up in front of Luke. He had won almost every game.

"Me mother must have been right after all. She said these cards would be lucky for me one day, this must be the day."

As he dealt another hand, one of the cards slipped over the edge of the table and landed on the lino-covered floor beside 'Baggy' Hope's chair. Mr Hope bent to retrieve the card. As his head slowly reappeared above the tabletop he looked at each of his friends then back in Luke's direction. The stranger was grinning broadly, a black cheroot clenched between his teeth.

"What's the matter Jimmy? Cat got your tongue," he said, using 'Baggy's' real Christian name, which only his closest friends knew!

Mr Hope was deathly white. He drew in a deep breath and pointed a trembling finger towards Luke.

"Its… its… he's the… the… he's the bloody devil" he screamed at the top of his voice.

"He's got nee feet."

There were no questions from the others, only gasps of disbelief as they all charged towards the door as quickly as their unsteady legs would carry them.

Luke leaned back in his chair and roared with laughter; laughter that filled the whole house, almost deafening the four fleeing friends.

"Goodnight lads." He called after them.

"See you next Saturday," followed by another burst of raucous laughter.

Cannon Street seemed blacker than usual that night. Only one of the gas streetlights was working. The terrified quartet sprinted towards the light, which seemed to offer some sort of sanctuary.

"Whoa lads, whoa, howld on a minute," gasped Mr Aston, the smallest of the party.

"What am ah running away for? It's my bloody hoose."

"You're not gannin back there yah'sell the neet Dennis," said Mr Hope.

"You hord what ah said didn't yih?"

"What did yih mean Jim, he's got nee feet?" Asked Don looking slightly bemused.

"Ah just run 'cos ye buggers run, ah mean ah thought it was a raid or summick."

"Well why did any of us run anyway? If he's got nee feet he couldn't run after wih could he?" Reasoned a confused Slasher.

"Listen yih thick bugger, the devil doesn't need feet to run after yih, does he? He's the opposite to God, but he can do all the same tricks." Mr Hope remonstrated with his friend.

"Anyway, what makes you think he's the devil 'Baggy'?" Asked Mr Aston.

"He just might have two false feet, there's loads of blokes around here who've lost legs and arms and things in the pits."

"Aye that's true, but they div'ent have horse's hooves where their feet should be."

The three drunks seemed to sober up suddenly. They looked at their friend in disbelief.

"Whad'yih mean Bag, horse's hoofs?" They asked as one.

"When ah bent doon to pick that stray card up, ah couldn't believe me eyes. That bugger had two horse's hooves for feet. They weren't like ordinary hooves they were split in the middle like what they call cloven! If ah never move off this spot again ah swear there was even white hair hanging ower them, just like proper horse's legs."

Mr Hope's sombre tones made the others turn and look over their shoulders as he continued in his best posh voice in an effort emphasize the gravity of the situation.

"Just think aboot the night. A total stranger comes into the bar; he seems to know everybody but nee bugger knows him. He latches on to us four, pretending he cannit play cards; then after a few games he skins the lot of us. And what about them cards he got from his mother? And what aboot his name? Luke. Yi knah' what that's short for div'ent yih? Well think about it! Luke's short for LUCIFER!"

Dinky leapt into the air as Jimmy shouted the last word of his story, followed by his nasal laughter.

"Gerr away, I bet it was somebody playing a joke on them daft buggers," Dinky reasoned.

"Aye, that's possible, ah never said any other, but think about it. Mr Aston never came back to this house again. He moved into number sixty-one. Don and Slasher both became alcoholics. Mr Hope couldn't work down the pit after that. He said he'd lost his nerve. But what was even stranger, they never set eyes on Luke again! And neither did anybody else. And, nobody in the Hammer even remembered him being there on that Saturday night."

"Dih ye believe that Billy?" My friend asked.

"Well sometimes I think it's better to believe some things are possible, then you can always be on your guard, because if you just dismiss everything as fairy tales they might just jump up and surprise you one day!" I replied, trying to sound intelligent.

"Can you remember the story of the White Lady?" I asked Jimmy solemnly.

I could see Dinky was very nervous, so I thought it was a good opportunity to tell him my ghost story. Jimmy sniggered as I started to tell the tale. He had heard it before, but he played along with me and interjected with the occasional 'aye' or sharp intake of breath.

"We had all been playing 'Chasey' all night." I began.

"Trying to scare the wits out of each other by hiding in the old buildings and jumping out on anybody who came within range. All the streetlights were out as usual, except the one beside me Granny Robson's door. Tommy Casey had a black cloak on over his head and a white skull for a facemask. He had scared the living daylights out of half a dozen kids, myself included.

It was rather a damp night and there was quite a bit of chimney smoke mixed with the slight mist that seemed to be hanging at just above head height! At about nine o'clock several of us were gathered under the only streetlight, laughing and joking at each other's experiences during the past couple of hours. The breath from our mouths was rising above us like clouds of frosty mist as it made contact with the cold night air.

Tommy was head and shoulders above all of us and spread his arms out as he 'shushed' us into silence. He was staring into the darkness, beyond the glow of the gaslight, when his usually authoritative voice dwindled into a shaky whisper...

"It's a f... it's a ghost, look it's a ... am off."

With that he turned and ran in the opposite direction to where

323

he lived, yelling as he went…

"It's the 'White Lady' lads, run for your bloody lives!"

Well, I had never heard of the 'White Lady' before, but with all that had happened in the last hour or so and me being in a state of 'high alert' (or terrified) I ran like Tommy and everybody else, glancing over my shoulder as I went. What I saw made my blood turn cold.

As sure as day follows night I'm sure I saw someone in a long white flowing gown emerge from the gloom. She had a white veil over her head and face; she seemed to be floating rather than walking. I only glimpsed her briefly as she entered the reaches of the glow from the single gas mantle. There was no sound of footsteps or even the soft rustle of the white fabric, just silence.

Then fear and panic took over.

On reaching the end of the street we all stopped and peeped around the corner beside Mrs Buckton's house opposite Annie James'shop. There was no sign of the 'White Lady'! She had completely vanished. This scared us even more, so we decided unanimously to have an early night; but no one would walk along Cannon Street. Instead we made our way along Glue Terrace, then back down Edgeware Road and along the opposite end of the street to the sanctuary of our respective homes.

I can't remember ever being so scared before that night and even my mother noticed!

"What's the matter wih you? Yah as white as a sheet. What have you been up to? You look as though you've just seen a ghost."

"Ah have Ma," I admitted. "Ah have."

I told her the story of the 'White Lady'; how she just appeared out of the mist, floated down the street in our direction then disappeared completely.

"Where did this happen like?" Ma enquired.

"Just beside me Granny Robson's door," I replied.

"In fact she vanished just before she reached the lamp post."

"So she just appeared out of the mist, floated down towards yah Granny's door, then she disappeared." Ma repeated my story, smiling and looking inquisitive.

"Yih stupid sods," Ma said with a snigger.

"That wasn't a bloody ghost, that was Cilla Collins, she got married the day. It must have been her. 'Ah mother lives just a few doors up from yah Granny and she would have to go back there to get changed out of 'ah wedding dress. Wait'll ah tell her she frightened the life out of you daft buggers."

Well that certainly explained the appearance and apparent disappearance of the 'White Lady', but it did little to allay my fear of meeting her again. I gradually accepted my mother's explanation, but a nagging doubt remained in my mind. Had I seen a ghost or not?

"Hi that's a good one mind Billy," remarked Jimmy sounding impressed.

"Did you think yih really saw a ghost then?"

"Aye, ah was convinced it was a ghost, but me mother was right as well mind. Cilla had just been married that day, but nee body explained how she looked as though she was floating doon the street!"

"It might've just been an optical delusion." Dinky suggested, trying to sound intelligent.

"It's dead easy to think you've seen something when you're scared. Like that night ah thought ah saw 'Sandshoe Dick' run after you lot into Kelly's passage, ah turned to run the other way and ran right into the bugger!"

We were all sitting closer together in front of the flickering fire. Three brave teenagers alone in this dark derelict building. It was difficult to say who was the more scared between the three of us.

Dinky continued...

"He was a horrible bugger him mind yih. Ah'll never forget the stink of the stale beer and tabs as ah ran into him. Mind he didn't half clout me before ah got away from him..."

'Sandshoe Dick' was a mythical character who was created by parents, elder siblings or anyone who was trying to impress on their offspring or younger brothers or sisters that...

"If you don't behave yourself, Sandshoe Dick'll get you!"

We played a game of 'follow my leader' where everyone followed the leader into all the dark scary places. Inevitably someone would shout.

"Nit nit, its Sandshoe Dick!"

Whereupon we would all run for the nearest exit, followed by a hail of verbal abuse from the local residents and occasionally a bucket of water, or whatever happened to be in the bucket at the time.

One day 'Sandshoe Dick' stepped out of mythology and into reality. It was amazing. This poor unfortunate person suddenly took on the mantle of a legend. One of the most feared 'non-characters' of local folklore came to life.

He wore an old mac that had at some time in the past been white. It was far too big for him, but it obviously housed most of his scant belongings in its many pockets. His cloth cap looked quite new but his trousers were very worn and dirty. The last and most important part of the jigsaw was on his feet. How could it be anyone else? The enormous pair of dirty white sandshoes was a total give-away. He must be 'Sandshoe Dick'! He was 'Sandshoe Dick'.

All of the kids shouted after him.

"Nit nit it's 'Sandshoe Dick'."

But he didn't respond. He just carried on walking up Glue House Lane obviously making for the Loadman Street Mission, where he would find help, mainly in the shape of a meal and possible accommodation.

We didn't see him very often through the day but he paid regular visits to the 'Crooked Billet' pub, using the 'snug' as opposed to the main bar. When he emerged we would taunt him from a safe distance, never getting close enough to be in any danger, but still he didn't respond. One night some idiot decided we should try another ploy. Instead of shouting at 'Dick' we would sneak up on him and tap him on the shoulder, then run away as fast as we could hoping to get the luckless man to react. Well this worked a treat.

The first brave soul crept up behind him and tapped him gently on the shoulder, then turned and ran for safety. Too late! 'Sandshoe Dick' turned even quicker and grabbed his assailant by the scruff of the neck. He shook the youth violently, slapped him across the face and threw him into the gutter. Then he turned and ran towards the jeering crowd of tormentors who in turn scattered in all directions.

After that it became a nightly game. We would shout and jeer at the poor man and he would give chase. He often caught one of the slower kids whom he gave a clout or a kick up the backside, but he seemed happy with that, never becoming over aggressive. I think he probably enjoyed the chase as much as we did.

We never saw him leave Elswick. It just happened. One day he was there, the next he was gone. But that didn't change things all that much. We still had endless hours of fun running away from 'Sandshoe Dick', even though he wasn't there. It only needed someone to shout.

"Nit nit it's Sandshoe Dick" and we would be off like scared rabbits, often running for miles just in case it really was him.

He re-appeared on several occasions in the shape of Tommy Casey. Tom would dress up in his cloak and mask, don a pair of white sandshoes and for a night become 'Sandshoe Dick'. He chased us youngsters all over Elswick. If he caught someone, or when he caught someone, he gave them the traditional clout or kick, which he enjoyed much more than the recipient. Sometimes he enlisted the help of a couple of his captives to tie up and 'torture' the next person he caught. It was all good fun but sometimes the torture was quite realistic. On one occasion our house, number fifty-four, was used as the torture chamber. Four of us held one of our 'friends' down on our dining room table where 'Sandshoe Dick' proceeded to let hot wax from a candle drip onto his bare belly. This was followed by the plucking out of several pubic hairs. I'm pretty sure that in this day and age he would end up in jail for that kind of conduct.

"He did that to me once." Admitted 'Dinky'.

"He tied me up with hairy string, then he got Tomma Broon to pull me pants doon and he bornt me arse with hot candle grease! Ah mean, that wasn't funny. Ah think he was a bit twisted on the quiet."

Twisted or not we all took part in his mad games willingly, and no one ever complained about the pseudo 'Sandshoe Dick' or his tortures.

The ten o'clock buzzer from Vickers Armstrong jerked us back to reality.

"Bloody hell, that's ten o'clock. Me mother'll be out shortly screaming...'Billleeee' and ah'll be in for it if ah don't get me skates on!" I exclaimed. "She's only just started letting me stay out till ten

327

o'clock".

"Aye, you'd better keep an eye oot for Sandshoe Dick" as well, laughed Jimmy as we clattered noisily down the wooden stairs and out into the cold night air.

I watched 'Dinky' as he walked along our street. It was very dark and he kept looking around anxiously as he passed the end of each air raid shelter. When he reached the last one he let out an almighty scream. This was followed by the nasal laughter of Jimmy Walters who had raced along the other side of the street and leapt on my friend out of the darkness.

The tirade of abuse that followed was only slightly less audible than 'Football Final', but it was a lot more colourful!

Now that I was working for a living I was expected to contribute towards the family income. I say expected, but in truth it was obligatory. My wage packet was handed to my mother un-opened every Friday evening. She decided how much of the one pound, seven shillings and eleven pence she would keep and how much I would get. I didn't begrudge paying for my 'keep' and felt very proud of myself for being able to help now that my mother wasn't working. It was just the handing over of my pay packet that I objected to. I thought, 'If I worked for it I was entitled to dispose of it in whatever way I saw fit'.

I was given ten shillings pocket money and Ma kept the rest. She said she would feed and clothe me out of that but I thought she got the better deal. She bought me my first 'grown up' suit, but I hated it, so I suggested that I should buy my own clothes. I was amazed when my mother agreed, but I don't think she was prepared for my next coarse of action.

When my next 'pay day' arrived I opened the pay packet, took out what I thought I should have and gave Ma the rest!

"Ten bloody shilling, you must be joking. I'm still paying Dolan for your bloody suit." Ma said rather angrily.

"I'll finish paying for the suit." I replied.

"I'm getting measured for a new one at Jackson the Tailors

tomorrow, so I'll have the other one paid off before I have to start paying for the new one."

"Made to measure, mind you're getting big ideas, that'll cost a bloody fortune. And how are you going to pay for that? You can't get made to measure suits on weekly payments, you've got to pay cash as soon as they're ready," said Ma, with a hint of arrogance.

"Ah know that. Me Granda say's he'll get the money for me from a moneylender but I'll have to pay it back in twenty weeks. So ah'll save as much as ah can until the suit's ready then borrow the rest." I explained, getting a little impatient with this long-winded discussion.

"Bloody moneylenders at fifteen years of age! You're starting soon enough, getting yourself in moneylender's hands. Once they've got you, you'll never get away from them. Anyway you're not doing it and that's that."

"Oh well we'll see." I retorted, omitting the fact that I had already borrowed the eight pounds that the suit was costing.

"Yes we'll see you cheeky get. Don't think that 'cos you're working you're too bloody big to get a punch in the mouth." She said, her eyes starting to protrude rather dangerously.

I just smiled insolently.

"For two pins I'd knock that bloody smirk to the other side of your face."

She rushed towards me; her face distorted with anger but stopped short, knowing that it was just an empty gesture and that she had no chance of carrying out her threat.

"Why do you always start shouting?" I asked her quietly.

"I'm not bloody shouting," she shouted, louder than ever.

"You'll soon hear me when I start shouting."

"Aye and so will the rest of the street." I retorted.

Ma looked around for something to throw at me but I was already on my way out of the door.

"Yih better run yih cheeky bastard. If ah get me hands on you ah'll swing for yih. Wait'll ya father comes in, a'm letting him know the bloody cheek a'm having to put up with from you," she screamed after me as I retreated hastily.

I thought to myself. 'A'm not stopping in this bloody house

much longer. There just never seems to be any peace. If she's not shouting at me she's shouting at me Da or me sister. Well a'm not putting up with it. Ah'll join the army or something'.

My mother wasn't really a bad mother; she was just a bad tempered mother. When I was in trouble at school or with the Police she always stood up for me. She defended my innocence unreservedly. Then she would give me a good hiding for doing what she had insisted I hadn't done.

I recall one incident shortly after my fifteenth birthday. My Dad said some friends he had met in Liverpool had invited him and Ma to stay with them for a week's holiday during the summer. They would take my sister but as I was working I would have to stay at home. I was very happy with this arrangement. I would be able to sleep in their double bed. No making up my bed settee for a full week. Go to bed when I liked. Stay up as late as I liked. This would be more of a holiday for me than them.

It turned out to be a much longer holiday than anyone bargained for. My sister took ill during the first few days in Liverpool and quickly developed pneumonia. So I was on my own for about four weeks, until she was well enough to travel back to Newcastle.

When they returned I was out as usual. They hadn't bothered to let me know they were on their way back so I was quite surprised to see our front door open when I came home.

My sister looked very pale but she seemed to be over her illness and I was pleased to see her. My father was moaning about how much work he had lost and how much money it had cost him having to stay in Liverpool for four weeks. Not a word about how ill his daughter had been. Both of my parents seemed to be in a bad mood so I said I was going back out.

"Just a minute you."

Dad's favourite name for me was 'You'.

"Who've you had in this house while we've been away?" he asked, with a knowing leer on his face.

"Err, well nobody really, just the lads a couple of times but

330

we just listened to some records, what for like?" I replied nervously, wondering what I had done.

"What for like?" He mimicked sarcastically.

"I'll tell you what for like mister, there's blood all over the sheets in our bed, now what the hell do you think you've been up to?" he demanded angrily.

"What have you got in your bloody mind?"

Ma's voice was low and icy cold.

"Just what are you insinuating?" She continued, her voice rising slightly.

"Let him answer and I'll tell you what I'm insinuating." Dad replied nodding in my direction. He was smiling but it wasn't a pleasant smile.

"Well? I'm waiting. Where did that blood come from?"

"Well if you remember, before you went on holiday I had a boil on my forearm. A couple of days after you left it burst during the night and bled all over the bed, including the pillow." I said, looking him straight in the eye.

"Let me see your arm." Dad demanded.

I rolled up my sleeve to reveal the almost healed remains of the boil.

"That's healed quick mind, it looks more like a…"

"It looks more like a bloody what?" Ma shouted angrily.
" What are you trying to say? What's in your bloody rotten mind?"

"Calm down will you woman, calm down. I was just going to say it looks more like an old sore than a new one." He replied in a more conciliatory manner.

"Well it's not an old sore, anybody with half an eye can see that. Anyway it's nearly four weeks since it burst. It's had time to heal altogether, so what's yah bloody point?"

As my parents sparred up I quietly slipped out of the house. I knew this would turn into an almighty row and I wanted no part of it. I could hear Ma's voice rising in crescendo and my Dad defending himself, rather lamely.

Many years later he asked me, man to man, if the story of the boil was true. He seemed rather disappointed when I said it was. I got the impression that he would have been quite proud if I had deflowered some vestal virgin in his bed instead of bursting a boil.

Although my mother vigorously defended my integrity I could tell she wasn't totally convinced. I couldn't blame her really, I had told her so many lies in the past. Even I found it difficult to keep track of what was true and what was 'nearly' true.

I never told malicious lies; I merely bent the truth a little, primarily to avoid a good hiding.

I could never understand why everyone called a thrashing a 'good hiding'. I never experienced anything good about it. It was always very painful.

I had quite a painful experience one Saturday morning in Elswick Swimming Baths. I was desperately trying to teach myself to swim better but I was constantly being harassed by one of the 'Dunford family. The Dunfords had a reputation for bad behaviour, which they thoroughly deserved. George, one of the brothers who was about two years my senior was determined to half drown me and kept pushing my head under the water. I asked him to stop several times, but it was no use. His brothers were encouraging him and I was forced to leave the water for fear of drowning. As I tried to make my way to the stone stairs in the three foot six end of the pool my tormentor stood in front of me barring my exit.

"Where di yih think your gannin?" He sneered as I tried to push past.

"I'm going out," I replied, "'cause am sick of you ducking me."

"That's what ye think, yah gannin under again for a start."

He shouted as he lunged towards me. I managed to push him off but he was quite a bit stronger than I was and I knew he was determined to make a fool of me, so I just shouted at him...

"Now look, I want to get out of the water so cut it out and let me past."

"Oh, cut it out. A tough guy eh? Well let's see how tough you are."

Without any further warning I was head butted full in the face. If George had of been on his own I would have responded more positively, but seeing as how his brothers were with him and several cronies I knew I was on a hiding to nothing.

I made my way out of the pool to the jeers of his entourage all of who insisted they had 'had a go' with me before, and had 'done me up'. I was seething with anger. Head butted by a local bully, and did nothing about it. Branded a coward by his cronies. I felt like killing somebody, namely Geordie Dunford.

This incident was to haunt me for years.

About three weeks later, again on a Saturday morning, I was walking home from the baths when who should appear but another one of the Dunfords. On this occasion it was Teddy who had been present on that previous Saturday. My heart sank as he approached.

"Oh, so it's tough guy is it?"

He smirked, taking hold of my jersey and pushing me against the window of the local dole.

"Now listen Teddy, I don't want any trouble, so just let go of me jersey and ah'll go home."

I said patiently, trying to avoid another butt in the face.

"Yih might not want trouble but yah ganna get trouble," he growled as he made to throw a punch at me. I stopped the punch in mid flight, grabbed him by the throat, spun him around and crashed him up against the dole's plate glass window. He gasped in surprise but he couldn't do anything as I was almost strangling him. My little friend Billy was almost out of sight, but I heard him shouting.

"Go on Billy, duff him up!"

But I didn't 'duff him up'. Instead I just pushed him off and walked away in the opposite direction. He never responded. There was no torrent of abuse or cries of revenge; he just went on his way. I think his pride was hurt more than anything else was.

I came into contact with the Dunfords several times after that but I never experienced any more bullying. I think they got the message that collectively I was afraid of them but I was prepared to bide my time until the opportunity came along to confront them individually.

Many years later I was having a night out in the Pineapple

working men's club when I spotted 'brother' Geordie having an argument with a younger man. He was insisting that the youngster leave the club for some minor incident. Paul, (the young man) was trying very hard to convince Geordie that he was the innocent party and that he wanted to stay in the club with his friends and family. It was obvious that the pair didn't like each other and Dunford, being a club official was determined to remove the youngster. Suddenly there was a scuffle that lasted for about five seconds, followed by Paul agreeing to leave.

"OK. OK. I'll go. I don't want any more trouble," and he left the club.

My mind flashed back to Elswick swimming baths. But where was George? As the crowd dispersed, I saw him sitting on a chair shaking his head and holding his right cheek. He had tried to remove the young man by force, sadly he had underestimated Paul's response, namely a perfect left hook to the right cheek.

Next day Mr Dunford had a beautiful 'shiner', which complemented the fat lip that everyone said his wife Helen had provided as a reward for causing so much trouble.

Chapter Thirteen

Once you start working full time for your living I think your life becomes a sort of treadmill. I was spending so much time at work. We were expected to work overtime whenever Mr Johns deemed it necessary and that seemed to be almost every night. Saturday mornings were no longer part of our normal working week, now that we were down to a forty-two and a half hour cycle, but we still worked every Saturday morning, albeit for extra pay. The extra pay was a bit of a joke.

Although the unions had negotiated a shorter working week the employers had stipulated that to compensate for loss of production each employee would have to work the first hour and a half of overtime at the same rate as for single time. The next four hours would be paid at time and a quarter before finally reaching the magical 'time and a half'! For Sunday's we were paid 'double time', but you had to work up to that with single time, time and a quarter etc. So if you didn't work overtime before you started your Sunday shift, you rarely got double time. Believe it or not our union agreed to all of this.

Working extra hours was a lifeline in those austere times. A few extra hours per week was the only way of gaining extra income. Increases in wages were rare. The attitude of 'If you don't like how much we pay you, then leave,' seemed to prevail. Several good employees left David Allen's for higher paid jobs, but there was never any attempt to persuade them to stay. I found that very difficult to understand; surely if you had the best employee's in the trade it was of prime importance to make every effort to hold onto them. Mr Johns' philosophy was 'nobody is indispensable'. This was a short sighted attitude but it sparked off a chain of events that helped to develop the Industry into one of the four major forms of printing.

Although 'silk-screen-printing' had been around for over three thousand years, it still hadn't moved into the twentieth century. We were using the same method of printing that the Chinese had used when they first discovered how to weave silk from the silkworm (which isn't a worm at all; it's the caterpillar of the domesticated silk moth). But no one knew any better. There was very little information available. I personally scoured every bookshop and library in an attempt to gain more knowledge of my chosen profession, without success. I have the feeling today that the industry was never consciously developed. It more or less evolved, at least in the early days. I believe the movement of staff helped more than anything else, to create the changes that came about.

A major problem when printing multi-coloured posters etc. was registration. The pressure of the squee-gee on the surface of the mesh that was required to force the ink through the open areas caused a slight movement in the paper due to the air being trapped under each sheet prior to printing. The solution was to draw the air out through holes in the bench, which in turn held the paper down until printing took place.

Overnight the registration problem was solved. This was the embryo stage of modern vacuum bases. It was a closely guarded secret. Being able to confidently tackle complicated poster work was one step ahead of the competition, but the migration of employees from one company to another completely undermined the secrecy. Each printer who decided to seek new employment passed on whatever new ideas he had been exposed to, to his new employer. This inevitable breech of confidentiality more than helped to spur on company owners and managers to find newer and better ways to make the industry more efficient. With the new ideas came new equipment, new inks, new solvents new films and new jobs, but most important of all new thinking.

Setting up a screen-printing department was without exception, a natural progression for poster writers. A simple solution to handwriting half a dozen cinema posters, was to make a paper stencil and print them. This is where the industry had progressed to and where it had stagnated, until several screen printers decided individually that this trade had much more potential than anyone had previously imagined.

Small enterprises started to appear, 'one man' business's set up by former employees of David Allen and others. They started in old corner shops, garages, and disused railway arches, old Co-op dance halls and crumbling old churches. The capital needed to finance a basic screen-printing unit was so small anyone could afford it. The most important requirement was knowledge.

The bigger companies laughed at what they described as, ' the one day wonders'. They never considered that they could become serious competitors. To underestimate the fortitude and determination of these early entrepreneurs was a mistake. The 'no one's indispensable' brigade got it all wrong and the 'one day wonders' suddenly became a force to be reckoned with. In 1950 there was David Allen, David Burn, Young and Redshaw and Dawsons. These were the four main screen-printing companies in Newcastle.

By the 1960's there was a host of new enterprises started by former employees of these four. If my memory serves me correctly at least twenty new businesses were in operation in a space of ten years. Many of them were destined to become bigger than the four original companies put together.

I have to say that I never thought of leaving David Allen's. At fifteen years of age my only ambition was to stay with the company for the next fifty years, hopefully working my way up to foreman or manager. This outlook would change dramatically in the not too distant future.

I was always working overtime, the extra money being the main incentive. Then one day I suddenly realised how quickly time was passing. A week at school seemed like an eternity, a week at work was like a flash of lightning. One week just seemed to run into another, there never seemed to be enough time to do anything but work.

My family was growing bigger every day but I never seemed

to have time to see them. Grace was married with twins, Jean and Ronnie; Jenny was married with two boys, Ken and Alan; Liz was married with two daughters, Linda and Norma (and later two son's Steven and Malcolm). Dot was married and had a son and daughter, Raymond and June. So up until then I had eight new cousins, but I hardly ever saw them.

When you're young and selfish, you don't attach enough importance to these things. It's only when you get a little older (and more selfish) that you begin to realise how important your family is. The writer Jane Howard once said 'Call it a clan, call it a network, call it a tribe, call it a family. Whatever you call it, whoever you are, you need one'.

My surviving aunts and uncle are still like siblings to me. When I'm in their company I never cease to wonder at how little they've changed over all these years. They still have the same sense of humour and outlook on life. Although their memories are slightly clouded now, a few familiar dates and events can transport them back into the past in an instant. Sparking off nostalgic recollections of times happy, and not so happy. I have very happy memories of Monday nights at Brough Park with our Grace and the girls; watching our favourite speedway riders, Geoff Lloyd, Sid Littlewood and the very popular Ken-Le-Bretton, known as the ghost, because of his all white leathers.

In a recent conversation with Jenny I brought up the subject of my Nanna's death. It was inevitable I suppose, as she has never been out of my thoughts in almost sixty years. I was amazed at how quickly Jen turned the clock back to 1943. Her recall was almost instantaneous; she was working for 'Vickers' in twenty-nine shop at Scotswood when she got the phone call.

"I knew it was serious," she reflected. "No one got phone calls in them days, unless it was serious."

As teardrops began to highlight the sadness in her eyes, I too remembered that awful day. I lost my Nanna, but Jenny had lost her mother. How does a nineteen-year old girl cope with the loss of her mother at only forty-seven? I know how I felt, but I couldn't begin to imagine how she felt.

I don't believe that grieving is weeping and wailing. Neither do

I believe that you ever stop grieving. Grieving continues long after mourning stops. Talking about the loved one's you have lost, remembering their foibles. Enjoying the memories with happiness as well as sadness. I still find it extremely difficult to talk, or write about my Nanna, without shedding a few tears. But I sometimes wonder if they are really only tears of nostalgia, or as it is defined in the dictionary 'The sentimental yearning for a period of the past'.

9 781438 935775